The Outlaws of Medieval Legend

The swashbuckling mythical heroes of the Middle Ages have been the object of fascination for centuries. *The Outlaws of Medieval Legend* explores not only the notorious Robin Hood and William Wallace, but also some now forgotton rogues such as Gamelyn and Fulke Fitzwarin.

Apart from William Wallace, the heroes of the outlaw legends did not play a leading role on the historical stage. Nevertheless, this book reveals how they were remembered in tradition for generations. This intriguing book explains the popularity of these figures and how the stories appealed to the people of the Middle Ages. Maurice Keen discusses the origins, spirit and background of the tales as well as the real people on whom they were based.

In this edition of *The Outlaws of Medieval Legend*, the author provides a new introduction to set the book in the context of recent work on these exciting characters.

Maurice Keen is a distinguished historian of the Middle Ages and Fellow and Tutor at Balliol College, Oxford. His many books include *England in the Later Middle Ages* (Routledge, 1975), *Heraldry* (Yale, 1986) and *Nobles, Knights and Men at Arms in the Middle Ages* (Hambledon Press, 1996).

A mery geſte of

Robyn Hoode and of hys lyfe, wyth
a newe playe foꝛ to be played
in Maye games very pleſ
ſaunte and full of paſtyme.

The Outlaws of Medieval Legend

Maurice Keen

London and New York

First published 1961
Revised edition published in 1977
Revised paperback edition published in 1987
Revised edition published in 2000
by Routledge
11 New Fetter Lane, London EC4P 4EE

Simultaneously published in the USA and Canada
by Routledge
29 West 35th Street, New York, NY 10001

Routledge is an imprint of the Taylor & Francis Group

© 1961, 1977, 1987, 2000 Maurice Keen

Printed and bound in Great Britain by
T J International Ltd., Padstow, Cornwall

British Library Cataloguing in Publication Data
A catalogue record for this book is available from the British Library

Library of Congress Cataloging in Publication Data
A catalog record for this book has been requested

ISBN 0-415-23650-9 (Hbk)
ISBN 0-415-23900-1 (Pbk)

Contents

Illustrations

Preface to the New Edition

Forty years ago, when this book was written, I was a very young would-be historian, just starting out in academic life. Since writing it, my historical interests have developed in quite other directions, but for a time its subject played a part in my life that may explain why it is the sort of book it is.

In the summer of 1954 I had just completed my national service, and was waiting to go up to Balliol College, Oxford, to read English Literature. A letter from the College had suggested that in preparation I should try to read, among other things, all Chaucer's *Canterbury Tales*. There was a copy of them on my parents' shelves in Bell's old nineteenth century edition, and when I came to the *Coke's Tale of Gamelyn* I did not notice the footnote which explained that it was not by Chaucer, and plunged in. I emerged tremendously stirred and excited, and, realising how close this *Tale* was to that of Robin Hood, turned aside to the *Oxford Book of Ballads* to read the first versions of his story. Soon after, newly arrived at university, I attended some lectures by Father Gervase Mathew on fourteenth century romance, and when he spoke of the *Tale* and some other interesting analogues to it (including the *Romance of Fulk Fitzwarin*), I became newly excited. I promised myself that when I had time I would try to pursue the matter of outlaw stories further.

The chance came eighteen months later, when I had changed course to History, and the second year historians were all encouraged to compete for a College prize for a 'long essay', on a subject of their own choosing. Robin Hood was the subject of my (very long) essay, in which I sought to trace, through the stories of Hereward, Fitzwarin and Gamelyn an origin for his myth in literature of protest, and to relate Robin's robbing of the rich with the Peasants' Revolt (which had grabbed my attention in a tutorial under Richard Southern). I shared the prize with two contemporaries (one of whom, if I remember rightly, had written on the American Civil War and the other on coal miners), and came away the better for some £15 and a typescript of some 20,000 words.

Some three years later, when I was a junior research fellow of the Queen's College, I decided (at the instigation of Colin Franklin of Routledge) to try to expand that typescript into a book. I had besides been re-excited by a new article by R. H. Hilton in *Past and Present* (1958), in which he argued forcefully for the same sort of connection between the Robin Hood ballads and the Peasants' Revolt towards which I had been groping in my undergraduate essay. John Prestwich, my guide and mentor among the senior fellows of Queen's, encouraged me. I did not explain to him certain things that were in my mind; that I thought my doctoral research on the laws of war was not going well, that I was depressed about my prospects of getting a permanent academic job, and that Colin Franklin's suggestion seemed to offer a chance of leaving behind something between hard covers if I had to alter my career dreams. I embarked on some intensive further reading and then began to write, fast and excitedly.

I hope that some of that excitement shows in the book that is now being reprinted. As a broad treatment of the whole *genre* of outlaw stories and of literary relations between them, I hope also that it may still have some value. But I can now see plainly the marks of haste in writing, and of the fact that, when I wrote, I was a good deal less far into my apprenticeship in historical research than I supposed. My views on a number of issues raised in the book have altered radically, moreover, notably on the connection between medieval outlaw stories and class antagonisms, which coloured so much of what I wrote in youth. This is why the book is impossible to revise, and appears as it did in 1961, unaltered. To explain what I think now would mean writing a new book, and I have no urge to attempt that.

I do however owe it to my readers to clarify where I believe that I went wrong forty years ago, and where and why I have changed my views. That is what the Introduction that follows this Preface must seek to do.

MK

Preface

A great many people have helped me in the preparation of this book, and it is my first duty to acknowledge this. First of all my thanks are due to my colleague at Queen's College, Mr. J. O. Prestwich, who read the book in typescript and has given me invaluable advice and guidance, together with a great deal of valuable information—far too much, indeed, for me to acknowledge adequately in the text. I am also especially grateful to Mr. J. Wordsworth of Exeter College and to Mrs. Wordsworth for their advice and criticism, and to Father Gervase Mathew, whose lectures on fourteenth-century literature first interested me in the subject of this book. The Trustees of the British Museum I must thank for permission to reproduce three illustrations from printed books in their care. For their unfailing advice and kindness over the book's production I am grateful to Messrs. Routledge and Kegan Paul, and to the Editor of the Series of which this book is the first volume to appear.

The faults and mistakes in the book are of course my own. It is not, I fear, the product of extensive academic research, and for this reason I have tried not to write it as if it were. Because I have used no new sources and advanced no revolutionary theories, I have dispensed with the apparatus of learned footnotes, glossaries, and so on, and have tried to limit myself to telling the stories of the medieval outlaws in a form as near as possible to the original versions, and to fitting them into their correct historical context. This treatment leads inevitably to generalization, and to the omission from time to time of the cautious qualification. I can only hope that an effort to retain simplicity in discussion of a subject as endlessly debatable as the myth of Robin Hood has not resulted in a plethora of error and unwarranted assumption.

M.K.

Introduction to the Second Edition

Between 1900 and the late 1950s, when I was writing this book, there had not been much scholarly interest in Robin Hood or in outlaw legends more generally. Since the book first appeared in 1961, there has been a great deal of interest in both these matters, and what has been written by others has led me to re-consider, in some respects drastically, many of the views that I then expressed. The principal purpose of this introduction must be to explain where my opinions have altered, where I now think I went astray. But before that I need to say a word about some of the more important discussions of the outlaws and their stories that have appeared since 1961 (a fuller list of recent studies is given in the Additional Bibliography). All the outlaws whose legends I discussed in my book have attracted further investigation, but attention has, very naturally, focussed above all on the most famous of them, Robin Hood, and it is what I have written about his story and its context that requires most revision. I will therefore mention briefly some of the re-searches that have thrown new light on the earlier heroes of whom I have written before focussing more closely on the issues raised by the revived and very active scholarly interest in Robin Hood.

The earliest of the outlaws discussed below is Hereward the Wake. Cyril Hart, in the essay on 'Hereward the Wake and his companions' in his collection *The Danelaw* (1992), has added considerably to what we know of this Old English resistance hero. He has identified the Domesday Book holdings of Hereward and a number of his associates, some of whom (notably one Thurkill of Harringworth) had been substantial landowners in East Anglia before the Norman Conquest, and stood to lose dramatically by the Conqueror's policy of settling Norman knights on the estates of local monasteries, in particular Peter-borough and Ely. This probably contributed significantly to the sharpness of the resistance to the invader in this region. The next two outlaws of my book in chronological order are Fulk

Fitzwarin and Eustace the Monk (both born, probably, about 1170). Professor Glyn Burgess, in the introductions to his new translations of their two romances, *Two Medieval Outlaws* (1997), has brought together a much fuller and more informed account than I offer of the lives and landed interests of the historical figures on whom these stories are based. The collection edited by T. H. Ohlgren, *Medieval Outlaws: Ten Tales in Modern English* (1998), also includes modern translations of both these romances, along with a translation of the *Gesta Herewardi*. His introduction includes an invaluable discussion of tales of banditry and of the 'good outlaw' as literary themes, and of their sociological significance.

Ohlgren's *Ten Tales* includes modern English versions of the stories of three other outlaws whom I discuss, William Wallace, Gamelyn—and Robin Hood (a modernised version of the *Lytell Geste of Robyn Hode*). M. P. McDiarmid produced in 1968 a new edition of *Hary's Wallace*: the modifications to what I have written that are suggested by his masterly intro-duction are so major and so significant that I have set them aside for discussion at the end of this Introduction. The *Tale of Gamelyn* has also attracted attention, in two illuminating papers, the one by Richard Kaeuper ('An historian's reading of the *Tale of Gamelyn*', in *Medium Aevum*, vol. 52, 1983), and the other by John Scattergood ('*The Tale of Gamelyn*: the Noble Robber as Provincial Hero', in Carol M. Meale, ed., *Readings in Medieval Romance, 1994*). Both stress the pro-vincial social background of the romance: 'we have moved from the world of emergent high medieval chivalry to the late medieval English countryside where the country gentry and the yeomen are the actors' (Kaeuper). Both stress as the dominant theme of the *Tale* 'justifiable law-breaking', the justi-fication lying in the contemporarily perceived misdirections and corruptions of fourteenth century justice and local admin-istration. Both find parallels to its mockery of the law and assaults on court sessions and justices from the historical record of actual events. We see in *The Tale*, Scattergood argues cogently, a reflection of the conservatism of the minor country landowners in a violent society: 'it is a voice not so much from the greenwood as from the backwoods, resistant to a centralisation (of justice and administration) that it mistrusts'.

That same mistrust, and the same acceptance of violence in the course of justifiable law-breaking, colour likewise the stories of Robin Hood. As I have said, it is his legend above all among those concerning outlaws which has excited the widespread interest of scholars. The principal issues that their research has raised are well surveyed in two important books. One is the *Rymes of Robin Hood* (1978), a collection of the principal Robin Hood ballads brought together by R. B. Dobson and J. Taylor and introduced by a substantial discussion of their origins, audience and significance. The other is the magisterial study by Sir James Holt, *Robin Hood* (1982), which offers the most thorough, wide-ranging and coherent investigation of the subject to date. Besides these two books there has also been extensive discussion in learned journals. The most important articles that have appeared over the last two decades have been usefully included in the collection edited by Stephen Knight, *Robin Hood: An Anthology of Scholarship and Criticism* (1999). The most significant papers reproduced there, from the present point of view, seem to me to be those by John Maddicott, Douglas Gray, Peter Coss and Colin Richmond (for titles and bibliographical details, see the Additional Bibliography). This collection also reprints David Crook's important note, which first appeared in the *English Historical Review*, vol. 99 (1984), which takes back the first clear allusion to Robin's reputation as an outlaw to a note on the Memoranda Roll of the King's Remembrancer in the Exchequer, of April 1262. There is thus a very considerable literature in the light of which my opinions of 1961 need to be reviewed. In what remains of this Introduction I will do my best to explain where I now stand in the light of it, and how and where it has altered my opinions.

* * *

In 1961 I argued, emphatically, that the Robin Hood story rose to popularity in the later middle ages because it gave expression to the social grievances of the 'common people', and I equated the 'common people'—over-exclusively, I think— with the rural peasantry. The arguments with which I supported this view, in particular in Chapters XI and XIV, do not now seem to be satisfactory. In the first place I assumed too readily that the ballad form in which the Robin Hood story first found literary expression was a sure indication of its popular origin (pp. 96–7). In fact, there are good arguments for supposing that the origins of narrative 'ballads' such as those of Robin Hood are not to be sought, as I then thought they should be, in the communal story telling of country people—the accompaniment of their song and dance at rustic festivals—but were composed for recitation. Those who composed them in the form in which they now survive drew on diverse materials, which included full-scale literary romances. The Robin Hood ballads seem therefore in their origins to be closer to the medieval metrical romance than to the true sung ballad. Fulk Fitzwarin, whose story has affinities with Robin's (see Chapter IV) is known to have been the hero of a lost alliterative romance in English, and the *Tale of Gamelyn*, which is in so many ways so very close to the story of Robin Hood (see Chapter VII) is in form a metrical romance. These poems were certainly intended for a genteel rather than an exclusively popular audience, and so also must have been the lost romances about Ranulf of Chester, who is coupled with Robin Hood in Sloth's remark in *Piers Plowman*:

> I can not my pater noster as the prest hit saith
> But I can rymes of Robyn Hode and Randle Erle of Chester.

In 1961 I exaggerated the distance separating the Robin Hood ballads from stories such as these with an appeal to an aristocratic audience, from which in fact they seem to be at least in part derivative. I am therefore no longer inclined to argue for an exclusively popular appeal for the Robin Hood ballads, and am much more attracted by Sir James Holt's suggestion that the original focal centre for the dissemination of Robin's legend was the gentleman's household, 'not in the chamber but in the hall, where the entertainment was aimed not only at the master but also at the members (of the household) and the staff'.

In 1961, however, I assumed that ballads were a sure guide to the attitudes of the common people, and went on to argue that a significant relation was discernible between their attitudes, as expressed in the Robin Hood ballads, and the aspirations of the peasantry, as expressed in the demands that they put forward at the time of the Peasants' Revolt. Here my arguments, as set out in Chapter XI, appear on reflection somewhat specious. I relied chiefly on the fact that the kinds of people towards whom the peasants in 1381 revealed a special animus—officers of the law and ecclesiastical landlords—were also the favourite victims of the outlaws. But hostility towards grasping ecclesiastics and corrupt officials was not in any degree exclusive to the peasant class: for high and low alike they were two stock targets for complaint throughout the whole medieval period. Given this, it was rather special pleading on my part to suggest that, in order to relate the stories of the outlaws to peasant discontent, one does not need to look in them for references to the specific matters about which peasants were complaining in 1381, such as the exaction of labour services and of incidents of servile tenure like merchet and heriot, or the oppressive wage regulations of the Statute of Labourers. As a number of scholars have pointed out, agitation against unfree status is a theme conspicuous by its absence in the outlaw stories, and there is nowhere in them any sign of any sort of mental association between the outlaws' freedom in the 'fair forest' and emancipation from manorial serfdom. As I now believe, the appeal of Robin Hood's story owes much more than I once thought to the glamour that so easily attaches, in any age, to the activities of the 'gentleman bandit' whose misdoings are redeemed by the courage and generosity of his nature and of the manner of his robbing, and have nothing much to do with specifically class tensions, such as those which surfaced in the course of the Peasants' Revolt.

In this connection, Sir James Holt has also rightly stressed the origin of the Robin Hood ballads in the north, a region significantly untouched by the peasant movement of 1381. In the early ballads the centre of Robin Hood's activities is always Barnesdale, north of Doncaster in the West Riding of Yorkshire, rather than Sherwood, and it is here too that the Scottish chroniclers Bower and Wyntoun, whose references to Robin are earlier than any of the extant ballads, locate him. Barnesdale is close to the site of Robin Hood's Well which, as we learn from the Monkbretton cartulary, was already known as Robin Hood's Stone in the early fifteenth century, and is not far from Kirklees, the traditional site of his death and burial. Local references to the area in the *Litel Geste of Robyn Hode* are moreover specific to a point otherwise unparalleled in the early ballads: the 'Saylis' for instance, mentioned in stanza 18, can be identified firmly with a small landholding in the parish of Kirk Smeaton on the northern edge of Barnesdale. Robin's original connections with Yorkshire rather than Nottinghamshire are indeed so clear that it has been convincingly suggested that his story as we know it originated in two once separate cycles, one celebrating a Yorkshire outlaw and the other lampooning the Sheriff of Nottingham, and that these have been interwoven sometime in the course of its dissemination. This attractive theory is not demonstrable, but the originally more northern connection of Robin Hood is established firmly enough. The quest for the origin of his legend, in taking us into the north, takes us into an area where the community of the hall, where lord and followers and servants gathered together, remained a social reality longer than in the south. The north was too the great home of narrative balladry, that 'border minstrelsy' celebrating the deeds of Percies and Douglases and their ilk which has obvious literary affinities with the Robin Hood ballads, and which is clearly not to be associated with an exclusively peasant audience. Sir James Holt is I am sure on the mark in focussing attention firmly on a specifically northern context for the origin of Robin's story.

Virtually all scholars would now concur with Sir James, not only on this point but also in tracing back the origins of the story to the thirteenth century. By the fifteenth century, however, when references to Robin Hood become common and from which the earliest ballads about him date, it is clear that his legend was very widely disseminated, universally familiar in southern as well as in northern England. To what sort of audience did it now most strongly appeal, in a form that had been recast and re-interpreted over generations by nameless authors and minstrels? This issue has raised much controversy. As Sir James stresses, the Robin of legend displays many of the characteristics associated with fictional knightly heroes— courage, courtesy, generosity, a free and open bearing. This 'chivalrous' element is undoubtedly there in the ballads; but it is equally undeniable that in them Robin Hood's status is differentiated, explicitly and emphatically, from that of knighthood and gentility. Their Robin is always a yeoman: his 'good yeomanry' is indeed a recurrent theme. The object seems to be to present him as an independent commoner, no peasant indeed, but of humbler standing than a knight or squire.

Yeoman is a word that in the social vocabulary of the times can carry a variety of implications, but they are regularly—and more and more clearly as time goes by—sub-genteel. Sir James, in line with his preceding argument that the original focal centre for the dissemination of the legend was the gentleman's hall, stresses the use of the word to describe officers in both royal and aristocratic households, who 'were fed and liveried and were often drawn from gentle families'. Chaucer's description, in his *Prologue* to the *Canterbury Tales*, of his Knight's yeoman, his attendant servant clad in a coat and hood of green and with a mighty bow in his hand, might almost be a portrait of Robin Hood, he points out. Robin's legend, he concludes, reflects in its finished form 'the circumstances of the feudal household of the fourteenth and fifteenth centuries'. But 'yeoman' could equally be used to describe members of the rising class of lesser landholders, very often of peasant origin and regarded as of humbler rank than the genteel, who in the decades either side of 1400 were achieving a new measure of prosperity and independence, usually as tenant farmers. Robin's 'good yeomanry' can thus alternatively be interpreted as reflecting 'social aspirations based on the real economic progress' (Dobson and Taylor) achieved by persons of this status. Both Coss and Richmond incline toward this view, with individual modifications. In the increasingly literate society of the fourteenth and fifteenth centuries, Coss further and cogently argues, the 'downward dissemination' through local society of themes and matter drawn originally from romance owed as much (and perhaps more) to 'small group reading' as to oral diffusion. He thus leads the emphasis away from the hall and household setting that Holt has argued for. This opens the way, usefully as it seems to me, toward a view of the Robin Hood story's appeal to late medieval audiences that were characterised by their social breadth and variety, ranging from modest gentlemen through yeomen (of all descriptions) to 'apprentices, day labourers and journeymen, small proprietors and liveried merchants' (Ohlgren).

* * *

Any attempt to gauge the appeal of the Robin Hood stories in the late medieval period must clearly take account of the evidence that we have about real forest outlaws, the genuine analogue to which contemporary listeners and readers would have related the idealised fictional hero of the ballads. I have discussed below in Chapter XIII the activities of some of the outlaw bands of whose activities an historical record survives. Thanks to the researches of Sir James Holt and especially Professor J. G. Bellamy we now know a good deal more about men of this type than I did when I originally wrote. On the whole, the evidence they have uncovered seems to me to confirm the view that the essential historical context of the later fictional outlaw stories is the world of the lesser country gentry and yeomen, rather than the aristocratic world of hall and household in which Holt (rightly I think) locates their first, earliest popularisation. In terms of social status, the leaders of whom we learn from record sources are a diverse bunch. Roger Godberd, the Sherwood outlaw of the late 1260s (see below, pp. 195–7) and Eustace de Folville, north midland bandit of the 1330s (below, pp. 197–202), both came of knightly stock. James Coterel, the early fourteenth century robber of the Peak district whose career Bellamy has reconstructed might (but perhaps might not quite) have ranked as a minor gentleman. William Beckwith, who at one point in Richard II's reign was allegedly leading a band of several hundred men in the 'deep forest' of Knaresborough, would probably have been classed as a yeoman. Robert Stafford, *alias* Friar Tuck (below, p. 203), was a chaplain. What for present purposes seems probably more significant than the status of these men is the context in which they operated, which is that of local quarrels and of the regional enforcement of justice. Thus we find gangs being hired by local people of standing in order to protect their interests: the Coterels, for instance, were employed by the canons of Lichfield to put out the vicar of Bakewell from his church and to defend their jurisdictions in certain parishes of the Peak district where these had been challenged by Lenton Priory. Chief Justice Willoughby, who was put to ransom by the Folvilles, had judged a number of cases in which they or their associates were involved. William Beckwith seems to have taken to the woods and to violence because he had been passed over for an office in the forest of Knaresborough, to which he believed he had a right. Given that the activities of real outlaws seem thus so enmeshed in local matters, it seems reasonable to argue that romanticised versions of them probably had a particular appeal to people for whom local matters and their repercussions had likewise a direct significance—as they did for the yeomen and minor gentlemen of county society in the fourteenth and fifteenth centuries.

The activities of men like the Coterels and the Folvilles were not very savoury. Dobson and Taylor wisely caution us against making too much of a comparison between Robin Hood and gangsters such as they, whose disorderly violence does not seem to offer very promising matter for romanticisation. Nevertheless, as Bellamy points out, it is clear that mere profit was not always the object of their excesses: 'sometimes money was sought as a measure of revenge rather than material gain, to recompense the band for some wrong or imagined wrong once suffered'. William Beckwith's long running feud with Sir Robert de Rokely, steward of Knaresborough, is said to have disturbed the district to the point where the 'whole country-side' was divided by it: clearly he had achieved a measure of sympathy and Bellamy speculates that his and his family's cause may in the area have appeared as the 'popular' side, standing out against the associates of the powerful. In the disordered local conditions of late medieval England, as we are here reminded, it was not in the least uncommon for men to take to violence to defy the decisions of courts or to pursue imagined rights outside them, and it was not difficult for those who did so to appear, to some at least and from a local perspective, as the champions of justice. A certain analogy between the activities of real bandit gangs and those of legendary outlaw bands was undoubtedly perceived—witness the famous Parliamentary petition of 1439 complaining of the misdoings of Piers Venables of Derbyshire who, being out-lawed, drew to himself other miscreants and took to the woods 'like as it had been Robin Hood and his meiny'. In the cir-cumstances of the time, it was not a long or difficult step from the perceived analogy between men like Venables or the Folvilles and Robin Hood as disturbers of the peace, to the idealisation of the latter as a disturber of the peace in the cause of justice in local disputes and grievances.

* * *

There is much more that I would like to say here, in the way of modification of my earlier views about Robin Hood and comment on new issues connected with his legend that other scholars have raised. Space demands that what I have said so far, on the topics that seem to me most crucial, must suffice. There is one matter, however, that I must turn to briefly before concluding, the revisions that need to be made to what I have said about the legends concerning William Wallace's outlaw exploits in the course of his struggle against Edward I and the English in the early days of the Anglo-Scottish struggle, in the light of what M. P. McDiarmid has written in his introduction to his edition of *Hary's Wallace*. Significantly, they are in a number of respects closely analogous to some of those revisions which I have suggested need to be made to my earlier views about the Robin Hood story and its original literary origins, notwithstanding the fact that national confrontation, the underlying theme of *Hary's Wallace*, makes it the least locally focussed of all the outlaws stories that I have considered.

As McDiarmid shows, Blind Harry's long narrative poem is a much more sophisticated and interesting literary achievement than I appreciated in 1961. The author was a learned man, well read in the chronicles and French romances: his literary debts are very extensive and his skill as a narrator is considerable. He came from the Linlithgow area, and almost certainly had personal military experience, probably in the French service as well as in border warfare. He had aristocratic patrons and acquaintances, in particular Sir William Wallace of Craigie (who came of the same family as the great Wallace) and Sir James Liddale, both of whom took an interest in his poem. The poem itself is full of direct contemporary references to Harry's own time; part of its inspiration was the hostility that the patriotic author and his patrons felt towards the policies of James III in the 1470s, which they regarded as too anglophile. In the 1470s Scotland had been wholly independent of any measure of dependence under the English crown for well over a hundred years, and Harry's sentiments have therefore less to do with the experience of English oppression in the time of Edward I than I suggested in 1961, and much more to do with the tradition of national rivalry that had become deeply established by the fifteenth century, when Harry was writing. I went still further astray in treating Harry as a collector of popular traditions concerning Wallace. In fact, as McDiarmid shows, his sources were largely literary and he did not owe much to tradition (though there are occasional borrowings from that store). Harry's poem, therefore, does not really illustrate the relationship between popular stories told of heroes whose part was played in history and the 'later stories of men who belong to a greenwood of pure fancy' (as I suggested p. 77). Rather, since it can be demonstrated that some ballads concerning Wallace derive their matter from Harry, it illustrates the way in which narrative ballad is so often indebted to romance, whose audience was expected to be aristocratic— the point that Professor Holt has rightly stressed in connection with the search for the early literary origins of the Robin Hood ballads.

I ended the preface to the first edition of this book with a hope that my efforts to retain simplicity in discussion had not resulted in a plethora of error and unwarranted assumption. There seem to have been plenty of both. This time I will conclude merely by hoping that its reprinting may help to stimulate further interest in stories whose appeal will prove, I believe, to be perennial.

Introduction: some recantations

Since this book first appeared in 1961, there has been a good deal of interest displayed by English historians in the subject of medieval outlaws and the Robin Hood legend. My book, and the views that I have expressed in it, have been the subject of criticism, some of it harsh and much of it, as I now recognise, fully justified. This criticism has forced me to do more than modify some of my opinions: on certain quite central matters I have had to change my view completely. For this reason it is not really feasible to revise the book: I could not revise it without rewriting the whole *ab initio*, and since my historical interests are no longer centrally concerned with its subject, I am unwilling to attempt this. I do however owe it to the reader that I should make it clear where I think I went wrong in 1961, and where I stand now on the issues that I raised then. To this end the publishers have kindly allowed me to write a new introduction.

In 1961 I argued, emphatically, that the Robin Hood story rose to popularity in the later middle ages because it gave expression to the social grievances of the 'common people', and I equated the 'common people'—over-exclusively, I think—with the rural peasantry. The arguments with which I supported this view, in particular in Chapters XI and XIV, do not now seem to be satisfactory. In the first place I assumed too readily that the ballad form in which the Robin Hood story first found literary expression was a sure indication of its popular origin (pp. 96–7). In fact, there are good arguments for supposing that the origins of narrative 'ballads' such as those of Robin Hood are not to be sought, as I then thought they should be, in the communal story telling of country people—the accompaniment of their song and dance at rustic festivals—but were composed for recitation by professional minstrels. The materials on which such minstrels drew was diverse, but it certainly included full-scale literary romances. The Robin Hood ballads may therefore in their origins be closer to the medieval metrical romance than to the true sung ballad, and indeed there are some facts which point strongly in this direction. Fulk Fitz-warin, whose story has affinities with Robin's (see Chapter IV) is known to have been the hero of a lost alliterative romance in English, and the *Tale of Gamelyn*, which is in so many ways so very close to the story of Robin Hood (see chapter VII) is in form a metrical romance. These poems were certainly intended for a knightly rather than an exclusively popular audience, and so also must have been the lost romances about Ranulf of Chester, who is coupled with Robin Hood in Sloth's remark in *Piers Plowman* (which is the earliest known reference to the outlaw hero):

> I can not my pater noster as the prest hit saith
> But I can rymes of Robyn Hode and Randle Erle of Chester.

In 1961 I greatly exaggerated the distance separating the Robin Hood ballads from these stories with an appeal to an aristocratic audience, from which in fact they seem to be at least in part derivative. Reconsidering the position, I am therefore no longer inclined to claim an exclusively popular appeal for the Robin Hood ballads, and am much attracted by Professor Holt's suggestion that one of the focal centres for the dissemination of Robin's legend was the gentleman's household, 'not in the chamber but in the hall, where the entertainment was aimed not only at the master but also at the members (of the household) and the staff'. In 1961 I argued against this view: it now seems to me to have the ring of conviction.

In this connection Professor Holt has also rightly stressed the northern origin of the Robin Hood legends, which I very seriously under-emphasized. In the early ballads the centre of Robin Hood's activities is always Barnesdale, north of Doncaster in the West Riding of Yorkshire, rather than Sherwood, and it is here too that the Scottish chroniclers Bower and Wyntoun, whose references to Robin are earlier than any of the extant ballads, locate him. Barnesdale is close to the site of Robin Hood's Well which, as we learn from the Monkbretton cartulary, was already known as Robin Hood's stone in the early fifteenth century, and is not far from Kirklees, the traditional site of his death and burial. Local references to the area in the *Litel Geste of Robyn Hode* are moreover specific to a point otherwise unparalleled in the early ballads: the 'Saylis' for instance, mentioned in stanza 18, can be identified firmly with a small landholding in the parish of Kirk Smeaton on the northern edge of Barnesdale. Robin's original connections with York-shire rather than Nottinghamshire are indeed so clear that the plausible suggestion has been made that his story as we know it originated in two once separate cycles, one celebrating a Yorkshire outlaw and the other lampooning the Sheriff of Nottingham, and that these have been skilfully interwoven by some anonymous minstrel. This attractive theory is not demonstrable, but the originally more northern connection of Robin Hood is established firmly enough. The quest for the origin of his legend, in taking us into the north, takes us into an area where the community of the hall, where lord and followers and servants gathered together, remained a social reality longer than in the south. The north was too the great home of narrative balladry, that 'border minstrelsy' celebrating the deeds of Percies and Douglases and their ilk which has obvious literary affinities with the Robin Hood ballads, and which is clearly not to be associated with an exclusively peasant audience. In the light of these considerations my claim that the Robin Hood stories can be accepted as a sure guide to the 'thoughts and attitudes of a vanished common people', in England as a whole, will not stand up. Professor Holt is I am sure much nearer the mark in focussing attention rather on a specifically northern context 'of maintenance and misgovernment at its worst, of border and baronial warfare: later of medieval survivals, of the Pilgrimage of Grace, of the white coated tenantry of the Duke of Newcastle, of the expen-sive largesse and nostalgic reconstructions of Lady Anne Clifford'.

In 1961, however, I assumed that the ballads were a sure guide to the attitudes of the common people, and went on to argue that a significant relation was discernible between their attitudes as expressed in the Robin Hood ballads and the aspirations of the peasantry, as expressed in the demands that they put forward at the time of the Peasants' Revolt. Here I fear that my arguments, as set out in Chapter XI, appear on reflection somewhat specious. I relied chiefly on the fact that the kinds of people towards whom the peasants in 1381 revealed a special animus—officers of the law and ecclesiastical landlords—were also the favourite victims of the outlaws. But hostility towards grasping ecclesiastics and corrupt royal officials was not in any degree exclusive to the peasant class: for high and low alike they were two stock targets for complaint throughout the whole medieval period. Given this, it was very special pleading on my part to suggest that, in order to relate the stories of the outlaws to peasant discontent, one does not need to look in them for references to the specific matters about which peasants were complaining in 1381, such as the exaction of labour services and of incidents of servile tenure like merchet and heriot, or the oppressive wage regulations of the Statute of Labourers. As a number of my critics have pointed out, agitation against villein status is a theme conspicuous by its absence in the outlaw stories, and there is nowhere in them any sign of any sort of mental association between the outlaws' freedom in the 'fair forest' and emancipation from manorial serfdom. Once again, my arguments fail to stand up, and so, I suspect, will any other attempt to interpret the Robin Hood ballads in terms of attitudes exclusive to any one particular class. As I now believe, the appeal of his story owes much more than I once thought to the glamour that so easily attaches, in any age, to the activities of the 'gentleman bandit' whose misdoings are redeemed by the courage and generosity of his nature and of the manner of his robbing, and have nothing much at all to do with specifically class conflicts of the medieval period.

Questions concerning Robin Hood's status and about the historical context in which one should view his legend do remain, however, and some of them are intriguing ones. Professor Holt, developing his argument that we should look for the origins of the Robin Hood story in a tale with a conscious appeal to a genteel audience, has stressed that the Robin Hood of legend displays many of the characteristics traditionally associated with fictional knightly heroes—courage, courtesy, loyalty, generosity, a free and open bearing. This 'chivalrous' element is undeniably there in the ballads, but it is equally undeniable that the ballad minstrels separated Robin Hood as the hero of their story—and emphatically—from the gentility. True, they bid gentlemen who are of 'frebore blood' to listen to his story, but their Robin is always a yeoman, one who therefore, as the *Geste* explains, should not expect to pay for a knight's dinner:

> It was never the maner, by dere worthi God,
>   A Yomen to pay for a knight.

Robin's 'good yeomanry' is indeed a recurrent theme in the ballads. The precise implications of the word 'yeoman' are not easy to pin down, but in the later fourteenth century and the fifteenth it could be used equally to describe minor landholders, not gentry but a cut above the ordinary peasant husbandmen, and officials or servants of comparable status in the hierarchy of lordly households, feed to act as ushers or messengers or to keep the lord's bow or his dogs. Many of the former were prospering, even becoming socially ambitious (as references to the yeoman 'who araieth him as a squyer' attest); the latter performed tasks by no means servile, reminiscent of those performed for a knight by his squires in earlier times. For either kind of yeoman the path forward to gentility lay open, through thrifty farming on the one hand or through good and loyal service on the other. Whether in the household of a lord or in the local courts or at the local market the prosperous yeomen rubbed shoulders with the gentry; what more natural than that they should adopt some at least of the values of those who were their neighbours and, in economic terms, no longer always their superiors? So perhaps one should see the 'good yeomanry' of Robin Hood as a reflection of the eagerness of such independent spirits to make a kind of knightliness or chivalry their own. This would account for the popularity of the Robin Hood story among the 'common people', which is amply attested in early references to the vogue of his story, and will do so without loading his legend with implications which would make it unpalatable to gentry, some of whom (like Sir John Paston, who kept a man to play 'St Jorge and Robyn Hod and the shryff of Nottingham' before his household) certainly took an interest in it.

When we turn to look at the leaders of outlaw bands of

whom history has left a record (and whom I discuss in chapter XIII), we find a situation which is much what this re-examination of the ballads and their literary origins might lead us to expect, a preponderance of gentry, but some men of lesser status. Roger Godberd and Eustace de Folville were of knightly stock: James Coterel, the early fourteenth-century robber of the Peak district, might have ranked as a minor gentleman; William Beckwith, who at one point in Richard II's reign was allegedly leading a band of several hundred in the 'deep forest' of Knaresborough, would probably have ranked as a yeoman. Thanks principally to the researches of Professor Bellamy, we know a good deal more about men of this type than we did when I wrote in 1961. Some of the information which he has brought to light is of very great interest to the student of the outlaw stories. The activities of men like the Folvilles and the Coterels were not very savoury; nevertheless, as he points out, it is clear that mere gain was not always the object of their excesses: 'sometimes money was sought as a means of revenge rather than for material gain, to recompense the band and its members for some wrong or imagined wrong once suffered.' Chief Justice Willoughby, who was put to ransom by the Folvilles and the Coterels acting together (see p. 204), had, for instance, judged a number of cases in which they or their associates were involved. Again, we find that on occasion gangs were hired by local people of standing in order to protect their interests: the Coterels, for instance, were employed by the canons of Lichfield to put out the vicar of Bakewell from his church and later to defend their jurisdictions in certain parishes of the Peak district where these had been challenged by Lenton priory. William Beckwith seems to have taken to the woods and to violence because he had been passed over for an office in the forest of Knaresborough which his family had held in the past and to which he believed he had a right. Although his band included no men of substance, he made himself very formidable: his feud with Sir Robert de Rokeley, the steward of Knaresborough, and with Robert Doufbyggyng who acted as Rokeley's master forester, disturbed the district for five years, from 1387 to 1392, to the point where the whole countryside was said to be divided by it. Clearly Beckwith had achieved a measure of sympathy, and Bellamy speculates that his and his family's cause may in the area have appeared as the 'popular' side against the associates of the powerful and well born. Dobson and Taylor, in the excellent introduction to their collection of the *Rymes of Robyn Hood*, wisely caution us against making too much of a comparison between Robin Hood and gangsters like the Folvilles, whose disorderly violence does not seem to offer very promising matter for romanticization, but contemporaries could see some analogy—witness the famous parliamentary petition of 1439 complaining of the misdoing of Piers Venables of Derbyshire, who, being outlawed, drew to himself other misdoers and took to the wood 'like as it had been Robin Hood and his meiny'. In the disordered local conditions of late medieval England it was not in the least uncommon for men to take to violence to defy the decision of courts where the jury had been empanelled by a sheriff with hostile and powerful connections, and it was not very difficult for those who did so to appear, to some at least, as the true champions of justice. Just how great is the distance, we may ask, between the Coterels' protection of the rights of the Canons of Lichfield or William Beckwith's grievance at the loss of a hereditary office on the one hand, and Robin Hood's protection of Sir Richard atte Lee or the dispute over inheritance which is at the centre of the *Tale of Gamelyn* on the other? The outlaw of legend is an idealized figure, of course, but one can find some sort of historical analogue for him in the history of fourteenth- and fifteenth-century England, and the fact that one can do so helps us to understand why endemic disorder was such a problem in that age. To sum up. I believe that the social historian who is interested in the matter of the Robin Hood ballads will be best advised to view them in the context of an age plagued by lack of 'governance', when methods of enforcing law and order were still rudimentary and justice nearly always partial, and not in terms of class tensions.

There is much more that I would like to say here, in the way of modification of my earlier views about Robin Hood, but space demands that what I have said so far, on the topics that seem to me most crucial among those where I have been misled, must suffice. There is one other subject, though, that I ought to touch on before closing. My book includes a chapter on 'William Wallace and the Scottish Outlaws' (Chapter VI). Since I wrote, there has appeared M. P. McDiarmid's edition of *Hary's Wallace*, with a masterly introduction. As he shows, Blind Harry's poem is a much more sophisticated and interesting literary achievement than I appreciated. The author was a learned man, well read in the chronicles and French romances: his literary debts are very extensive and his skill as a narrator is considerable. He came from the Linlithgow area, and almost certainly had personal military experience, probably in the French service as well as in border warfare. He had aristocratic patrons and acquaintances, in particular Sir William Wallace of Craigie (who came of the same family as the great Wallace) and Sir James Liddale, both of whom took an interest in his poem. The poem itself is full of direct contemporary references to Harry's own time; part of its inspiration was the hostility that the patriotic author and his patrons felt towards the policies of James III in the 1470s, which they regarded as too anglophile. In the 1470s Scotland had been wholly independent of any measure of dependence under the English crown for well over a hundred years, and Harry's sentiments have therefore less to do with the experience of English oppression in the time of Edward I than I suggested in 1961, and much more to do with the tradition of national rivalry that had become deeply established by the fifteenth century, when Harry was writing. I went still further astray in treating Harry as a collector of popular traditions concerning Wallace. In fact, as McDiarmid shows, his sources were largely literary and he did not owe much to tradition (though there are occasional borrowings from that store). Harry's poem, therefore, does not really illustrate the relationship between popular stories told of heroes whose part was played in history and the 'later stories of men who belong to a greenwood of pure fancy' (as I suggested p. 77). Rather, since it can be demonstrated that some ballads concerning Wallace derive their matter from Harry, it illustrates the way in which narrative ballad is so often indebted to romance, whose audience was expected to be aristocratic—the point that Professor Holt has rightly stressed in connection with the search for literary origins for the Robin Hood ballads.

I ended the preface to the first edition of this book with a hope that my efforts to retain simplicity in discussion had not resulted in a plethora of error and unwarranted assumption. There seem to have been plenty of both. This time I will conclude merely by hoping that it may help to stimulate further interest in stories whose appeal will prove, I hope, to be perennial.

M. K., 1977

I

<hr>

The Matter of the Greenwood

<hr>

It was said in the days of medieval romance that there were three matters which were worth a poet's consideration, the matter of Britain, the matter of France, and the matter of Rome the Great. In England one might almost add to these a fourth, the matter of the Greenwood. The stories of Robin Hood and his outlaws have the same childhood fascination as the stories of King Arthur and Merlin, and they are a good deal more familiar to most of us than the stories of Roland and Oliver, or of Brut the Trojan, the legendary founder of the British kingdom. Their legends, like those of the Round Table, are part of the great medieval legacy to modern nursery story, and command the same attention from those who find a compelling interest in the quest after the origin of twice-told tales.

The Greenwood is the familiar back-drop to much medieval romance. This is not surprising: in an age when thick forests clothed wide tracts of the country, their shade was the natural setting for all sorts of unexpected adventure. Arthur's knights seldom strayed long in them before they encountered the Black Knight or dwarf or enchanted hart whose appearance heralded some new and startling crisis in their affairs. The infinite credulity of the middle ages instinctively peopled woods and waste places with all sorts of marvellous beings. Saxon saints, who had retired to the depths of the Fenland to live as hermits, found their retreat infested with elves and nicers, strange spirits who swarmed like mosquitoes in these unhallowed wastes. Foresters of the twelfth century saw among their trees mysterious knights, riding in torchlight procession, whom they took to be the followers of Arthur. Even when Shakespeare wrote his *Midsummer Night's Dream*, the forest still seemed the natural setting for a tale of the spirit world.

The stories of Robin Hood and the outlaws, however, belonged to the forest in a special sense. In other stories, in the courtly romances, for instance, of the Round Table, it was little more than a useful and engaging stage-prop. The opening of such stories was in court or castle, and their themes remained inextricably linked with the life that was led there. But to the stories of the outlaws, of Robin Hood and Little John and Gamelyn, the forest background was essential. The forest was their home; its beasts were their food; its peasantry their allies. Within its bounds their whole drama was enacted. If they ventured outside it, it would be only on some brief expedition to avenge wrong done, and to return to it, when right had been restored and whatever sheriff or abbot was the villain of the piece had been brought low. If they left it, it would be with the king's final pardon, and their tale would be thereby ended. For once they had come again within the law's protection, men had no more to tell of them: their fame was as outlaws of the wild and they returned to obscurity when they left their calling.

For Arthur and his knights the Greenwood was a dangerous no-man's land: for Robin Hood it was sanctuary. The reason for this is that, although their stories belong to the same age, knights of the Round Table and forest outlaws were men of a very different stamp. For Arthur and his knights the forest marked the boundary of an unknown world where the laws did not run and where wicked men and strange spirits found a refuge. But Robin Hood was an outlaw, a man whom society had placed outside the law's protection: for him it was an asylum from the tyranny of evil lords and a corrupt law. For he and Arthur belonged to opposite poles of society: the one was a king, the beau-ideal of a chivalrous aristocracy; the other was a yeoman, the champion of the poor against an aristocracy which failed to conform to its ideal.

2

This is why the champion of chivalry and the outlaw never met face to face in medieval story, though they adventured in the same forests. Robin Hood lived his life too close to the soil to attract the attention of the authors of high-flown courtly romance. Though they turned as readily as any to popular myth, which was the great source book of all medieval story-tellers, in order to deck out their narratives with trappings of the marvellous and supernatural, his tale was not really suitable for adaptation to their purposes. Their appeal was to an aristocratic audience: Robin Hood was the hero of the people, and popular class hatred played too big a part in his story for their public to stomach. The ballads about him were sung by men quite different from the courtly poets, obscure minstrels whose names are one and all forgotten, and only a fragment of whose repertoire remains to bear witness to the tastes and ideas of their peasant listeners. What survives is however enough to show what the average peasant thought about the whole train of corrupt officialdom which hung about the loins of their masters, and what they would have liked to do to them.

The streak of class violence which runs all through the stories of Robin Hood and the other outlaws is perhaps their most striking feature. This may be at first surprising, for it is an element in the story which time has, perhaps wisely, censored. The Robin Hood of medieval legend steps a good deal nearer the realities of his time than the emasculated version of him which we remember from nursery tales. In the ballads we are up against a full-blooded medieval brigand, who, even if his conduct is redeemed by a courtly generosity to the poor and deserving, is a brigand nevertheless and can be called by no other name. He is a desperate man, and he has recourse to desperate and violent remedies. It will not do to forget this, for if one does one will forget what an outlaw really was.

Revelling in the blood of one's enemies is now an outmoded pleasure, but to the middle ages it appeared natural and almost justifiable. There is nothing sinister, therefore, in the violence of the outlaw ballads, but ruthless it certainly is. They reveal in their heroes a cold and callous brutality as regards whole classes of their fellow men. Sometimes they seem almost to exult in bloodshed, even in the death of peaceful citizens going about their lawful business and only involved in the adventure by cruel mischance. At the pinch of necessity Robin's merry men spared neither man nor child. When Little John and Much the Miller's son surprised the monk who had betrayed Robin Hood to the sheriff, murder was the order of the day and they had no scruples about their manner of dealing with the boy who rode with him:

> 'John smote off the munkis head,
>   No longer wold he dwell;
> So did Much the litull page,
>   Ffor ferd lest he should telle.'

So much for the innocent child; but even the dead had scant respect from the outlaw. When Robin slew Guy of Gisborne he cut off his head and put it on his bow's end. Not content with that:

> 'Robin pulled forth an Irish knife,
>   And nicked Sir Guy in the face;
> That he was never on woman born
>   Could tell whose head it was.'

Robin Hood's life was a long struggle against the forces of tyranny and injustice, but his victory was only achieved in the blood of his enemies, and his admirers rejoiced to see it run.

It is the same in the stories of other outlaws. The three outlaws of 'mery Carlisle', Adam Bell, Clym of the Clough, and William of Cloudisley, whose tale is told in an early ballad, spared neither principals nor their accomplices. When William was taken by the sheriff and imprisoned in Carlisle, it was guile and murder that opened the gates of the city for Clym and Adam when they came to rescue him:

> 'They called the porter to consell,
>   And wrang his neck in two,
> And cast him in a depe dongeon
>   And took his keys him fro.'

In the *Tale of Gamelyn*, written just over a hundred years earlier, almost exactly the same incident occurs. When Gamelyn, the Outlaw King, came to the home of his wicked brother, he found that the porter had barred the gate against him. When he broke his way in his method of settling accounts with the man were swift and direct:

'Gamelyn overtook the porter, and his teene (vengeance) wrak,
And gert him in the necke, that the boon to-brak;
And took him by that oon arm and threw him in a welle;
Seven fadmen it was deep, as I have herd telle.'

At the end of the *Tale of Gamelyn* the villains all hang on the
gallows they had designed for the outlaws. At the end of the
ballad of *Robin Hood and the Widow's Three Sons* the sheriff and
his officials are hung on three gallows. Gone is the picture of the

The outlaws rescue a companion from execution.

discomfited sheriff, caught by the outlaws, who, having had his
valuables removed and having undertaken henceforth to mend
his ways, is set down by his captors to a hearty meal of the
king's poached venison. These tales have a ruder finale.

No doubt this conscious and deliberate ruthlessness of the
outlaws is in part just a reflection of the violence of the period
in which the ballads about them were composed. The middle
ages were rough times, and their woods and fens concealed
more tangible threats to the peace of the wayfarer than Pucks
and Questing Beasts. In a lawless and violent era, when the
king could by no means make his power felt in all places and at
all times and when the arm of justice was all too often short,
they could prove a refuge for desperate and unfortunate men of
all sorts. Common thieves, fugitives from justice or the lack of
it, sons of poor families who in time of want could not be
supported at home, gentry discredited or dispossessed in the
endless political upheavals of the age: any in fact whom a tough

world had reduced to extremities, might be the kind of person to be found eking out a wild and probably lawless living in the waste places of the earth. If he could gather about him a band of kindred spirits such a man might be very secure. When at last his double-dealing turned both Matilda and King Stephen against him in the time of their civil wars, Geoffrey de Mandeville, the Earl of Essex, took to the fenland, the old haunt of outlaws since the time of Hereward the Wake, and there lived as an independent war-lord, spreading terror and devastation far and wide from his headquarters in Ely and Ramsey. Geoffrey died, killed by a chance arrow, less than a hundred years after the Norman Conquest, but at the end of the fifteenth century, the last and perhaps the most lawless of our medieval history, we are still hearing shrill complaints of armed bands which, in the fierce days of the Wars of the Roses, lurked in the forests, stealing the deer and committing murders and homicides, and which the authorities were powerless to put down. Whenever the government was weak or the country divided by civil wars— which in the middle ages was all too frequently—we begin to hear of the activities of these lawless denizens of the forest and waste who have set the laws at nought, and whom it might be unwise for the wealthy clerk or citizen to encounter unprotected on a lonely road.

The violent tone of the outlaw ballads is therefore true to life. It reveals their authors as realists : their forests are peopled with brigands who really did exist, not with imaginary goblins and enchanters. But this is not by any means the whole story. The outlaws of legend, if they undeniably belong to the world of mortal men, have equally undeniably been enlarged and romanticized to more than life-size in the minds of the people who heard and loved the ballads which recounted their deeds. Indeed, though their activities are corporeal enough, their stories do not have quite the ring of true history. The theme of the righting of wrong done, of the lightening of the load of the peasant and the defeat of social injustice, which invests all the outlaws' acts with a kind of chivalry, does not really belong to the history of highway robbery. No robber ever could have lived as the Robin Hood of legends did; he is an ideal, not an actual figure. In the ballads it is always summer in his forest; and the sufferings and despair which must have been the lot of any true outlaw in the frozen winter woods are passed over in significant silence. Robin Hood's forest is no doubt closer to reality than that in which Arthur's knights wandered, but he and it belong all the same to an imagined never-never land of legend.

Legend is largely born of the working of popular imagination on the situations of the workaday world, but in the process of weaving them into myth it changes them. They become tinged with the beliefs and aspirations of those who tell the story. This is why popular legend is so useful to the historian: it can tell him what his records so often conceal, what it was that men really believed in and what they really desired. It is this that makes the violent tone of the outlaw legends so striking. For, turbulent as they were, the middle ages had as great a respect for law as any period before or since. For them all authority was in the end derived from God; the ultimate validity of the law was therefore upheld by divine sanction. In an age of faith this made for a stubborn conservatism in social thinking. Ancient usage and the established order of things, hallowed by time, were sacrosanct; custom had the force of law. In such a world revolutionary ideals were disreputable, and lawlessness of itself could command no admiration. It would do the orderly thought of the middle ages injustice to suggest that it was merely their dashing and defiant spirit that won the outlaws their place in popular esteem.

Whence then the violence of the outlaw legends? Why was it that the popular imagination of an age with an exaggerated respect for authority chose to personify its aspirations in the stories of men who had set the law at defiance? Is the fact that it did so just the consequence of literacy being the preserve of a small educated class, so that the written records conceal the revolutionary ideas which were surging beneath the upper crust of the social world? These are the problems which the popularity of the outlaw legends set us. If they are to be answered, there are various lines of inquiry which suggest themselves. The social and historical background of the stories clearly claim attention. History should be able to tell us what it was that roused the indignation which their violent tone indicates; the cast of contemporary social thinking alone can tell us whether their ferocious idealism was typical of its age or not. The literary origins of the stories also demand examination, for it will be much easier to see why the popular imagination idealized the outlaw if we can tell whence it got its picture of the outlaw hero. If these three things, the origin, the spirit, and the background of the outlaw stories, can be explained, enough will have been said. But first we must hear more of the stories themselves.

II

◇◇

The Story of Hereward

◇◇

BEFORE plunging into the matter of the outlaw legends, it is necessary to say something of what the word outlaw really means, for it is a word which has now slipped from our legal vocabulary. When the form of law which the process of outlawry embodied was abolished in the 1880s, there had long been no outlaws in England, and the idea of the outlaw, understood only through historical memory, had acquired a romantic flavour of forest adventure which had nothing to do with its original meaning.

Outlawry meant originally nothing more nor less than the putting of an individual outside the protection of the law of the land, by a legal decision of the King or his courts. By that sentence the outlaw was denied henceforth his ancient inherited privileges at law, which were part of every man's birthright, and of whose authority the medieval king was but the guardian and temporary repository. He became thus an outcast from society; he had no more rights than a hunted beast. Indeed, the price upon his head was originally as that upon a wolf; whence it was said commonly that an outlaw 'had a wolf's head', and so in the *Tale of Gamelyn* we hear that Gamelyn's wolf's head was cried about the county. Another favourite phrase to describe the outlaw was that he was civilly dead (*civiliter mortuus*); hence he could be killed with impunity. This was the old rule, but by the thirteenth century it had been softened; the outlaw in Bracton's day forfeited his chattels and his rights at law, and his revenues were for the time being taken into the Crown's hands, but he did not lose all his claim to his inheritance, nor was the man who killed him free of the charge of homicide. Nevertheless, he remained an outcast, a man with no defence except by force against those who committed trespass against his goods or his person. His one hope of survival was his own skill in eluding the authorities; his only hope of restoration lay in suing for a pardon from the same men who had condemned him. He was a fugitive whom his fellows aided at their own peril; for the time being he must live by his wits.

The sentence of outlawry was therefore one to be dreaded. All the same, the very sentence implied an admission of weakness on the part of the law itself. You have defied us, the law said to the outlaw, therefore we will disown you. In saying this, it confessed that it had proved incapable of bringing him to justice. It revealed a failure on the part of the government; the sentence uncovered the inability of medieval society to curb its own unruly elements. If a man was powerful enough, or if he could retreat to some distant and deserted place, he could defy the law, and if it appeared to be in his interest to he would do so. The sentence of outlawry for this reason passed into desuetude after the end of the middle ages, because the law and the government became strong enough to enforce their own decisions. It belonged to the old, disordered age of society, when a strong castle or a forest retreat could put a man outside the reach of authority.

The sentence of outlawry was thus a kind of banishment from society. So it is not surprising to find that the first outlaws of literature were the exile-heroes of certain early sagas and romances; indeed, even in the later, true 'outlaw' legends some remark occasionally recalls this literary ancestry. Certain incidents in the stories of Robin Hood recall the legend of the exile King Horn, and Hereward, the first of the English outlaws, was called in his own day not Hereward the Wake but Hereward the exile. Indeed, the stories of his early life, after he had been banished from his country by Edward the Confessor, and before he had returned to England to lead the last hopeless resistance to the Norman invader, are much closer to the stories of the saga heroes than to those of the outlaws of Barnesdale or of Sherwood Forest.

Nevertheless, Hereward is the lineal ancestor of the later English outlaws. Halfway through the story of his life, as it is told in the fullest of the accounts, the *Gesta Herewardi*, the tone of the story changes. The first half records the romantic adventures of a young exile, but with Hereward's return from banishment to his native land, to combat William the Conqueror and his Normans and to claim the English inheritance which the slaughter of his kindred has left him, this warrior who resembles the saga heroes is forgotten and the outlaw appears on the scene. We hear no more of the life of kings and courts or of the pageantry of the pitched battle; we are introduced to the wild life of fugitives among the fens and to a new war of tricks and disguises and ambushes laid in waste places. Cooks and potters and fishermen, who have so far had no part to play in the story, assume the central roles. There are still, of course, occasional reminders of the aristocratic, almost chivalrous tone of the first half of the story, in the gathering of the last English nobles about Hereward in the Isle of Ely, or in Hereward's visit to the last English Abbot of Peterborough to receive knighthood at his hands after the ancient Saxon manner. But the change is real; Hereward's life has come closer to the soil, and his companions are no longer courtly youths, but are drawn from all classes; one may find side by side amongst them a dispossessed English earl, and a peasant who has fled after killing a Norman with the scythe which he was carrying to mow his field. At the same time, the story has somehow come alive; the pride of Englishmen in their compatriot who defied the great Conqueror revivifies the dry bones of the tale, and commands a new interest.

It would take too long to recount the whole story of Hereward as the author of the *Gesta* retails it. Much of it, like so much medieval narrative, is merely episodic, and the earlier part of it is quite clearly fictional. There is plenty here to attract the reader who goes to medieval literature in search of the marvellous. There is the tale of the fantastic bear which Hereward slew, which was endowed with human intelligence; its parent had, it was said, carried away a princess, and fathered upon her Bearn of Norway, who had a bear's strength, and this beast

11

which had a man's mind. There is the tale of how Hereward killed the giant of Cornwall, saving the King's daughter from his embraces, and of how the jealousy of the King's knights forced him to flee to Ireland. There is the story of how in Flanders Turfrida, the wisest and most beautiful of women, fell in love with him and how he won her in marriage; there is the tale of his wars in Scaldemariland and of his vonderful mare Swallow. These stories throw no light, however, on the character of the outlaw, and for those who are interested in him from this point of view they are important for one reason only. Their very existence indicates the extent of the fame and popularity of the outlaw. It was his struggle with the Conqueror that originally made his reputation, but that reputation soon made him the kind of figure about whom all kinds of bogus legends collected. It shows at once how widespread the fame of a dangerous outlaw could soon become, and also how chary we should be of accepting any but strictly contemporary evidence about his life as factual.

The historicity of Hereward is beyond doubt, but of the facts of his life history has remarkably little to tell us. Hugo Candidus mentions that he held lands of the Abbey of Peterborough, and 'Domesday' shows him holding lands of the Abbey of Crowland, though strangely enough Bourne, always his ancestral home in the legends, was not apparently his. He also, or someone bearing the same name, had lands in Warwickshire, which a Hereward was still holding when the 'Domesday' survey was compiled. At some time before his revolt he had apparently been banished, though there is nothing to show definitely that this was by the sentence of Edward the Confessor. We can say nothing certain of his ancestry or of his descendants. He emerges into history in fact only for a brief moment in 1070, when the fenland rebels combined with the Danish fleet and fell upon Peterborough, where they burned the monastery and took away its treasures and relics to save them—this at least was their excuse—from the hands of the new Norman abbot. Among those who were at the sack of Peterborough were, says the *Anglo-Saxon Chronicle*, 'Hereward and his gang', a phrase which indicates that the outlaw was already well known in the Fens. After this raid the Danes took their leave and sailed, not to reappear in the fenland, and the English rebels retreated to the stronghold of Ely on its island. There amongst them were the last of the English nobles to be found in arms, Earl Morcar and Siward Barn, perhaps others and, of course, Hereward. For nearly a year they resisted the siege of King William. At the end of that time, when the whole island was surrounded both by land and water, the treachery of the monks placed the monastery and all who had taken refuge in it in the hands of the Conqueror. All, that is, 'but Hereward alone', who, with a few companions, made good his escape. With this he disappears from history, and what his ultimate fate was only legend records.

Legend, of course, is not to be despised as a historical source, and there need be no doubt that the stories of Hereward found in later chronicles do contain some substratum of fact. But it is equally clear that by the time that they came to be written down traditions had become confused; both Geoffrey Gaimar and the author of the *Gesta*, for instance, have muddled their dates and placed the sack of Peterborough after, not before, the siege of Ely. Certain of the persons who are asserted by them and by the *Ely Book* to have been among the rebels at Ely could not possibly have been there; Earl Edwin had been killed in Scotland, and Stigand, the deposed English Archbishop, was in prison at Winchester. Though we know something of the sources available to these authors, this does not really help us much in assessing the reliability of their account of any single incident. The *Book of Ely* records that there were many songs of the deeds of Hereward current among the peasantry when it was compiled; it also refers to a life by one Prior Richard, who seems to have flourished in the third quarter of the twelfth century. Geoffrey Gaimar tells us nothing of the sources of his information. The author of the *Gesta Herewardi* claims to have found some part of a book of Hereward's life written in Anglo-Saxon by one Leofric the Deacon who was one of Hereward's companions; he had been told, he says, that there were many such accounts to be found extant in the fenlands, but every story he heard of some great book stowed away in a monastery proved an empty myth, and this was all that he could uncover. He had talked, he however declares, to men who could remember Hereward and even to some of his companions, and from these combined sources he has put together the story he retails. That there were plenty of traditions preserved in songs and ballads of Hereward there need be no doubt, and the authors must have used them. But whether Leofric's book ever really existed, whether it was really by Leofric, and just what persons it was that the author of the *Gesta* spoke with, we shall probably never know. As the story of Hereward is told, therefore, it must be remembered that one cannot tell what truth there is in it; one can only be certain that whatever truth there is has now been exaggerated and romanticized out of its historical perspective, and confused by illiterate memories.

The story as it shall be told here is more or less that of the *Gesta*, which is the fullest account, expanded where this is necessary. I have done my best to render it connected; it remains, however, incurably episodic. Omitting the early accounts of Hereward's wanderings abroad, it opens with his return to England in the year 1068, having heard some rumour of the Conquest and anxious to find if any of his kin survived. He left behind him in Flanders his wife Turfrida and his two nephews; it was accompanied only by a single servant that he finally arrived one evening at his ancestral home of Bourne, and, not yet revealing his identity, entered the house of one Osred, who had been his father's thane and who now offered him his hospitality. He found the household in deep mourning. Only the day before a Norman lord and his men had come to the village, to demand from Hereward's mother the land and all that belonged to his family. Hereward's younger brother was there, and when two of them laid rough hands on her he slew them, whereon he was surrounded and killed; they had cut off his head and placed it over the door of his own home in token of their revenge. Hereward heard the news in silence, still concealing his own identity; as he went to bed, however, he caught sounds of singing and shouting from somewhere in the village. Wrapping himself in a cloak and taking his servant with him, he went out to investigate. It was the Normans celebrating their victory in his own house. As he entered he took down the head of his brother, which he kissed and wrapped in a cloth. Penetrating further, he found his enemies; they had been feasting and were now all drunk. They had brought in some of the women of the village, in whose arms they lay, while a dancer amused them, singing insultingly songs about the English and imitating their crude manners. Hereward remained unobserved in the shadows; soon one of the girls, whose spirit had been roused by the

14

jester's insults, protested. 'If our lord's other son Hereward
were here' she cried 'you'd have changed your tune before
tomorrow morning.' The Norman lord silenced her; 'That
particular rogue' he said 'is not likely at the moment to show his
face this side of the Alps'. The jester took up his words, and
began his songs again, but at this moment Hereward leapt into
the room and cut him down with a single blow of his sword.
Then he began to lay about him; the Normans were too drunk
to resist; some he killed himself, others his servant, whom he
had left at the door, cut down as they tried to escape. No one
was left alive. In the morning their fourteen heads grinned down
in the place of his brother's at the doorway. The other Normans
who had come to the district took warning and fled.

As the news of his deeds and of the flight of the French
spread, his countrymen soon came flocking to join Hereward.
For the moment, however, he contented himself with choosing
out a small bodyguard, mostly from among his own kin, with
whose aid he finally drove out such Frenchmen as had dared to
linger in the lands of his inheritance. At the head of this band he
seems to have gone as far afield as Peterborough, for it is said
that he was there knighted after the Saxon manner by Brand, its
last English abbot. Already his fame as an outlaw must have
spread far, for Frederic, brother of the Earl of Warenne, took
an oath to hunt him out, and rode off at the head of his men in
quest of him. But when, late one evening, he met Hereward and
his people, it was he that met his end; and thus it was that the
outlaw earned the undying hatred of the Earl of Warenne. After
this adventure, the *Gesta* tells us, Hereward decided to return to
Flanders to revisit his wife and nephews. He disbanded his men,
but promised that he would be back within a year, and that they
should have a sign when he returned.

Within a year Hereward was back, this time with Turfrida
and his relatives, and had given the signal by setting fire to
three villas on Brunneswald above his manor of Bourne. Since
his last visit no Norman had dared to set foot on his land, and
soon he had gathered about him the stoutest of the Saxons.
Many of them were old rebels; there was Leofric the mower,
who had, armed only with his scythe, driven off twenty Normans
who had attempted to take him when he was harvesting alone
in the field; there was Leofric surnamed the cunning, because of

the many times he had, by one ruse or another, escaped from captivity; there was Wulric the Black, who, having once disguised himself by blackening his face with charcoal, had penetrated unobserved among his enemies and killed ten of them; and Wulric Hraga, who had once rescued four brothers from unjust execution, and slain their guards. There were others too; Leofric the Deacon, who afterwards wrote Hereward's life in English, Utlamhe (the outlaw), Hereward's cook, Winter, Hurchill, and Grugan, besides, of course, Hereward's two nephews, Siward the White and Siward the Red, who had come with him from Flanders. Soon Hereward was at the head of a fierce and powerful band, his 'gang', as the *Anglo-Saxon Chronicle* has rightly called them.

About this same time another group of rebels had shut themselves up in Ely, supported by the monks who feared that the Conqueror would after his custom set a Frenchman over them. With them, says the *Gesta*, were Morcar and Count Tosti and their abbot, and later legends tell of others, Earl Edwin, Stigand the one-time Archbishop, Frithric, an exile from St Albans, even the last of the English royal house, Edgar Atheling himself. When they heard of Hereward's return, these men were not slow in sending for him to come and join them, and to conduct the defence of their island. Hereward came by water, the safest route, but even so his journey was eventful. The Earl of Warenne, having heard of his coming, marched to cut him off at Herbeche, where the water was narrow. But Hereward was there before him; the Earl found his enemies on the far side of the water, and was himself struck down by an arrow from Hereward's bow; though it glanced upon his armour, he was almost unconscious and had to be assisted from the water's edge. Meanwhile, Hereward and his men slipped away among the fens they knew so well, and reached Ely in safety the same day.

Ely, at this time, was an island among the fens, and it was all but impregnable. As long as its garrison could live upon what they could grow or catch upon their own island, there was every prospect of their being able to hold out indefinitely. The most promising line of attack lay through the village of Aldreth to the south-west; even here, however, it was necessary to construct a bridge across the marsh. Here accordingly, when he had once surrounded the island, the Conqueror launched the first attack. It failed dismally, for his bridges could not bear the weight of marching troops; the leading men were plunged into the bog, and many perished. The author of the *Gesta*, forty or fifty years later, could remember having seen their skeletons, still in their rusty armour, retrieved by fishermen from the fen. Only one Norman soldier, the legend records, reached the island, one Deda, who was led on by the rewards the king had promised to those who should be first in the assault. He was taken prisoner and led before Hereward, who treated him with the greatest courtesy. After he had been some time in the island, its commander sent him back to William, to whom he gave a full account of the manner of life of the besieged garrison.

Deda's picture of life on the island is one of the best passages in the *Gesta*; quite undramatized, it is probably near enough the truth. These men were desperate, he told the King; they were prepared for any hardship, when servitude was the alternative, and, well defended, the place was strong enough to stand four sieges. They were prepared for attack at any moment, and the monks were as ready to take arms as any of the outlaws. All dined together, monk and soldier side by side, each with his arms hung by him upon the wall, handy to be seized at an instant's notice. The Abbot and the three earls dined at a high table together with the two foremost outlaws, Hereward and Thur-kill. Each day was busily occupied, and they had put up strong defences. The island was fertile and all co-operated to till the soil; besides, they could all but live by hunting alone. The waters abounded in fish, and the woods in wild beasts and herons; the waterfowl they trapped (no doubt by netting, as for many ages was done in the fens), especially at the time of the moult, when they were not hard to catch. Deda said he had seen as many as a thousand birds taken at one time from a single marsh. There were plenty of fenmen among the garrison, who knew well enough how to live off the marshes. The place was strong, Deda warned the King; it would serve no purpose to keep it surrounded year in and year out; and since the outlaws would never be strong enough to drive him away, he advised him to offer them terms.

Having heard Deda's story, King William was inclined to make a peace with the rebels, but the Earl of Warenne and Ivo Taillebois urged him to fight them to the finish. Ivo had a new plan; he knew, he said, of a sorceress, who by her powerful enchantments would still the courage of the garrison, and so terrify them that the King could enter the island unopposed. Though at first unwilling, William in the end agreed to the plan, and began to gather in his forces, all in the greatest secrecy, lest the garrison should hear of it and also fall back on the black art to counter him. Even so, however, rumours of some new plan of attack reached the rebels on the island, though what it was they were unable to discover. They decided it would be necessary to send some spy to the enemy camp, and after some debate Hereward himself agreed to take on the task.

Hereward set off upon his mare Swallow, which, though the fastest of beasts was ill-favoured to look upon, and leant colour to the disguise of a rustic. As he rode he met a potter, and this gave him a new idea; he persuaded him to lend him his pots, and decided to penetrate the camp peddling his wares. He reached it before night, and managed to obtain lodging at the cottage of an old woman, in which, by the merest chance, the same witch whom Ivo de Taillebois had hired was also housed. As he was about to sleep, Hereward overheard the two women talking over her plans; they were speaking in French, which they supposed he as a mere peasant could not understand. When therefore they rose, he too got up and followed them. He watched them make their way to a certain spring, and heard them address many questions to its unseen guardian; he saw them wait each time for an answer, though he heard nothing. He slipped away before them, and in the morning he left their house for the camp.

When Hereward reached the camp he began to cry his wares, and soon some of the servants from the King's kitchen came to examine them. One of the soldiers who was passing, however, remarked on his resemblance to Hereward, and a crowd began to gather as many were anxious to see a man who resembled the famous outlaw; there was a good deal of discussion as to whether such a warrior could really be a short, stocky little man such as this potter. They questioned him eagerly as to whether he had ever seen the outlaw; 'Indeed I have' he replied 'and I have reason to remember it, for it was he who stole my cow and my four sheep, all that I had bar my pots and this old horse, and me with two sons to support.' The general excitement caused by the potter's appearance encouraged the cooks to invite him round to their quarters while they prepared the King's meal; there they plied him with drink, in the hope of more stories. They themselves, however, were not abstaining, and when one of them suggested a practical joke which involved shaving the potter's beard and crown with a kitchen knife, the party began to get exciting. Hereward became extremely angry; a single blow laid the instigator of the idea unconscious, but he soon found himself surrounded by equally angry cooks, armed with knives and forks, and decided the best policy was to come quietly. As they were leading him off, however, he suddenly broke loose, seized a sword from one of his guardians, cut him down, and, rushing down the steps of the house into the lower court (the King appears to have lodged in some kind of mansion) found his horse Swallow and leapt upon her. A group of young knights, who were passing, gave pursuit, but Hereward made for the fens, and they were soon lost among the marshes, where only he knew the hidden paths. Only one ever caught up with him, and he, already exhausted, soon yielded to the outlaw, who sent him back to King William with the news of who the potter had been who had caused such stir in his kitchens.

With many more ruses Hereward and his men continued to defy the King's assaults. When he marched his army forward, led by the witch who cast spells from a wooden siege-tower, the outlaws set light to the dry sedge, and as the wind fanned the flames, watched the King's army retreat in confusion. The witch and her tower were both consumed. On another occasion Hereward, once more disguised, this time as a fenland fisherman, joined the King's labourers and worked with his men on the pontoons, until one night after they had left their work he fired them all. At length, however, the monks of Ely began to tire of the struggle; they heard that their lands outside the island were divided among the King's vassals, and they feared for their possessions. Secretly they entered into negotiations with William and finally it was agreed that the island should be surrendered on condition that they should continue to enjoy all their lands. So, with their guidance, William's men began the march into Ely.

Hereward was out on a raiding party when he heard the news (at least so the version in the *Gesta* goes), but he immediately turned his men back. His intention was to burn the place before the Conqueror could reach it; he should find only the empty shell of a monastery in which to celebrate his triumph. One of the monks, however, met them as they were returning, with faggots upon their shoulders; he besought them to abandon their scheme, pointing out that the King's army was already too near to give much chance of success. Hereward was at last persuaded; he changed his plan and made for his boats on one of the great marshes; there he took to the water with his men and retreated into the heart of the fenland. This is one story; Geoffrey Gaimar's tale is still more dramatic. It tells how Hereward with only five companions escaped from Ely, and slipped past the King's guards concealed under the nets of a friendly fisher, who had sold his catch to the King's soldiers. Both accounts agree again, however, on his subsequent movements; they take him to his old haunt of Brunneswald, whence he raided far and wide, sometimes based there, sometimes in the thick Northamptonshire forests near Peterborough.

Here he continued his career as an outlaw, using every trick and stratagem to elude capture. Sometimes his men reversed the shoes of their horses, so that their pursuers would never be certain, when they lighted on their tracks, which way they had been travelling. On one occasion Hereward was all but surrounded by the men of Ivo de Taillebois and Abbot Turold; he and his men, however, managed to cut themselves out. In an ensuing fight Turold actually fell into Hereward's hands; he only freed himself at a ransom of thirty thousand pounds. Even then the treacherous abbot would not keep his word; thus he brought down the wrath of Hereward who fell on Peterborough, burning the town and carrying off the treasures of the monastery. Only a midnight vision of St Peter, as a terrifying sage brandishing an enormous key, induced him to return his spoil. His piety was not unrewarded. Lost in the woods at night as they made their way back to Brunneswald, his men were led by a great white hound, which appeared suddenly and all through the dark hours went before them, while at the same time unearthly lights, like the fairy will o' wisps, played about the lance points of his soldiers. It was only with the coming of the dawn that they disappeared; they saw now, too, that what they had taken for a hound was a white wolf, which vanished into the forest, having led them safely many miles on their road home. Once secure again in Brunneswald, they continued their war of raids and skirmishes, and Hereward had more than one encounter with the King's champions. He was still as strong as ever, for his fame had attracted many, even some Frenchmen, to his service. One tradition even has it that he joined the revolt of William's earls in 1072.

Even so Hereward was tiring of the struggle. He had fallen in love again, with a woman of his race, famous for her beauty, Alfthrida, and she undertook to make his peace with the King. So he was betrothed to her, and the faithful Turfrida retired to a monastery; but the tale tells that Hereward was never so well off again after she had left him, for he never had wiser counsel than she in her time had given him. In due course his new wife reconciled him with the Conqueror, and his lands were returned to him. His presence at the Court was clearly an embarrassment; he had too many enemies, and at one time the intrigues of the Earl of Warenne and Ivo de Taillebois caused his imprisonment. It was not long, however, before he was rescued by his old companions, and again admitted to the peace of the Conqueror. In the end he returned to his lands at Bourne, and there, according to the *Gesta*, ended his days in peace. Gaimar tells a sadder story; how his enemies had never forgiven him, so that he went always guarded, fearing sudden attack. In the end they surprised him one day when at table; his sentry had slept at his post and they came upon him unawares. In a tremendous struggle Hereward was at last struck down, killing with his last blow the man who had slain him.

Had there been four such men as Hereward in England, says Gaimar, the Conqueror would never have won the land. This points a moral; Hereward's stand was not really the isolated defiance of a casual outlaw, but a last pocket of organized resistance. He was a warrior and a soldier, and this sets him in at least one sense apart from the Robin Hoods and Gamelyns of later legends, who were not the men to organize the defence of besieged garrisons or to fight on equal terms with the King's knightly champions. It is important to remember this, that if Hereward was the lineal ancestor of Robin Hood, he was also the lineal descendant of the aristocratic heroes of Anglo-Saxon history, Byrtnoth and Alfred the Great. One must not expect to find in his story all the trappings which later became traditional to the outlaw legends, or to diagnose identical reasons for his popularity. Nevertheless, on the legal definition he was an outlaw, a man who had placed himself outside the protection of the lawful King of England, and it was as an outlaw that he was remembered; 'under his command' says Gaimar 'assembled all those who were outlaws'. Moreover, there are strong family resemblances between his story and personality and those of later outlaws, and this must be the theme of the next chapter.

III

The Historical Background
of the Hereward Legend

THERE is plenty in the legend of Hereward which has little or
no connexion with outlaw mythology—the long opening passages in the *Gesta* with their heroic flavour, the fights with the
champions, the magic which conjures up will o' the wisps and
spectral wolves to conduct his men through the dark forest.
Nevertheless the affiliation with Robin Hood is clear enough.
It is not merely his way of life that is so similar, the forest lair,
the enmity of rich lords and abbots, the living off the wild,
which stamps Hereward as of the same breed. It is more than
this; it is more too than the name and fame of outlaw; it is
rather, for instance, the fact that whole incidents of his story are
shared with his later counterpart, that another age attributed to
Robin Hood the precise exploits that the twelfth century
attributed to Hereward. The story of Hereward and the potter
has been recounted at length here, perhaps tediously, but there
was reason for this. *Robin Hood and the Potter*, one of the
earliest ballads of Robin Hood that has survived, tells of him
just this story; the *dramatis personae* are changed, and the
Conqueror has become the Sheriff of Nottingham, but the plot
is identical. What makes the coincidence the more striking in
this case is that it is recounted also of a third character, the
Boulonnais outlaw, Eustace the Monk. His story, like Hereward's,

has other close similarities to those of later outlaws. Already, therefore, in the legend of Hereward, we are beginning to come across a stock of incidents common to the legends of this type, which suggests that we may expect to find other affinities, and at the same time cautions us against attaching any direct historical value to an exploit recounted in the ballads.

It is dangerous, of course, to build too much on this instance of the potter. The medieval literary public seems to have had a passion for concealment; whence the pigsty prince, and a host of cavaliers, who, whether from innate modesty or a perverse inclination to keep people guessing, triumphed in innumerable tournaments under equally innumerable disguises. In any case medieval authors were seldom original, and the same stock

The Sheriff's wife entertains Robin Hood disguised as the Potter.

incident can appear in a whole series of unconnected cycles. But in this case behind the similarity of incident there lies a more basic similarity of theme. The popularity of the outlaws and their reputation did not rest, as in the case of their later counterparts, the 'gentlemen of the road' like Dick Turpin, upon the mere glamour of courteous thieving. Their stories were popular because they were part of a literature of popular protest. They were not just defying accepted authority, they were fighting against it because it was unjust, and it was this that made them heroes for the common people who were the victims of this same injustice. In the case of Hereward one does not have to look far to see the nature of the injustice against which he was protesting. The Norman Conquest had not just meant a change of dynasty for England, as had Cnut's conquest forty years earlier. It was a national catastrophe, which affected rich and poor alike. As late as the fourteenth century the extent of the disaster was still remembered; a popular preacher could still then remind his listeners of the death-bed prophecy of Edward the Confessor, that for the sins of the country retribution should follow when he was gone, when for a year and a day the land should lie at the mercy of enemies, and demons should haunt the soil. Its awful fulfilment was familiar to them.

What, in a few words, did the Norman Conquest mean for England? It meant, in the first place, the harrying of great tracts of land; twenty years after the Conqueror's arrival, when the 'Domesday' survey was compiled, a trail of wasted villages still marked the line of his march upon London. In the north, devastation had been systematic; where once Earl Tostig had held sixteen manors near Preston it is reported that the land was now deserted, and the jurors summoned for the survey could not say who dwelt there or whether anyone did. It meant also the disinheriting, by main force or by slow stages of depression, of the whole class of English landowners. There are only two English names surviving among those who, in the Domesday survey, are listed as tenants-in-chief of the king. The case of those Englishman who do still hold their land is more usually that of, for instance, Ailric of Marsh Gibbon, who, as the book tells us, held his lands freely in the time of King Edward, but in 1086 was holding it 'at rent, heavily and wretchedly'; or the Warwickshire Hereward, once a free man, but now the man of Ogier the Breton. Ailnoth of Canterbury, an English exile who was writing at much the same time at the court of the King of Denmark, says that the English nobles had all been slain or imprisoned, driven from the land, disinherited or reduced to public servitude. For the many the Conquest meant the substitution for old, often beloved masters of new lords, of a foreign race, who spoke a strange tongue and obeyed unfamiliar laws. For the monasteries and clergy it meant new, foreign, and no doubt often unsympathetic superiors. For the peasant again it meant new masters, and in many areas, especially East Anglia, the loss of old freedoms. The Domesday survey shows more and more of the free sokemen of the Danelaw, who had held land freely in the villages in the time of King Edward, being depressed into the ranks of the unfree villeinage. It meant new and harsh laws; above all, and significantly from our point of view, the introduction of the Forest Laws.

The object of the Forest Law was to preserve the king's game. It ran in all those places which William the Conqueror chose to call his forest, and these included wide areas of cultivated land as well as woodland and waste. It protected at once the beasts of the wood and their covers, and the peasant who was rash enough to interfere with the animals which trampled his crops or to clear bushes on a plot of waste land rendered himself liable to awful penalties. It was an arbitrary law, founded in the king's will; this meant that the poacher could be arrested on suspicion and left to linger years in gaol awaiting the convenience of the Forest Justices for his case to be tried. He could seek no redress at common law for the hardships he had suffered, for affairs of the forests were not subject to the common law. The Conqueror enforced this new law ruthlessly. Even the Norman chroniclers, whose purpose was to sing his praises, wring their hands in horror over the destruction of entire villages and the eviction of their inhabitants when he claimed the whole New Forest as his game reserve. Such were the results of William's and his son's inordinate love of the chase, for 'he loved the tall stags as if he were their father'. Little wonder that men saw in the death of William Rufus, killed out hunting in his father's New Forest, a direct judgement of God.

There was no class in the community, in fact, but felt the dire and immediate consequences of the Norman Conquest. That it had brought benefits to compensate for these is doubtless true, but for our purpose this is not relevant. What is important for us is that the old order of things had been swept away overnight, a native aristocracy expelled and a native culture driven underground, with immense accompanying hardship for a whole race.

This in itself would be enough to explain the popularity of Hereward and his kind, the last Englishmen to be found in arms against the new order. But one must remember what manner of men the Anglo-Saxons were. They were a proud race with a distinguished history, arrogant, like all the Teutons, of their descent and of the deeds of their ancestors, with an insular culture of their own which, if it had lost some if its one-time vigour, was still a long way from degeneracy. Though it is dangerous to speak of nationalism in this period, an intense tribal loyalty was one of the most important legacies of the Germanic world to the Middle Ages, and the Anglo-Saxons had their full inheritance of it. There is no sign that this spirit was weakening appreciably in the last years of Anglo-Saxon history; the famous poem on the Battle of Maldon, written about the year 1000, is every whit as imbued with it as any earlier work, and a poem which appears in the *Anglo-Saxon Chronicle* on Edward's death on the very eve of the Conquest tells the same story of loyalty to the homeland—or rather, perhaps to the race. It tells how Edward, after Cnut had overcome Ethelred's kin and ruled the 'dear kingdom' for twenty-three winters, had returned to rule his own people, 'the Angles and Saxons, mighty in battle'. This prowess in war was no boast based on the memory of long past victories; Harold's brief reign in 1066 had seen enough time for the overthrow of Tostig, the rebel Earl, and of Harold Hardraada, saga hero and King of Norway. The housecarles of Harold's bodyguard at Hastings lived up to their Germanic code of military honour; they died, almost to a man, in a last stand about the body of their fallen King. This spirit of loyalty to native lords was strongest, no doubt, among the upper classes, down to the lesser nobles, so many of whom lost their land in the upheaval of the Conquest. But it was felt lower in the social scale too; we must not forget Dunnere, the simple churl, who in the Maldon poem was as ready to die with his lord as any of his superiors. There is nothing to surprise us in the fact that Hereward should have become a hero for all classes of the conquered English people. All alike, or almost all, had suffered in the disaster, and all, or almost all, shared in that pride of race that his last stand, at Ely and after, enshrined.

Of his popularity and its extent there is evidence enough. The endless proliferations and variations of his story make it clear that it had been told a hundred times and a hundred different ways. The tradition in the *Gesta* of his putting away of Turfrida and of his second marriage is almost certainly only a clumsy effort to reconcile two different accounts. We have three different stories of his end; in the *Gesta* he lives to die in peace; in Gaimar he is surprised by his Norman enemies in his own home; in another account he is killed in a quarrel with his own son-in-law, Hugh de Ewermouthe. The accretions to his story are all designed to enhance a popular fame; he becomes a hero of romantic adventures, and his eulogists find for him kinship with the highest aristocracy of the Anglo-Saxon race; in one account he is the grandson of the Confessor's famous Earl of Mercia, Leofric; in another, the nephew of Ralph the Staller. His fame among his own people was not only widespread, moreover; it was lasting. In the thirteenth century men still went to visit the ruined wooden structure in the Fens which was called Hereward's Castle. The *Book of Ely*, written a hundred years after his exploits, says that songs of him were still sung in the taverns by the common people. Ingulph tells the same story; 'his deeds are still sung to this day on the king's highway'. Ingulph is a fraud of the late fourteenth century and his evidence must not be taken at its face value. It may be that the author is following up, with the instinct of a skilled forger, a chance remark in some earlier chronicle which will lend his story that kind of antiquarian touch which he knows will render it convincing. This is possible; but Crowland, where he wrote, is near enough to the scene of Hereward's exploits to make it more probable that he had heard such songs himself, and that the outlaw's fame had lasted, at least locally, for something like three centuries.

As we might expect, Hereward was not the only leader of the Anglo-Saxon resistance to become a hero of popular stories. Twice the *Gesta* makes reference to one Brumannus, who captured a Norman abbot and ducked him in the sea in a sack. The author seems to expect his readers to find the story familiar enough, but no other traditions concerning this obscure figure survive. About Eadric the Wild, who was in revolt in the marches of Wales between the years 1067 and 1069, legends also seem to have collected. In the chronicles of Wygmore Abbey we find apocryphal stories of his struggles with the Norman lord, Ralph de Mortemer. In Walter Mapes' *Book of Courtiers' Trifles*, written at the end of the twelfth century, we find Eadric, like Hereward, becoming the hero of romantic adventure. Walter tells how Eadric, wandering in the forest by night, came upon a house in the remote woods, within which a group of beautiful girls were playing. Eadric entered, and before the morning he had won one of them to be his bride. So they left the forest, and for a few years lived together, until one day Eadric asked her whether she did not wish ever to revisit her sisters. Hardly had he spoken than the fairy-wife vanished; nor was he ever able again to find the house in the forest. The story is not original; it is a country tale told, with a few variations, a hundred times of different characters and in different places. It reveals at once how all kinds of extraneous matter began to enter the legends once they were popularized, and how Hereward and Eadric and their like soon became, for the country people, suitable heroes for every kind of story, even though their principal fame was as outlaws.

These are the only three Saxon leaders whose reputation as outlaws has survived. No doubt there were others of whom ballads were also sung, but their names are sunk without trace. Probably their stories were never put into writing, but passed down from father to son in the country until they went out of fashion. Their disappearance from recorded history is hardly surprising; after all, no single ballad of Hereward or Eadric in the native language has survived, the reason no doubt being that they were the literary property of the conquered and oppressed. In any case resistance after the first few years cannot have risen above the level of sporadic brigandry. Later chronicles are equally silent about the doings of local outlaws, though we know from other evidence that such men must have existed. These few indications suggest that in some places there were restive elements for years after the Conquest; the murdrum fine, for instance, which the Conqueror ordered to be levied on any township within whose bounds a man was found killed and which could not produce a culprit. If the inhabitants were unable to prove that the man was English, the fine rose to the enormous sum of forty-six marks. One imagines that the aim of this measure can only have been to discourage local populations from conniving at the crimes of those who bore ill-will to the French.

Otherwise we have to imagine for ourselves the history of resistance to the Norman from a few scattered and quite general remarks in the chronicles. There is one of these, however, that is so illuminating that it seems to be worth quoting exactly. It comes from a late source, the thirteenth-century chronicle known as the *Flowers of History*. The passage is describing the end of William's reign and the peace which he established; nevertheless, it declares, to the last there were pockets of resistance. 'Those of the English who were of gentle birth were driven from their lands; they could not dig, to beg they were ashamed. So with their kindred they took refuge in the woods, living by what they could hunt, and only falling back on raiding when all else failed them'. A few sentences later the author elaborates; 'in their lairs in the woods and waste places . . . they laid a thousand secret ambushes and traps for the Normans'. Two things are significant about these statements. Firstly, the writer seems to have been aware of traditions of widespread, if disorganized, resistance to the Normans. Secondly, his picture of the way of life of these Saxon nobles is an almost perfect description of that of the traditional outlaws. Cut out his references to Saxon and Norman, and he might just as well be writing of Robin Hood. All the correct elements are there. The Saxons take to the woods and live by hunting just as did the later outlaws. They too are not mere brigands; their enemies are those who represent the forces of injustice, the Norman lords and abbots, whose tyranny and usurpations justify any nemesis that may overtake them. To their own people, the chronicler implies, the outlaws would be, except perhaps at the pinch of extreme necessity, courteous enough. Outlawry, we see, is already justified by its own internal code. The incidents in the life of Hereward, the only outlaw of whom any connected stories survive, bear out the description of the *Flowers of History*. Hereward never lived by indiscriminate plunder. Those he fought were the captains and instruments of the new tyranny, whose characters were revealed in their actions; the Normans who had slain his brother and usurped his lands; the French abbot who had secured succession to Peterborough, among the proudest of the old English monasteries; Ivo de Taillebois, who could unhesitatingly stoop to enlisting the aid of sorceresses against his enemies. On the one occasion on which Hereward did fall to plundering, his eulogists show him returning his treasure freely to its owners (though this is quite mythical; the treasures of Peterborough were carried away by the Danes and lost, with most of their fleet, in a great storm on the North Sea). All through his story Hereward conforms to the morality of the later, mythical outlaws, and for the same reason, that his acts of violence are acts of protest against injustice. This is why he is a popular hero, and it is this basic theme in his legend that links it most closely with that of Robin Hood.

The basis of the fame of Hereward, which was lasting, is, as we have said, the reputation of a native hero struggling against a hated conqueror, yet historians have little to say of hatred of the Norman or resistance to him. Reasons have been suggested why the exploits of isolated outlaws might have escaped the notice of the chroniclers, but if the popularity of the stories of Hereward and Eadric were the only evidence of the sentiments of the conquered race, this interpretation would rest on tenuous ground. Most historians have on the whole been inclined to write down the longevity of racial malaise after the Norman Conquest; it did not endure long, they tell us, after the turn of the eleventh and twelfth centuries. They can quote in their favour evidence; Henry I's strategic marriage with Edith-Matilda, who had inherited the claim of the English royal house of Cerdic's descendants; Ailred of Rievaulx's complaint that Stephen's usurpation had once again broken the ties of the crown with that same royal family; Richard FitzNeale's statement in his *Dialogue of the Exchequer* (dateable to about 1180) that 'today the two nations are so mingled that one can barely tell apart who is of Norman, who of the English blood'. If this is the whole picture, Hereward can hardly be claimed as enjoying a lasting popularity as the hero of a downtrodden race.

There is, however, other evidence. Down to the end of the reign of Rufus, the *Anglo-Saxon Chronicle* with its continuous references to the French makes it clear that they were thought of as a race apart, and these kinds of distinctions do not die overnight. The scornful English nicknames which the Normans found for Henry I and his wife, 'Godric and Godgifu', show that at least in his reign the feeling was not just one-sided. The words which Ailred of Rievaulx puts into the mouth of Bishop Walter Espec, when he rallied his forces before the Battle of the Standard, fought against the Scots in 1139, witness that on the Norman side these feelings had lasted. It was not to English, but to Norman pride and Norman history that he appealed: 'It was our fathers' he cried 'who conquered this island and imposed our laws upon it . . . and who was it but your Norman who over-ran far kingdoms, Apulia, Calabria, Sicily?' This appeal to the Norman blood becomes less startling when we read in *Orderic Vitalis* that a bare two years previously, in 1137, a plot had been discovered to kill all the Normans in England on the same day and to hand over the kingdom to the Scots. As late as the first years of Stephen's reign, clearly, some embers of the old English resentment of the Frenchmen's yoke were still smouldering.

Orderic's brief notice of this plot is sadly vague, and one is left wondering who were these Englishmen who, so many years after the Conquest, were planning still the downfall of the foreign lords? The first half of the twelfth century is generally said to have witnessed the nadir of native English fortunes; the men whom Henry I 'raised from the dust to do him service' were almost all, despite his English marriage, men of French extrac-tion, though there is some evidence that in his time already a slow native recovery seems to begin. It is at this point that one is reminded of an important reservation on the passage quoted from Richard FitzNeale's *Dialogue* a little way back, in which he describes the mingling of the two races. 'I speak of freemen' he says. We should read this in the light of Ailnoth of Canter-bury's statement that many of the old English lords had been reduced to 'public servitude'. Among the class whom Richard would describe as unfree, that is to say, there were plenty who were not born to bondage, but whose fathers had been reduced to it by hard fortune in the dark days of the Conquest. Very few English families, Stenton writes, can be traced from 1066 into the later middle ages; this applies even to the remote areas in Mercia and Northumbria. Among the unfree classes of the twelfth century, the peasants whom King Henry I saw in his troubled dream threatening him with scythes and pitchforks, there must have been many whose hatred of their French masters was embittered by memories of generations of freedom before 1066.

There are other scattered pieces of evidence. Ailnoth of Canterbury speaks of the great hope and desire of many Englishmen in East Anglia, where most were of Danish stock,

that the Danes would invade England in 1085. Clearly there
were then still lively aspirations among the English that they
might be delivered from the burden of conquest. The twelfth
century was well begun, it appears, when the *Gesta Herewardi*
was written, yet there are passages in it which still pulsate with
racial feeling. There is the account, for instance, of Hereward's
rising anger as he listened to the Norman jester 'pouring
ridicule on the English and attempting to imitate their crude
dances', and the exultation of the story-teller in the flight of all
the Normans of the country round at the rumour of Hereward's
deeds. Right down to its last entry at the end of Stephen's reign,
moreover, the *Anglo-Saxon Chronicle*, the last fragment in the
tradition of old English prose writing, preserves a different tone
to the other chronicles of its age. Even its account of the
anarchy of the civil wars between Stephen and Matilda seems to
preserve a native flavour. It is always 'they' who are at fault;
'*they*' made dire taxes which *they* called tenseries'; '*they* built
castles and *they* filled them with devils and evil men'. It is true,
of course, that the reign of Stephen saw a new influx of for-
eigners, the Flemish mercenaries whom both sides used indis-
criminately. But these surely are the 'devils and evil men'; *they*
are the Norman lords, the alien, irresponsible feudality whose
worse characteristics the failure in a line of strong kings and the
subsequent anarchy had but now fully revealed.

The *Peterborough Saxon Chronicle* is the last major piece of
English writing in the old tradition which has survived, but this
does not mean that it was the only literary work in English of
its day. It is no mere archaic survival, and linguistic scholars
can trace in it and the other contemporary fragments of English
writing signs of developments in forms of speech and modes of
expression which were to come into their own in the later
Middle Ages in the great revival of vernacular literature. The
Norman Conquest could not destroy English culture; what it
could and did do was to force it underground. English literary
composition did not cease, but a great deal of it was subsequently
lost because it was never written down; it was designed for a
public that had lost touch with literacy. So English songs of
Hereward do not survive, but we know they existed, and we
know also of other lost English works of the period. The traces
of their existence form a few more fragmentary links in the

chain of evidence which suggests the survival, long after it had ceased to attract the attention of chroniclers, of English racial feelings. For the subject matter of a great deal of the lost English literature of the twelfth century suggests that throughout this period the heroes of Saxon history remained the most popular figures for those who formed the literary public of authors who wrote or composed in the native tongue.

The traces of this lost literature survive mostly in chance references in chronicles, as in the case of the songs of Hereward. Among the most popular heroes are, as we should expect, the Saxon kings. In East Anglia, at any rate, the fame of Cnut was long remembered; Cnut's rowing song, with its opening line, 'Mury sang the muneches binnen Ely', is one of the oldest snatches of genuine popular poetry to survive from the post-Conquest age. William of Malmesbury tells us that in his time ballads about the marriage of Cnut's daughter Gunnhildis to the Emperor Conrad were still sung in the streets; Matthew Paris writing the best part of a century after him, bears him out:— 'to this day men in their songs in taverns and at gatherings strive vainly to recapture the pomp of that wedding feast'. From what follows in his account it is clear that he is not just following William; there really were ballads of Cnut and Gunnhildis which were still popular in the thirteenth century. Athelstan too caught the eye of William of Malmesbury; 'so far I have written upon good authority' he says suddenly in his account of that king's reign, 'what follows I have learnt rather from ballads and songs handed down through succeeding ages than from books compiled for the enlightenment of posterity'. He embarks then on the strange romance of Athelstan's birth; of the beautiful shepherd girl who saw in a vision the whole of England proceeding from her womb, and was afterwards got with child by King Edward and brought forth a son who was in the end to succeed him. But above all the other old English kings it is Alfred who is celebrated. It is in the twelfth century chronicle of Henry of Huntingdon that the famous apocryphal story of the burnt cakes first appears. In the '*Brut*' of *Layamon*—a surviving English poem from the end of the twelfth century—he is 'England's darling.' For the rest, he seems to have come to be regarded by English people as a sort of native Solomon. His so-called proverbs were collected, and circulated for edification;

in the poem called *The Owl and the Nightingale,* one of the few
literary productions of the thirteenth century which is English in
tone as well as language, a host of sage remarks quoted by the
disputant birds are attributed to his unfailing wisdom. It is clear
that throughout the twelfth century and into the thirteenth the
memory of the Saxon kings was kept alive in oral tradition by a
special reverence for them on the part of those among the population whose language remained English—especially, that is to
say, among the common people.

Kings, however, were not the only Saxon heroes to be kept
in remembrance. The memory of other champions was preserved in song too; the details of the deeds and death of Byrtnoth, for instance, which are preserved in the *Book of Ely* were
probably culled from some later and longer poem than the one
which has survived. Waltheof, the last of the English earls,
whom the Conqueror executed at Winchester, was also long
remembered; miracles were said to have been performed at his
tomb. But perhaps the most interesting of all are traces which
survive of a saga of Earl Godwin, Harold's father, which are
preserved in a whole series of authors. The fullest version is in
Walter Mapes' already quoted *Book of Courtiers' Trifles*; it is,
alas, incomplete. It recounts how King Ethelred, while out
hunting, strayed from his companions, and, wandering by night,
sought shelter at length from the cold in the house of a cowherd.
There he was hospitably entertained, and especially by the
herdsman's son Godwin, a boy 'better and more comely than his
parentage might have argued'. In the end he so charmed the
King that he took him into his own service and in due course he
became Earl of Gloucester (there was no Earl of Gloucester in
Saxon times; this shows how the tale has been brought up to
date by successive generations of raconteurs). The story here
unfortunately changes suddenly; it degenerates into the tale of
how Godwin raped the nuns of Berkely and cheated the Archbishop of Canterbury of his lands at Bosham. What in fact has
happened is that Walter has lost track of the English story and
that we are now getting the other side; 'the splendid youth of
epic legend has become the crafty and greedy politician of
Norman calumnies'. This is most significant; we are finding at
the end of the twelfth century a story which has two contrary
versions which are specifically English and French. The

evidence for the English epic is borne out by passages from the *Knytlinga Saga* and from *Radulphus Niger* which tally with the first part of Mapes' story; the tale was clearly well enough known. Taken together with the Norman tale, it is a striking instance of the survival of racial feelings in literature.

What all this rather literary information suggests is that racial feelings which spelt resentment of Norman lordship lasted longer than has often been supposed. This, after all, is only what we should expect; the memory of the common people is the longest on earth, the Norman Conquest had been a disaster for their race, and the everyday world preserved endless circumstances to remind men of it, in new laws resulting in unfamiliar inconveniences and inhibitions, for instance, and in the domination of men who spoke a different tongue. That past misfortunes and present discomforts and indignities should be resented was only natural. This does not of course mean that for a century or more after the Conquest the embers of an English revolt needed only the breath of a leader to fan them into flame. It does, however, provide a background for the legends of Hereward and the other outlaws, of a fond admiration for men who had once had the courage to defy the injustices which most men had sullenly accepted. It reveals their popularity not as some isolated phenomenon, but as in tune with sentiments which were probably for many years very general among the conquered race. It was to be the same later; many peasants may have listened wistfully to the songs of Robin Hood, and resentment at the injustice of the legal system was spread wide enough, but very few ever had the courage to follow him into open revolt against their lords.

Literary evidence, however, when historical evidence to back it is not forthcoming, cannot suggest more than lingering sentiments, and by the end of the twelfth century the Norman Conquest and the hardships it brought with it must have been passing out of mind. The present circumstances of the average peasant were hard enough; there was no need for him to hark back to long-past grievances to find matter of complaint against his lord. Richard Coeur de Lion was, significantly, the first English king after the Conquest to become in course of time a popular hero. Chronicle memories of the deeds of Hereward and other Saxon leaders become, after the turn of the new century, vague and perfunctory. Matthew Paris remembers a name and the siege of Ely, little more. In due course, no doubt, the common people too forgot their one-time favourite; by the time that the compositions of ballad-writers begin to survive in any number, his name has lapsed from the list of popular heroes. It would be attractive here, having reviewed the many similarities that link the legends of Hereward and Robin Hood, to try and relate more closely their background, to suggest that it was the Norman Conquest that first set the fashion for outlaw legends, and that, as time passed, it was merely the racial element that was forgotten, while the struggle against tyrannous lords was remembered. So Hereward's fame as an outlaw would last until new favourites eclipsed him, while his fame as a Saxon would pass out of memory. There are a few scraps of evidence which might be taken to confirm such a view. There is for instance the fact that as time went on the Saxon heroes seem to have been more and more associated by the peasantry with themselves; Athelstan and Godwin find for themselves in twelfth-century legend peasant pedigrees, and Alfred is found wandering among his common people disguised as a countryman. The constant appeals of those who felt themselves injured in their liberties to the ancient laws of Edward the Confessor seem to reflect the attitude of a generation which looked back to the pre-Conquest era as a golden age. Much later again, in the time of the Peasant's Revolt, we find the rebels appealing to ancient charters of the Saxon kings which, they declared, had long ago guaranteed their liberties which lords in subsequent ages had usurped. The men of St Albans appealed to a lost charter of Offa, those of Bury to one of Cnut. Surely, it might be said, here is an indication that as time went on pre-Conquest memories became associated with the social grievances of the common people which seem to have grown steadily as the middle ages progressed. So Hereward would become in memory the champion of popular rights, and thus the ancestor of Robin Hood not only in his literary genre but also as the hero of the oppressed poor. In the end, however, the evidence is too slight to support more than a very tentative suggestion. Others than the poor looked back to the Saxon period to find justification for supposed liberties. Even men of baronial rank appealed to the Laws of Edward. The remote history of the old English period was also a fruitful source for the spurious claims of, for instance, acquisitive monastic houses and bishops anxious for metropolitan priority; the forger of Ingulph, of whom we have heard, found space for some useful, if apocryphal, Saxon charters granting lands to his abbey of Crowland in his *soi-disant* ancient chronicle. One cannot with any safety go further than pointing to a similarity of theme in a literature which appealed to the oppressed when the oppressor was a conquering Norman and one where the oppressor was a corrupt lord or sheriff. The evidence is too uncertain to allow this parallel to be developed into a more direct connexion.

For the moment it must be enough to have shown that there is a connexion between Hereward and the later outlaws, not only on account of the manner of their lives and actions as recounted in the histories, but also because their popularity resulted from the same sort of situation. In both cases their popular appeal was as men who had set themselves openly against the forces of injustice. We have seen how far legend founded in this reputation romanticized the historical Hereward, the fenland robber who plundered Peterborough, until he is barely recognizable. If there was a Robin Hood, we should therefore hardly expect to recognize his true features from the character credited to him in legends which have been elaborated to enhance the fame of an idealized outlaw.

IV

The Romance of Fulk Fitzwarin

THERE are two sides to the character of the Hereward of legend. There is the romantic hero who grapples with overgrown bears and wins the hearts of princesses, and there is the fenland robber, the idol of the oppressed Saxons. When, a hundred and fifty years after his time, in the reign of King John, we hear once more of two outlaw heroes, Fulk Fitzwarin and Eustace the Monk, we find the same themes interwoven in their stories. Already, however, the two elements, Round Table romance, and stories of chivalrous brigandage, are beginning to find literary partnership uncomfortable. In the story of Fulk Fitzwarin magical encounters and chivalrous adventure, though introduced as episodes, really provide the main interest; his outlawry and his long struggle with King John are only the background theme, lending its unconnected incidents some shadow of continuity. In the story of Eustace the Monk, on the other hand, the magic is cut to a minimum: it provides a burlesque beginning and an epic end to the tale. Clearly, we are coming near to a parting of the ways; in the later stories, of Gamelyn and Robin Hood and Adam Bell, chivalrous adventures in a world of enchantment find no place. The gradual disappearance of this element from the stories is striking, when one remembers how later writers have tried to see in Robin Hood

39

the devotee of a witch religion or the folk memory of a pagan god.

There is no question here that this last possibility may lie behind the popularity of the outlaw legends, for both Fulk Fitzwarin and Eustace the Monk were, like Hereward, real historical characters. Fulk was one of the many unruly barons of John's reign: indeed he was among those whose rising in 1215 ultimately forced the King to grant Magna Carta. He came of a family whose lands lay in the Welsh Marches, always a wild and dangerous area, and the story of his disorderly career then dated back to the very beginning of the reign. It was indeed his adventures as an outlaw in John's first years of kingship that supplied the historical basis about which his legend grew up, and though we do not know much of his doings, there is no doubt that he was at that time the head of an outlaw band. It was the favour shown to his marcher rival, Maurice of Powis, that led him to defy the King and put himself outside the law (here the dry records of the Exchequer bear out the details in the later legend); this probably came about early in the year 1200. Shropshire was his usual haunt as a brigand; in 1201 one Simon de Lenz was being paid by the King to hunt down the outlaws there. But he ranged far and wide; in 1202 he was besieged by men of the county in Stanley Abbey in Wiltshire, but he seems to have escaped, perhaps through their lack of vigilance. He certainly by now had a compact band of his own; when he was pardoned next year, thirty-eight persons were also forgiven who had been outlawed for being in his company, and we know there were others who had been outlaws even before Fulk's time and had joined forces with him. This is all we know of his doings as an outlaw, but it is enough for our purpose. Though Fulk lived many years into Henry III's reign, to die full of years and prosperity, the story that he was once a forest outlaw has its foundation in fact. We have no grounds to credit the historical Fulk, a rough border baron, with any specially admirable characteristics; his apotheosis into a romantic hero helps to show how in the outlaw legend the realities of history have been idealized.

The legendary story of Fulk Fitzwarin which later grew up has come down to us through a romance in French prose which survives in a single manuscript, probably of the reign of

Edward I. This must, however, have been based on an older version, for verse rhythms keep breaking through the style. Leland, the great Tudor antiquary, knew the story from a poem in English alliterative verse, doubtless intended for a less sophisticated audience, but this poem has, alas, disappeared; already in Leland's time the manuscript was imperfect, for he had to supply the ending from a French version. 'Here lakkyd a quire or two in the olde Englisch booke of the nobile acts of the Guarines' he wrote 'and these things that folow I translatid owte of an olde French historie or Rime.'—perhaps the verse original of our story. Once upon a time, clearly, the fame of Fulk was familiar enough in English legend, but time and the accidents of history which preserve one manuscript and mislay another, have obliterated the memory of his former popularity.

Fulk's great fortress, over the possession of which he first fell out with King John, was Whittington, or, as the French romance has it, Blauncheville in Blauncheland. The story of how it came to his family had become the stuff of legend already when the romance was written. Payn Peverel, who came with the Conqueror, wrested it from the power of an evil spirit, who walked in the body of the dead giant Geomagog, whom one of the followers of Brut the Trojan had flung from a rock into the sea. This evil spirit, when he was driven from the land, granted to Payn the lordship of 'all the honour of Blaunche Lande', and revealed to him in an enigmatic prophecy the future of his race there. But it would never reveal to him the whereabouts of Geomagog's treasure. The Giant had possessed, he told Payn 'swans, peacocks, horses, and all other beasts moulded in fine gold; and he had a golden bull, which . . . was his prophet, in whom he placed all his faith. . . . Twice in the year the giants were wont to honour their god, which is the golden bull, by whom all this marvellous store of gold was collected.' The discovery of that, said the spirit, was reserved for another: it remains, as far as we know, buried in Blaunch Launde to this day.

William Peverell, Payn's son, left a beautiful daughter, Mellette of the Blaunche Tour, and in a great jousting before the King, Fulk's grandfather, Sir Guarin de Meez, won her hand and all the inheritance of Whittington. For a long while the story-teller lingers over the wars with Welsh princes and with the other barons of the Welsh border which Sir Guarin and his son, Fulk le Brun, waged, and how they became the trusted councillors first of King Henry, and later of his son, Richard Coeur de Lion. Fulk le Brun married Hawyse, daughter of Sir Joyce de Dinan, who brought him half her father's lands. They had together four sons, Fulk, William, Philip the Red and Alan, who were brought up at the Court of King Henry.

With Richard the young Fulk got on well enough, but with John, whose proverbial badness seems to have started early, he fell out from the first. With a charming contempt for the idea of historical cause, the writer of the story ascribes their bad relations to a nursery quarrel during which John broke a chessboard over Fulk's head, for which he received a whipping, which he never forgave. So when Richard died and John came to the throne Fulk's rising fortunes were reversed. His old enemy of the Marches, Morys Fitz Roger, was quick to seize the opportunity; he sent to the King a warhorse and a white gerfalcon, and he begged him in return to grant him Fulk's honour of Blauncheville. John promised that whatever Morys should put in writing he would seal with his great seal, and Fulk, after a stormy interview, renounced his homage to him. He and all his relatives took flight for Brittany.

The story of Fulk, as it follows on from this point, is long and has the same aimless episodic quality as the story of Hereward as it is told in the *Gesta*. I shall not, therefore, attempt to recount all its unconnected incident, or even to observe strictly the order of the narrative, but shall try to give enough to convey the quality of the story and something of its atmosphere.

Fulk was long in flight from the wrath of King John. Sometimes, with a few companions, he was living in the forests, wandering from one waste place to another, always eluding pursuit by a thousand stratagems, and preying meanwhile upon the tyrant's lands and his men. Sometimes he found an asylum in the courts of other princes, with Llewellyn the Prince of Wales or with Philip Augustus the King of France, John's arch-enemy. Twice he sailed to distant lands, and there it was that there befell him many marvellous adventures, which savour more of the deeds of a Knight of the Round Table than of those of an unruly border baron of the thirteenth century. On his first journey he sailed with Mador de Russie, whose ancestors to the third and fourth generations had been drowned at sea, and his voyage took him north to the Kingdom of Orceanie beyond Scotland and south to the dukedom of Carthage. In Orkney he rescued the King's daughter from the hands of seven robber chiefs, the sons of a witch, who lived in a rich cavern on a remote island. In Carthage he overcame a monster or dragon that lived upon human flesh in a mountain on the sea, which had carried off the daughter of the Duke of Yberie. The writer seems to have got well confused as to the nature of this beast. When Fulk is fighting with it he describes a huge winged reptile, like the traditional dragon of St. George. Elsewhere, however, it appears as a half human monster, more like Grendel whom Beowulf, the hero of the old English poem, slew, and which also preyed on human flesh. It lived in a house upon the mountain with a great door, and the duke's daughter told Fulk how 'when his hideous face and his beard were smeared with blood, then he would come to me and cause me to wash with clear water his face and his beard and his breast.' When he had killed the dragon, Fulk took the cool gold upon which alone it could sleep, because of the hot fire in its belly, and having returned the princess to her father, sailed back to England.

Later, when he was again hard pressed by John's followers and had been wounded in battle, Fulk went back to his friend Mador, and set out on his second voyage. This time his ship broke adrift while his companions were ashore on the coast of Spain, and he finally came to land in a Kingdom of the Saracens. By them he was courteously received and healed of his wounds, and finally, after fighting for them in single combat with a Christian knight—(who turned out, by one of those coincidences which could only occur in the romances of chivalry, to be his brother Alan, now the Champion of the Duchess of Carthage)— united their country with that of Yberie, married their King to the same lady whom he had once saved from the dragon, and converted them to Christianity. Having dealt briefly with this fairly heavy assignment, he and his companions took ship again with Mador, and returned to England and to the serious business of fighting King John.

For these voyages to distant lands were no more, really, than colourful interludes in the tale of Fulk's long battle with the tyrant who was reigning in his native land. Throughout this part of the narrative he plays the part of a real outlaw, wandering with a few faithful followers in wild places, always on the move, for John's vindictive anger pursued him everywhere. At one time we hear of him in the forest of Babbyng, near his own Blaunchville, laying ambush for Morys Fitz Roger; at another moment he is in the forest of Kent, and then next we find him lurking in the waste places of the Scottish Marches. Twice John's hunting parties fell in with him and his outlaws; once it was in the New Forest, the other time in the woods of Windsor. Of the three children his wife bore him while he was an outlaw, two were born in the Church's sanctuary, the third, another Fulk, 'was born upon a mountain of Wales, and was baptized in a stream which came from the Maid's Well.' Often Fulk and his men were succoured by friends and sympathizers, for none cared much for the evil king, and he counted among his kindred the greatest lords of the land; indeed it was said among John's foreign favourites that 'all the English nobles were cousins to Sir Fulk, and therefore traitors to the King, and would not take these felons'. But for this, they could never have faced the king, and indeed in his struggle with him, Fulk was reduced to a war of stratagems; the story of it is a tale of ambushes and disguises, of daring rescues and flight into the thick forest. It is all very reminiscent of Hereward's war in the Fenland, when after the fall of Ely he with only a handful of Englishmen held his own against the Conqueror in the recesses of the marshes and woods. Fulk's men too, like Hereward's, preyed only on their true enemy, King John and his servants. They were no brigands; and when the northern robber, Piers de Bruville, took Fulk's name to cover his banditry, a terrible revenge overtook him. Surprised by Fulk in the hall of a house which he was raiding, he was forced to bind his men in their seats and to behead every one of them with his own hands; when the ugly task was finished, his own head was struck off, for, said Fulk, 'none should ever charge him falsely with theft'. In all this we see an outlaw of the traditional stamp, observing his own rules in a war against oppression.

Fulk's private code of robbery is best illustrated in the incident of his plunder of John's merchants, one of the two or three episodes of his story which seems really to anticipate the deeds of Robin Hood. Fulk and his companions had made their lair in 'the forest of Bradene', and, while they were there, there passed that way under a strong escort ten burgesses, 'merchants who had purchased with the money of the King of England the richest cloths, furs, spices and dresses'. Fulk sent his men to summon them to come to speak with their master in the forest, and though they refused at first, they soon surrendered, and were led away into the woods. 'Fulk took them into the forest, where they told him they were the King's merchants. When Fulk heard this he was much pleased, and he said to them "Sir merchants, if you lose this property, on whom will fall the loss? Tell me the truth." "Sir" said they "If we lose it through our cowardice, or by our own want of proper care, the loss will fall upon ourselves: but if we lose it otherwise, by danger of the sea, or by force, the loss will fall upon the King." "Are you speaking the truth?" "Assuredly, Sir," said they. When Fulk understood the loss would be the King's, then he measured the rich cloth and the costly fur with his lance, and he clothed all who were with him, little and big, in this rich cloth, and to each he gave according to his degree, but everyone had a liberal allowance. Of the other goods, each took what he liked. When evening came and the merchants had dined heartily, he recommended them to God, and asked them to salute the King in the name of Fulk Fitzwarin, who thanked him much for their good dresses.'

This same story is told later, with only a little variation, in the *Lyttel Geste* of *Robin Hood*. There it is the cellarer of St. Mary's Abbey who travels by the forest, and who is overcome, he and his escorts, by Little John, who leads him to Robin in the woods. In his house in the forest, Robin bids the monk welcome, for he must, he says, have brought him the money which Our Lady owes to him, for:

> 'She was a borowe (surety)', sayd Robyn,
>   'Between a knyght and me,
> Of a lytel money that I hym lent
> . Under the grene wode tree.'

How much money, asks Robin, has the monk in his coffers?

> 'What is in your cofers?' sayd Robyn .
>   'Trewe than tell thou me.'
> 'Syr', he said, 'twenty marke
>   Al so mote I the (prosper)'.

So, at his master's behest, Little John empties the coffers, and there is revealed eight hundred pounds and more. Robin takes from the monk all but the 'spending money' he has claimed; then he bids him to drink with him, and sends him on his way with a message of thanks to Our Lady who has made repayment, for there is none more prompt in paying her debts in all England.

> 'Fyll of ye best wine, do hym drynke,' sayd Robin,
>   'And grete well thy Lady hende (kind);
> And yf she have nede of Robyn Hode,
>   A frend she shall hym fynde.'

So the monk rides on, with the same bitter vows and ironical greeting for his master, the Abbot of Our Lady's monastery, which Fulk Fitzwarin sent by the merchants to King John.

One other adventure of Fulk's is almost identical with a story told later of Robin Hood. This is the episode in Windsor Forest, where Fulk had learnt from the peasants that John would be hunting. So when he and his men heard outside the wood the horns of the hunters, they determined to get the King into their power. Fulk left his companions in ambush, and proceeded alone.

Fulk went on and met an old collier, with whom he exchanged his clothes, and he soon busied himself about tending the man's fire with his great iron fork. By and by the King came past with three knights and saw the man working, and Fulk threw himself on his knees and saluted him with exaggerated humility. ' "Sir villein" said the King "have you seen any stag or doe pass this way?" "Yes my lord, some time ago." "What beast did you see?" "Sire my lord, one horned, it had long horns." "Where is it?" "Sire, I can very easily lead you where I have seen it." "Go on then, sir villein, and we will follow you. . . ." So Fulk took the great fork of iron in his hand, and he conducted the King to shoot, for he had a very fair bow. "Sire", said Fulk, "would it please you that I should go into the thicket, and cause the beast to come this way"; "Yes" said the King. Fulk hastily leaped into the thick of the forest, and ordered his band hastily to take King John "for I have led him here with only three of his knights, and all his retinue is in the other part of the forest." Fulk and his band rushed out of the thicket and saw the King, and took him immediately. "Sir King," said Fulk "now I have you in my power; shall I pass such a sentence upon you as you would upon me if you had taken me?'' The King trembled for fear, for he had a great dread of Fulk, and Fulk swore that he should die for the great damage and disinheriting he had done upon many a good man in England. The King cried him mercy, and begged his life for the love of God, and swore that he would restore to him entirely all his inheritance and whatsoever he had taken from him or any of his; and that thereto he would give him in all things such security as he himself could propose. Fulk granted him well all his demands, upon condition that in presence of all these knights, he would give his faith to keep this covenant. The King pledged him his faith that he would keep covenant with him, and was glad enough to be able to thus escape.'

Neither Robin Hood nor any of his men, it is true, ever changed clothes with a charcoal burner: it was Eustace the Monk, who had something like a mania for disguises, who did that. But otherwise the story in the *Lyttel Geste* is substantially the same. John's role is played by the Sheriff of Nottingham; Little John takes the main lead, having disguised himself earlier and served the Sheriff under the name of Reynold Grenelefe. So when he meets the Sheriff his master hunting in Sherwood, he like Fulk falls on his knees before him. He has seen 'as fair a sight as ever yet he saw', a great horned stag:

'Yonder I se a ryght fayre hart
His colour is of grene'

The Sheriff, by some miracle of gullibility, misses the ironic reference here to Robin Hood, and like John, he lets himself be led right into the lair of the outlaws. But Robin, for the love of Little John, consents to spare him, though he tells him he shall be his prisoner for a year. But the Sheriff casts himself on Robin's mercy, and in the end he swears the same oath as John and is released:—

'Let me go, then' sayd the sheryf,
'For seynt Charyte;
And I wyll be thy beste frende
That ever yet had the.'

'Thou shalt swere me an othe', sayd Robyn,
'On my bryght brand,
Thou shalt never awayte me scathe
By water ne by land.

And thou fynde any of my men,
　　By night or by day,
Upon thyne othe thou shalt swere
　　To helpe them that thou may.'

It is the very same oath in fact as Fulk made the King swear,
down to the condition that all his men shall be under the same
pardon. There is a moral in this. No doubt there is a good deal
in the legend of Fulk Fitzwarin that is historically true or at
least has some basis in fact (the author is, for instance, sur-
prisingly accurately informed about Fulk's relations), but it is
clear in the light of these shared episodes that there is a good
deal of stock incident as well. In the case of Robin Hood, one
may well wonder whether there is anything more than elaborated stock incident in the whole of his history. We are already
beginning to find too many of his adventures undertaken by
older heroes, to give them much credit as containing even a
residue of fact.

Fulk's fortunes as an outlaw ebbed and flowed; like Robin
Hood, he always ultimately escaped from peril, but at times he
was hard enough pressed. Once he was wounded in battle with
the King's men, almost to death; twice faithful followers from
his company fell into John's hands. These catastrophes set the
stage for two great rescue scenes; and here again there is a
distant reminiscence of the adventures of later outlaws, of the
rescue of William of Cloudisley from Carlisle in the ballad of
Adam Bell, or the rescue of Robin Hood, after he had been betrayed coming to Nottingham to hear the Mass. The hero of
these two incidents in Fulk's legend is the strange figure,
Johan de Rampaygne, 'a Soothsayer, a jocular, and minstralle',
a man of a thousand ruses, who knew distant lands and langu-
ages, and had learnt the strange qualities of plants for healing
and other purposes, so that he was to Fulk almost as useful as a
private magician. The first of these two incidents is the rescue of
Ardulf de Bracy, who had been unhorsed and taken in a skirmish
with John's knights and carried to Shrewsbury Castle, where he
was kept under close guard by Sir Henry de Audelee. John de
Rampaygne made his way alone into the castle, having stained
his skin jet black 'so that there was nothing white, save only his
teeth', and dressed as an Ethiopian minstrel. King John he
charmed with fulsome flattery, telling him that the noise of his

deeds had reached even to Abyssinia (though he added in an undertone that it was not the King's more attractive qualities which had achieved such widespread renown). Then he played before the King on his tabor, and, by and by, Sir Ardulf was brought in between two guards to hear music for the last time, for he was to die next day. While the cup was being passed round after dinner, John found his opportunity to slip a certain powder into the wine, and soon all who had drunk of it were overcome with 'a deadly slepe'. When they all lay at last in drugged slumber, John de Rampaygne unloosed Sir Ardulf, and they placed between the knights who had guarded him the King's fool. They escaped from the castle by a rope of sheets from a high window, and fled through the night to Fulk in the forest near Blauncheville, where they were received with joy.

The other rescue was that of Fulk's brother, William Fitzwarin, who had been severely wounded, and fell into the hands of his pursuers while the whole band was in flight. His prison was harder than Sir Ardulf's, for Fulk had to put to sea, and he was left in John's power while his brother was adventuring among the Saracens. The Lord, however, looked after his own, for by some curious whim the King spared William's life and contented himself with keeping him a perpetual prisoner. King John seems to have taken little trouble to keep himself informed of Fulk's distinguished exploits abroad: so he had no suspicions when a strange ship put into London, and its master, a rich Eastern merchant, came ashore to visit him and charmed him with compliments in bad Latin and still more winning gifts. By lavish distribution of treasures won by Fulk and his companions among the Saracens and at Carthage, John de Rampaygne, for it was of course he, soon made himself one of the most popular characters about the court, and was free to go where he would. He soon learnt of the manner of William Fitzwarin's prison, and so it was that shortly afterward his guards, taking him back to his cell from his meal, found themselves surrounded by a group of unusually muscular merchants, and were quickly overpowered. Fulk had brought his ship up the river as far as he dared; before the King could organize a proper pursuit the galley had put out, and William Fitzwarin and his brother were on their way to Brittany.

It was not long after this, that John and Fulk were ultimately reconciled, and the tale closes after one more short adventure in Ireland, where Fulk overcame a black giant, whose hatchet he carried home to hang as a trophy in his hall at Blauncheville. The prophecy was fulfilled which the evil spirit had made long ago to Payn Peverel and which Merlin had made before him, for all its strange references to the lèopard and the wild boar and the wolf of Blauncheville were realized in the blazonry of the shields which Fulk and his rivals bore. The hero could now lay aside his sword, to face the domestic worries of his later years, a second marriage, a heavenly vision and the blindness which afflicted him in the last seven years of his life.

Fulk's fame as an outlaw, and the basis of it, was the long war which he maintained against the tyrant John, just as Hereward's fame rested on his struggle with the Norman and Robin Hood's on his struggle with the Sheriff of Nottingham. At the same time, it is no good pretending that he was a man of the same stamp as Robin Hood. He was not a hero of the people; no more need be said of this than that the story which we have of him is in a language which a peasant would not have understood. How much the English version which Leland saw popularized the tale we shall, alas, never know; with a few minor variations, however, the gist of the story which he recounts is so similar to the French one that one must suppose it to have shared tone as well as content. And the tone of the French version is that of chivalrous romance. Fulk is a knight, born to a rich heritage of military adventure, a latter day Lancelot who is at home in the world where tournaments and crusades and the rescue of well-born young women from giants and dragons and robbers are the stuff of existence. His fights with King John reach the dimensions of pitched battles; he could put seven hundred men into the field, armed and horsed, and his weapons were the sword and lance, not the peasant's pike or his bow. Robin Hood, though one old chronicler stated that it would have taken four hundred armed men to dislodge him and his outlaws from Barnesdale, never aspired to undertaking military operations on this scale. Fulk belongs to a different world to the peasants' hero; he is an aristocrat, and the tone and content of his story is in the aristo-cratic tradition.

In two respects, however, there is a family similarity between the stories of Fulk and those of the later and more famous outlaws. In the first place there is the general similarity of plot and incident. In both cases, the main themes of the narratives are the adventures of men who, for one reason or another, set themselves against the accepted powers, and took themselves to the forest to live as outlaws. There is nothing overdrawn about this picture in Fulk's case: we shall see later that the idea of rebels taking to the woods was just as familiar to the history of the thirteenth century as it was to the age of Hereward. Just how similar two particular incidents in the legend of Fulk are to stories related of other outlaws we have already seen. Over and above these two most striking examples, there are plenty of other echoes: in the rescue scenes for instance, or in Fulk's marriage to the beautiful Matilda which saved her from John's lust, which recalls Robin Hood's rescue of the love of Alan-a'-Dale, who had been 'chosen to be an old knight's delight'. Fulk was a baron, and no doubt the English poem of his life had more in common with such English romances as Sir Bevis of Southampton or Sir Gawain and the Green Knight than with the ballads of Robin Hood. On the other hand, the various common incidents reveal a distinct relationship and indicate the kind of source the ballad-writers drew on to decorate their songs of Robin Hood and his ilk, merely adapting the incidents to suit a different mood.

The other respect in which the two legends are akin is in the *raison d'être* of their heroes' outlawry. There heroes were outlaws because of the wickedness of the powers that were, not instinctive lawlessness, for Robin and Fulk both repudiated the name of robber, and each observed the same strict moral code in their brigandage. Robin would 'do no housbonde no harm', and the yeoman and the good squire were safe from him. 'In all the time he was a banished man' says the romance 'neither Fulk nor any of his did damage at any time to anyone, save the King and his knights'. It was for this reason he was always loved of the best men of his age, Randolf Earl of Chester, the famous William the Marshal, Hubert Walter, Archbishop of Canterbury. He was, too, a good lord to his people: 'this Fulk was a good purveyor and a liberal, and he caused the royal road to be turned by his hall at his manor of Alleston, so that no traveller should pass without food or other honour, or good of his'. Both he and Robin had the common weal at heart, and fought for the side of right; it was against tyranny that they took up arms. It is true that the tyrannies against which they battled were of a different nature: Robin Hood's enemy was the whole legal and economic system—Fulk's was the individual will of a single evil-minded King. Robin fought for the oppressed peasant and the poor knight cheated of his lands at a corrupt law; Fulk for nobles whose inheritance had been seized or laid waste, or whose wives and daughters had been violated. In both cases, however, the tyranny is the most genuine part of the story. The black character of John, his ill faith, his vindictive anger and his insatiable lust, all find ample historical authority in the chronicles of his reign, just as the estate accounts and legal records of the fourteenth century bear witness to the misery of the labouring poor in the age when Robin Hood first became famous. The difference, in fact, is really only the difference between the age of Magna Carta and the age of the Peasants' Revolt. Though they may come from different social worlds, the Fulk of fiction and Robin Hood have this essential thing in common, that both claim justification for their wild acts as the upholders, albeit unofficial, of the liberties of their race.

V

The Romance
of Eustace the Monk

Eustace the Monk, like Fulk Fitzwarin, flourished in the time of King John. In legend he takes on the combined roles of Fulk, Friar Tuck and John de Rampaygne, for he was at once a renegade monk, an outlawed knight and a distinguished magician. In spite of these relations, however, he was not an Englishman (though he was long in the service of the English king), and it is only because some of his adventures were so similar to those of Robin Hood that he deserves notice here. Indeed Michel, who first printed his story, refers to him as 'a sort of Robin Hood of the Boulonnais'. In fact, his story is if anything nearer to the legend of Fulk Fitzwarin than that of Robin Hood, for it was as a knight fighting the tyranny of his feudal overlord (in his case Rainald of Dammartin, the famous Count of Boulogne) that he won his fame as an outlaw. As in the case of Fulk, moreover, a good deal of the story is devoted to recounting adventures on a larger scale than those of the average outlaw of that time, when as a sea captain he served first King John and later Prince Louis of France.

We know more of the life of the historical Eustace than we do of any of the other outlaws, for of all of them, it was he who made the deepest impression on the history of his times. Two kings, those of England and France, thought enough of him to vie for his services; he was a man who had haunted royal courts and led diplomatic negotiations, and he was probably the greatest sea captain of his age. His name was enough at one time to strike terror into the hearts of Channel seamen, and the English chroniclers regarded his final defeat at sea and their land's deliverance from him as a direct act of God. How great was their dread and dislike of him we may judge by the tone in which they spoke of him; he was 'the Archpirate', 'the apostate', one who 'from a black monk became a demoniac', and they saw in his invincibility clear evidence of his magical powers. Time added to this reputation; a hundred years after his death he had become for Walter of Hemingford, who wrote under Edward II, a tyrant of Spain surnamed Monachus, who had wasted many lands until at last, hearing that England was ruled by a child (the infant Henry III) he aspired to conquer that country also. These legends, which grew up after his death and increased his stature to that of a foreign prince, bear testimony to the vivid impression which his career made upon Englishmen of his day.

We first hear of Eustace as a monk of the abbey of Saumur, which he left, putting aside his order, to claim the inheritance of his father. After this he seems to have entered the service of the Count of Boulogne, and by 1203, our first firm date, he had become his seneschal. Soon after this he must have quarrelled with his master, for the chronicle of the Dukes of Normandy tells us that he warred long with him, and by 1205 we know that he had entered John's service. His main reason for this seems to have been that the count had now definitely joined the King of France; indeed, Eustace seems to have kept up intermittently his struggle against him while he was serving John as a sea captain. We find him now campaigning off the Channel Islands; on one occasion he is said to have sailed up the Seine on a daring raid which took him beyond Rouen. He stood well for a time with the English king; and for his services he received of him lands in Norfolk. But in 1212 John and the Count of Boulogne, after drawn-out overtures, entered into alliance, and Eustace, when he learnt that his old enemy had become the king's man, turned to the service of France. Promotion came fast. To all intents, he was admiral to Prince Louis when he invaded England in 1215; it was he who in that year managed to land the French siege machines at Folkestone, but for which they would have been hard pressed in their campaign; and when Louis sailed from Calais in person it was the ships of Eustace which carried him to England. Eustace's naval operations went far toward saving the Prince from disaster in the Winchelsea campaign, early in 1217. The great English naval victory off Sandwich, in which he lost his life, spelt the end of the war itself. From an outlaw of the Boulonnais Forest, he had by then made a name for himself as one of the ablest commanders of his time.

The French poem about Eustace is one of the testimonies to this fame and in its general outline of his life it seems fairly accurate. It must, however, have been culled from various sources; the first part, for instance, is devoted to celebrating his powers as a magician, but when he quarrels with the Count of Boulogne and becomes an outlaw, this side of his character seems to be completely forgotten. In his war with the Count he relies on cunning, not conjuring, for his success. The story ends with an account of how he lost his life in the battle off Sandwich, historically of very fair accuracy, and this sea captain of the closing lines seems to have not much connexion with either the magician or the outlaw; in all probability he is a good deal more like the real Eustace than either of them. Clearly the poem drew on widely differing accounts of his life, some perhaps purely traditional.

The magic of the opening part of the poem has nothing to do with the enchanted fairy world into which the Romance of Fulk Fitzwarin led us. It is pure burlesque, savouring of the horse-play scenes in Marlowe's *Dr. Faustus* rather than of chivalrous romance. Like the Doctor, Eustace had learnt the magician's art from Mephistopheles himself. For love of necromancy he had travelled to the great centre of all magical study, Toledo, and there for a summer and a winter he sat at the feet of the devil his master in 'an abyss beneath the earth'. When he returned, he was so accomplished a pupil that there was none to match him for magic in all France. He had not lingered putting his knowledge to the test. He and another magician had enjoyed an uproarious return from Spain, casting spells on surly landladies who demanded payment, enchanting the horses of an intractable carter into galloping in reverse, and setting the townsfolk where they passed against one another in indecorous mêlées. Eustace's return to his monastery meant the end of all order in the cloister.

Everything was put to confusion: the monks found themselves fasting when they should have been eating, going barefoot when they should have worn shoes, and swearing under their breath when they were supposed to be reading the hours. The abbey cook was terrified out of his wits when a side of bacon leapt to its feet and took on the shape of a little ugly old woman who pranced about his kitchen. Meanwhile Eustace was wasting his substance in the town, drinking in undesirable company and gambling away his crucifixes, images and monastic books in the tavern.

This splendid existence was unfortunately to be short lived. Eustace's father, Baudain Buskues, was a peer of the Boulonnais, and died suddenly, killed by his long-standing rival, Hainfrois de Meresinguehans: so passed to Eustace with his father's lands and his peerage the sterner inheritance of his feud. He left his abbey and his monk's habit, and it was as a peer of the county that he appeared before Rainald of Dammartin to demand justice against his father's murderer. In reply Hainfrois threw down his gage, claiming his right of trial by battle before the lords of the Boulonnais: and in the judicial duel which followed Eustace's champion was killed. By then he had already warned the count that he would not abide by the decision if it went against him; Hainfrois, too, had not forgotten the quarrel and lost no opportunity of poisoning his lord's mind against Eustace. When Eustace refused, for fear of treachery, to appear before Rainald at Hardelot, the latter seized his lands and burnt his gardens. In revenge, Eustace fell on the Count's newly built mills while the latter was celebrating the marriage of his son Simon, and burnt them, sending the miller to his master to tell him that Eustace the Monk had lighted two great candles for his wedding feast. After this he took to the woods and to the life of an outlaw.

Eustace's deeds as an outlaw continue the burlesque mood of the opening passages of the story. There is nothing particularly heroic about them: the tale is of how, in a multitude of disguises, Eustace fooled and cheated the Count and generally put him to loss and ridicule. Sometimes he would appear before him as a monk who had come to plead with him on behalf of Eustace, or in a group of pilgrims fresh from Rome, men of worthy appearance, who would infallibly help themselves to some of the Count's property if he lingered for a moment in their company.

Or he would be a leper on crutches begging for alms on the highway, who would accept a few pence from the Count as he passed, and then wait to knock down the stable boy who was following with his lord's finest horse, and escape upon it to his companions in the forest. If the Count set out with his men to pursue him, he would invariably meet with some peasant or workman who had seen Eustace passing only minutes before and would send him several leagues out of his way, giving the outlaws a chance to ambush his rear-guard or raid his houses. Once, disguised as a merchant coming to bribe the count in a lawsuit, Eustace succeeded in palming off on him a present of fresh baked pastries, containing a mixture of tow, pitch and wax, which caused considerable embarrassment at the comital dinner table. On another occasion he appeared as a charcoal burner carrying a great fork (as Fulk Fitzwarin had done): on yet another he was a potter crying his wares (as were Hereward and Robin Hood in their tales). At the end of one long pursuit the Count could find nothing for it but to arrest on suspicion everyone he encountered. His men came in with a motley bag, first, four monks, then four pedlars and a pig; then three poultrymen and a brace of ass-drivers, a group of fishermen with their wares about them, and finally four clerks and an arch-priest. While, however, he was investigating their credentials, Eustace had penetrated to his stables disguised as a woman and was making improper advances to one of his sergeants. The man was found subsequently in a bog, and two of the Count's best horses disappeared. Some of Eustace's pranks were of a more brutal nature. Once he cut out the tongue of one of the Count's pages and sent him back, speechless, to his master, who could only guess the story the boy might have told. On another occasion, in reprisal for the Count's acts of violence, Eustace cut off the feet of four of his sergeants whom he had surprised. A fifth, who was with them, was glad enough 'to save his trotters' by carrying back the outlaw's compliments to their master, with a full explanation as to why his companions had been able to proceed no further. On the other hand, it is true, Eustace spared the Count's life on the one occasion when he fell into his hands. This scene is similar to those in which King John, in one case, and the Sheriff of Nottingham in another, were lured into the power of outlaws: it was Eustace, disguised as a plundered merchant, who led his enemy into an ambush in the middle of the forest. The sequel, however, is different. Eustace demanded peace and pardon, but his suit was steadily refused, and in the end he let the Count go in peace, for, he said, as the Count had come there following him in good faith, in good faith he should be allowed to depart also. Hainfrois de Meresinguehans also was spared when he fell into the outlaw's hands, and sent back with a contemptuous message from Eustace.

All through this part of the story passages here and there are reminiscent of the ballads of Robin Hood. Two incidents, however, are almost identical in both legends. Strikingly enough they form part of the same adventure as we have already seen recounted both of Fulk Fitzwarin and Robin, only the similarity here is even closer. It is the scene where the outlaw chief questions his prisoners as to what they have with them, and will take only what he regards, in accordance with their answers, as his rightful spoil. This incident occurs twice in the *Lyttel Geste*; once in the encounter with the high cellarer of St. Mary's Abbey, which was detailed in the last chapter, and once when Robin first meets Sir Richard Lee, who was not despoiled because he gave a truthful account of himself. In the tale of Eustace also the incident is introduced twice, and again the reply of the prisoner is in one case true and the other false. The first occasion was when a certain merchant of Flanders fell into Eustace's hands, who admitted to the forty pounds he was carrying with him though he was in fear and trembling of being plundered. Eustace sent him on his way with his blessing; 'Go and God protect you; but remember that, if you had lied to me in anything, you would not have carried hence a penny'. Eustace, indeed, gave him one of ten stolen horses to take to the Count with his compliments. There was a real irony here, for in France a soldier owed to his lord the tenth part of all booty taken in war: the outlaw, with feigned punctiliousness, was sending back to his suzerain, as a tithe of spoil, his own property which had been plundered.

Later in the poem, the Abbot of Jumièges, like the cellarer of St. Mary's after him, had the misfortune to fall into the hands of the outlaws. Four marks of silver, he told them, was all that he and his men had about them, just as the cellarer later said to Robin he had but his spending money with him. But when

Eustace lifted up his gown to search him, there were thirty marks about the Abbot's person; so the four silver marks were returned him, while Eustace kept the rest, as Robin kept what he called in jest his loan to Our Lady. Once again we see the strict code of the outlaw in action:—

'If the abbot had said the truth
He would have had again all his property.
The abbot lost what he had
Only because he lied.'

Robin Hood and his men capture the abbot of St Mary's.

Even Eustace, for all the opprobrium of the chroniclers, and the sale of his soul to the devil, observed the rules. Right was on his side. Though in the burlesque of the tale we find nothing of his protecting peasants, we find the other knights of the Boulonnais his sympathizers, warning the Count, when Eustace falls into his hands, that he may not kill him outright but must observe the forms of law, so giving the outlaw his chance for escape.

Knight as he was and a friend of knights, the story of Eustace the Monk has little of the aristocratic tone of the romance of Fulk Fitzwarin. Though its flavour is more popular than that tale it cannot on the other hand be said to be much of an anticipation of the ballads of Robin Hood, except as regards isolated incidents. The author toes the line as regards the outlaw code by putting Eustace in the right, by the tales of the murder of his

father, of the Count's tyrannical confiscation of his land, and
readiness to disregard the law in his just cause. Eustace's callous
indifference to bloodshed is again typical of the outlaw legends,
but it is typical also of the medieval age of which violence was a
primary characteristic. What the writer is really interested in
are the ludicrous pranks by which Eustace, whether as magician
or outlaw, manages to score off all those who cross him. By the
end of the poem these begin to lose their point by mere repetition, and there is nothing much to be gained from retailing any
more of them in detail. One can find enough of their genre of
humour in the pages of Rabelais or in Elizabethan comedy, and
it is a good deal funnier.

We can thus dismiss the French poem about Eustace the
Monk, but we cannot thus dismiss him. For it is by no means the
only evidence of the legend which grew up about his name.
Indeed these other accretions to it, preserved in later chronicles,
are perhaps the most interesting feature of his story, for they
show very clearly how in a brief hundred years the facts of
history could become overlayed with legend and how, behind
the wildest story, there may always lie a residue of truth. It is in
the story of Eustace's death at Sandwich that this development
is most clearly illustrated.

Eustace died at sea, as the devil at Toledo had told him that
he would do, in the great naval battle off Sandwich on 24 August
1217. Our accounts of the battle are very circumstantial. Though
he was in command of the fleet this defeat was not one which
could be laid at Eustace's door; he is said to have warned Robert
de Courtenay, the French lord who was his nominal superior,
against turning from his course to follow the feigned flight of
Hubert de Burgh who, with a few fishing boats, had come out to
lure the French fleet to battle. But Robert would not be over-
ruled, and by going out of his course he let the English get to
windward of him. The fight was close in to the harbour, and he
had clearly miscalculated the size of the English fleet; for his
ships, laden as they were with horses and tackle for Louis in
England, the mistake was a fatal one. Eustace's ship, in the van,
struck the second ship in the English column; the other English
ships came up with the wind, but the French could not manoeuvre to assist their leader. He was soon grappled with four
English ships, one a great cog; his men were blinded with the

lime which the English flung from their mastheads, and then their vessel was boarded. There was a great slaughter among his men; only the nobles were spared for their ransoms. Eustace himself was taken in the hold; though he offered a great sum for his life, it was refused, for orders had been given that he was to be treated as a traitor. Stephen Crabbe of Winchelsea, a mariner 'who had been long with him' when he was in the service of King John, struck off his head upon the rail of the ship. It is some sign of the faith his men had in Eustace that the capture of his ship was the signal for the whole French fleet to turn in retreat; the English carried on a running fight with them all the way to Calais, and it was only a remnant that regained the port. Eustace's head was afterwards fixed upon a lance and borne by the victors to Canterbury.

This is the account, as it stands in the contemporary sources, the *History of the Dukes of Normandy*, the *Song of William Marshal*, and the chronicles of Paris and Wendover. Just a hundred years later, in the early years of the fourteenth century, two further accounts were written of this same battle. By then the true events seem to have been quite forgotten, and about their almost obliterated memory a whole miraculous history had been built up. In the 'Polistorie' of John of Canterbury we have a story just about as far-fetched as is possible to imagine. It was on the day of St. Bartholomew, in the year 1217, he tells us, that there came towards Sandwich a great fleet led by a monk named Eustace. He was accompanied by many lords of France, who were confident of success because of his deep skill in magic; some had brought their cows and even their children in their cradles, so sure were they that with his help they would conquer the land. As they came up to the harbour of Sandwich their whole fleet could be seen, except for the ship of Eustace, for he had cast a spell so that it was invisible. The people of the town were so stricken with fear that they despaired of all success, except by God's help; they fell upon their knees and implored him, for the love of St. Bartholomew, to deliver them, vowing that if their prayer was granted they would raise a chapel and in it endow a chantry to his perpetual honour. Their prayer was soon granted. It chanced that there was at this time in the town one Stephen Crabbe who had once been the intimate of Eustace, who of love for him had revealed to him many of the secrets of his magic. It was he who now came forward to reveal their unknown danger to the citizens and to offer his aid. 'This Eustace' he warned them, 'who is the leader of our enemies, cannot be seen of one who is ignorant of magic, and I have learnt from himself this enchantment. I will give today then, my life for the sake of this land, for I know well that, in entering his ship, I cannot escape death from the multitude of soldiers who are with him.'

So Stephen embarked in one of the three vessels which were all the defence the harbour of Sandwich boasted, and put out to sea. As he drew level he leapt from it into the ship of Eustace, which to him alone was visible. The English, who saw him standing and fighting, as it appeared to them, over the water, raised a great shout of dismay, for they concluded that some evil spirit had taken his form. But Stephen, defying numbers, fought his way to Eustace, and cut off the magician's head. In that instant his ship became visible to all. Stephen, even as his companions watched, was seized, cut down, and his corpse thrown into the sea. Meanwhile, however, a hurricane was gathering; the trees on the shore were rooted up by the wind, and as it entered the harbour every ship of the enemy fleet was upset. As this storm raged the people of Sandwich saw in the air a man in red garments, and they heard a voice crying: 'I am Bartholomew and I am sent to assist you: fear nothing.' With these words the figure vanished in the clouds, and was heard no more. The entire French fleet was destroyed.

The version in Walter of Hemingford is more succinct, but only somewhat less extravagant. It is he who has the story of the tyrant of Spain, surnamed Monachus, who had resolved to conquer England and set out on this quest at the head of an enormous fleet. When he was still far from the coast, the rumour of his approach was heard and all feared greatly. 'If he lands' the sailors declared, 'he will devastate everything, for the country is not prepared and the King is distant. So we will take our lives in our hands and meet him at sea: valour is not all, and aid will come to us from on high.' So they put out, and as the fleets closed a volunteer was called on to climb the mast of the tyrant's ship and cut down the sail, so that the fleet would lose the guidance of its leading vessel. This daring manoeuvre succeeded and God gave the enemy into English hands. With a huge booty they returned to the shore and the kingdom was saved.

Hemingford's account remembers then the key factor in the battle, the capture of Eustace's ship, after which the others fled. John of Canterbury's account is wilder, but we, with the older records before us, can see that it too contains a substratum of fact. It has remembered correctly not only the name of Eustace, which in Hemingford is forgotten, but also the name of his executioner Stephen Crabbe, and even that he was an old companion of the monk's. The story of the tempest also has some historical foundation. It seems to represent a conflation of two famous incidents, the Battle of Sandwich in 1217, and the great storm in 1215 which destroyed a French fleet under Hugh de Bove. But upon this slight residuum of fact a new and unrecognizable history has been based.

If we did not possess trustworthy accounts of the Battle of Sandwich, if indeed Crabbe's name had somehow slipped out of them, the whole story would seem to be pure invention. Any sane historian would be justified in rejecting every detail but the name of Eustace. Yet barely a hundred years had passed since the battle when John of Canterbury wrote. We shall do well to bear in mind this example of the mushroom growth of legend when we come to consider the speculations of those who have tried to uncover a substratum of genuine history in the incidents of the Robin Hood ballads. We shall have learnt, by then, that in dealing with legendary material, though after a century a few small historical details may survive, it is plain foolish to take on trust whole episodes unless they can be compared with explicit statements in earlier and reliable authorities.

VI

William Wallace
and the Scottish Outlaws

I T is largely on account of accretions which have grown into his
story, in the same way as they did with that of Eustace the
Monk, that William Wallace the Scotsman earns a place in the
history of outlaw literature. His true story belongs rather to the
annals of patriotism than of outlawry, and it is therefore with
hesitation that I have included a chapter about him. It was his
spectacular victory over the English at Stirling Bridge and the
brief hour of his triumph which followed it in the year 1297 that
made him a hero of legend. Subsequent story magnified his
achievement out of recognition: he became the hero of a ten-
years' war against the English, who had three times rescued his
country from their yoke; he became the leader of the Scottish
forces in immense pitched battles at which either he was not
present, or which were not fought at all; and the lives lost in the
struggle against him ran into hundreds of thousands. He became
a muscular giant whose strength was all but irresistible: he took
part in battles upon the sea and in Gascony, concerning his role
in which history remains silent. He became the chosen champion
of Philip the Fair of France, and held parley with the Queen of
Edward I of England, who was dead before his historical career
opened. As in the case of Eustace, there is a residue of history
buried beneath this welter of fiction: he really did visit France,
and there really were more battles in the war between England

and Scotland than he ever took part in. But the wishful thinking of ardent patriots has added so much to the tale, that it has become hard to say with any certainty just what kernel of truth is concealed under it.

By the middle ages themselves this half-fictional hero was associated with the traditional outlaws. A note in a fifteenth-century hand beside a poem written by an English monk who was an actual contemporary of Wallace calls him 'the Scottish Robin Hood'. Their names are again coupled by an anonymous Scottish poet of the sixteenth century :—

'Thair is no story that I of hier
Of Johne nor Robene Hude
Nor yit of Wallace wicht but weir
That me thinkes halfe so gude.'

There is no accident involved here. The lost author of these lines had good reason for his association of Wallace with Robin Hood rather than with other national heroes of Scottish history, such as Robert the Bruce, whose fame in history also attracted all kinds of legends. For among the stories recounted of Wallace were many which had their origin not in the magnified reverberation of historical event, but in tradition. Amongst these were many which were very similar to those told of Robin Hood and other outlaws. In essence, indeed, they are the same stories, merely associated by different authors with the name of a different hero.

That this sort of story should have been told of the patriot Wallace, who in his time made himself guardian of the realm of Scotland, is due to the peculiar circumstances of the struggle in which he achieved renown. The war between Edward I and the Scots in which he won it arose, after a long period of peace between the two countries, as a result of the former's claim that the realm of Scotland was no more than a fief of the English crown. This was not gainsaid by any of the three claimants to the Scottish throne between whom he was called on to arbitrate in 1290, partly because all three of them held estates in England and partly because a denial of the claim might have put in question the hereditary right of any one of them to inherit the crown. The Scottish aristocracy, most of whom were of Norman extraction and many of whom also held lands in

England, were in any case ready to compromise with Edward. This had two important consequences. In the first place it meant that Wallace, as an open rebel against the acknowledged superior lord of his country, was technically an outlaw. The English records therefore refer to him as a 'public robber', and at his mockery of a trial the law of outlawry was invoked: he was not allowed to speak because it was 'contrary to the laws of England that any outlaw should be allowed to answer in his own defence'. The fact that most of the Scottish baronage tended at the push to side with the English meant further that Wallace's struggle was largely a guerilla war. He appeared as a leader of a motley gang of peasants, townsmen and small landowners like himself, who for most of the time lurked in the forests like the traditional outlaws and preyed upon the English and their supporters. In his first recorded exploit, the assassination of the English Sheriff of Lanark, Thomas Hazelrigg, Wallace commanded a band of a mere thirty men. The army which he led to victory at Stirling was mustered in the forest of Selkirk. For seven years after his defeat in 1298, he remained at large, finding refuge in the woods and mountains, and constantly skirmishing with the English soldiers. Like Hereward, he used the opportunity which a wild countryside afforded him to rally men to the cause of a nation *in extremis*, in face of the tyranny of a foreign ruler whose legal title to sovereignty he refused to recognize.

Considering the impact which his career made on the imagination of his countrymen, we know remarkably little about the historical detail of the life of William Wallace. The date of his birth is unknown. He came of a family of small landowners whose estates were in Ayrshire, and who seem to have been of Welsh origin. Nothing certain is known of him until after the outbreak of war between England and Scotland in 1296. In 1297, as has been said, he slew the Sheriff of Lanark, according to tradition to avenge the death of his beloved, Marion Bradfute, the heiress of Lamington, who had been executed by the English for harbouring her outlawed lover. This deed made him immediately a hero in the eyes of the common people, who had suffered bitterly by the ravages of the English soldiers and the tyranny of the officers to whom the English King had entrusted the administration of his subject kingdom, and they began to flock to his banner. He soon found himself at the head of a powerful irregular force. It was his genius that converted this undisciplined horde into an army of foot soldiers. In July 1297 he joined forces with another patriot, William Douglas 'the hardy'. They had by then cleared the English from Ayrshire and Annandale, and now mustered a force to besiege Dundee. When the English under the Earl of Warenne marched their army against them, they were overthrown in a great battle at Stirling Bridge by Wallace and Sir Andrew Murray.

In the wake of this victory almost the whole of Scotland was recovered from the English. Dundee fell, and so did Edinburgh and even Berwick. Wallace led his men across the border, and

The defeat of Wallace at Falkirk.

raided throughout Westmorland, Cumberland, and Northumberland. He and Murray made themselves 'guardians of the realm of Scotland', and when the latter died Wallace acted as sole governor, granting lands and making treaties in the name of John de Balliol, the King whom Edward had deposed. But though he had made himself a master of the realm and had become a popular hero, Wallace was still cruelly hampered by the equivocal attitude of the Scottish aristocracy. Resistance was anything but united when in the summer of 1298 Edward of England marched north in person. When Wallace drew up his men at Falkirk against him, there were bitter quarrels over the leadership of the army, and John Comyn seems to have refused to fight. When the English advanced the Scottish knights took to their heels, and Wallace and his rude foot soldiers were left to face the English cavalry outnumbered. The battle which followed was hard fought, but it ended in a massacre. More than a thousand Scotsmen lost their lives, and it was with only a remnant of his army that Wallace retreated through Stirling.

For seven years after the disaster of Falkirk Wallace remained in arms, but he never recovered the position which he then lost. He resigned his guardianship soon after; but the title was already an empty one. The war continued, complicated endlessly by the rivalry of Bruce and Comyn for the throne, and Wallace seems to have taken part in it as an independent guerilla leader. When he went abroad in 1299 it was without the leave of the guardians; he visited Philip of France, and probably also the Pope, but he does not seem to have had any official part in the negotiations which then took place between Scotland and the Holy See. At just what date he returned to Scotland is unknown, but when in 1304 Edward I at last forced the majority of her lords into fresh submission, Wallace was excluded from the terms of the peace. The English were clearly determined to hunt him down, for large sums were expended on his pursuit, and several rebellious Scotsmen were offered free pardons if they could succeed in capturing him. He was at last captured, through the assistance of one of his followers, Ralph de Haliburton, who had been made a prisoner by the English. He was sent to London where he was tried, and condemned without being allowed to speak in his own defence. He was beheaded, disembowelled, and quartered, and his remains were hung on gibbets at Newcastle, Berwick, Stirling and Perth. The savagery of his sentence bears witness to the bitterness of the struggle in which he had made himself famous.

Wallace's renown grew over the generations while the feud between England and Scotland lasted. All sorts of stories were told of him, both in poems and in popular tradition:

> 'Off his gud dedis and manhad
> Grete Gestis, I hard say, are made;
> But sa mony, I trow nocht,
> As he in till his dayis wrocht.
> Quha (who) all hys dedis of prys wald dyte,
> Hym worthyd a gret buke to wryte.'

So wrote the chronicler Andrew of Wyntoun, who died in 1424. It was probably about fifty or sixty years later that the various stories were gathered into a 'grete buke' by Blind Harry the minstrel, who seems to have died in the time of James IV. Little is known of this obscure singer of the great age of Scottish poetry. He is one of the dead 'makaris' whom Dunbar laments in his great poem, *Timor mortis conturbat me*; and John Major mentions him, saying he was blind from infancy. The royal accounts show a series of payments to him, the last in the year 1492. He is familiarly called in them 'Blin Harry', but it is not even clear that he was blind. The delightful descriptive passages, which are among the finest in his poem, could certainly hardly have been written by one who was blind, as Major says he was, from infancy.

The most striking feature of Harry's poem is its extreme length. Its literary merit is slight, and its historical accuracy is even slighter. I shall therefore give only the briefest synopsis of its contents. The chronology in it is hopeless, and Harry is quite inconsistent with himself about Wallace's age; it is therefore impossible to attach dates to any events except those which are historically known. He starts by describing his hero's childhood; his first exploit mentioned is the killing of the son of the English constable of Dundee. This is followed by an incident in which he kills a group of Englishmen who had attempted to take from him his catch while he was fishing in the River Irvine. As a result of this he was taken prisoner by the English, and thrown into a dungeon in the Castle of Ayr, where he was fed on 'barrell herring and wattir'. As a result of this he was seized with a 'flux' and thrown on a 'myddyn' for dead. He was however merely unconscious; a kindly woman found him, and seeing he was alive took him to her home and nursed him back to health. While he was recovering, a prophecy was made concerning him by the famous seer, Thomas of Ercildowne, who was said to have lived seven years in Elfland, and who declared that he should thrice be the deliverer of Scotland from her enemies.

Once recovered, Wallace returned to fighting the English, whose tyrannies were rousing a whole proud people to indignation:

> 'Alas, that folk, that evir was fre,
> And in fredome wount for to be,

> Throw grete myschance and foly
> War tretyt than sa wykkitly,
> That thar fays (foes) thar Judges war;
> What wretchitnes may men have mar?'

Thus John Barbour, the biographer of Bruce. Blind Harry at this stage describes his hero's part as the leader in an endless series of encounters with the English, which are recounted with a wealth of bloodthirsty detail. The story he tells is of a guerilla warfare; he pictures his hero and his followers moving from wood to wood, now under 'Shortwood shaw', now in Meffen Wood, now in the forest of Clyde. Their war is one of surprises and stratagems: we find Wallace adopting, like Eustace, a host of disguises to spy upon his enemies. He appears now as an old woman with a distaff, now as a potter, now as a monk, and uses all the advantages which cunning, a wild countryside, and the sympathy of its oppressed inhabitants affords him. Against this background Harry also tells the story of his love; of how his lady harboured him in the hour of need; of how she put into his power the English who had tried to force her to betray him; and of how in the end, after they had become man and wife, she was taken by the Englishman Hazelrigg and put to death. This part of the story culminates in the entirely fictional Battle of Biggar, after which Wallace was chosen to be guardian of Scotland, and a truce was arranged.

We now come to a series of incidents which have a certain historical basis. This section of the poem begins with the horrifying incident of the burning of the 'Barns of Ayr', the quarters in the town where the English soldiers were sleeping, in revenge for the hanging of fourteen Scottish lords against the terms of the truce. Here Blind Harry's story rises to horrid eloquence in his description of the fate of the men whose houses Wallace had fired:

> 'Sum nakyt burnt, bot beltless all away;
> Sum never rais, but smoryt whar thai lay;
> Sum ruschyt fast, till Ayr yff thai mycht wyn;
> Blyndyt in fyr, thar dedis were full dym.
> The reik melyt with fylth of carioune,
> Amang the fyr, rycht foul off offensioune.'

This incident, which is based in history, is followed by the events which led up to the Battle of Stirling, and Wallace's

70

raid into England. With characteristic exaggeration Blind Harry magnifies this into a major campaign which brought the Scots to an encampment at St. Albans, where the Queen of England came in person to Wallace to plead with him for peace, which in the end was granted her. This is followed by an entirely imaginary tale of his hero's visit to France, and of how he captured at sea the 'Red Rievar', a French pirate, to whom he granted his life and who became his firmest friend. According to the poem it was his high deeds against the English in Gascony, where he fought for Philip the Fair (his peace had been for Scotland only) which stirred Edward I in his absence to muster a new army, and march again toward the north at the head of one hundred thousand men.

This news brought Wallace hurrying back to his country. He had soon raised men, and with his army he overthrew the English who were already in Scotland at the great battle of 'Blak Yrnside Forest', another imaginary engagement. Once again the English were driven out of much of Scotland. But Edward was meanwhile approaching, and when Wallace went to meet him at Falkirk his quarrel with Comyn was fatal to the cause. Outnumbered by tens of thousands, he yet succeeded in hacking his way out of an untenable position, with the usual terrific slaughter of 'Southerons', that is, Englishmen. This was in reality the downfall of Wallace's cause, but Harry manages to bring him out triumphant again, telling a story of how he surprised Edward's army in the camp at Linlithgow and put it to flight. Yet once more the English were thrust out of the land; and Wallace came again to Edinburgh as guardian, and governed the land:

'Thus in gud pece Scotland with rycht he stad' (established). His task seemed to him to be now accomplished. In a great council at Edinburgh he resigned the guardianship, and took ship for France to seek new adventures.

After another brush with pirates upon the sea, in which he slew with his own hands their captain, John of the Lyn, we find Wallace levying war on the English in Gascony as Philip the Fair's most trusted lieutenant. His other adventures in France included the killing of two 'champions' who had been hired by jealous rivals to assassinate him, and a triumph in single combat with a mentally disordered lion, which he tackled without armour in order to keep the odds even. Wallace in fact polished it off at a blow, and was able to turn to the amazed crowd with the insolent question:

'Is thar ma doggis that ye wald yet haff sleyne?'

These deeds, however, aroused such envy among the eclipsed Frenchmen that he thought it better to return to Scotland, which the English had once again in his absence overrun.

There was little resistance left in Scotland when Wallace landed at the Firth of Tay. For a while he lay concealed in the house of his cousin Crawford at Elchok; there he assembled a small band and defeated 'Young Butler' and his English soldiers by a clever stratagem. For the moment he was reduced once more to his old forest existence, and to a war of skirmishes, but this was a fair beginning and men began again to rally to him. Soon he was able to put an army into the field, to undertake sieges and win back cities. St. Johnston, Glasgow, Kircud-bright, Lochmaban, these and the other key points fell one by one into his hands. Bruce himself was ready at last to break his peace with King Edward and to come back to lead his people. Wearied out with disastrous war, the English fell back on treachery to bring down the Scottish champion. It was John Menteith who accepted their gold and the shameful task. He surprised Wallace when he was asleep, unarmed and with only one servant, in Glasgow, whither he had come to a secret assignation with the Bruce. With a romance about the house being surrounded with English soldiers they wheedled him into letting himself be bound, declaring that he had no hope of escaping with his life unless he appeared as their prisoner. Once in their power, he was soon on the road to London, where his end awaited him. He died a martyr for Scotland, his death attended with monastic visions of his being carried into heaven with only a few ritual hours' delay in purgatory.

So ends Blind Harry's tale of William Wallace. History would be hard put to it to find a champion to hold a candle to his hero: his repeated triumphs against overwhelming odds could only be paralleled in some child's story. For those parts of the story which have no known historical basis the minstrel's own teeming and unrestrained imagination is clearly to some extent responsible. Some, however, probably represent magnified versions of incidents which actually occurred, but which the chroniclers of the day thought too trivial to be worth notice in their annals. Harry claimed that he based his account on a Latin life, now lost, by one John Blair, who was Wallace's priest. Other parts are purely traditional. Among these is the celebrated story of the potter, which now makes its third and penultimate appearance in the story of an outlaw. Many of these traditional episodes are quite easily recognizable, for they are different in tone from other incidents. They are simple, straightforward interludes, representing the workings of popular fancy: the others are detailed, sometimes complex elaborations, introduced to bring out some point about the hero. So the incident of the Queen of England and her ladies' embassy to Wallace reveals that he is the flower of chivalry:

'Wallace to sic did never gret owtrage.'

Others resemble those episodes introduced in earlier stories to exalt the stature of the principal character: so the stories of Wallace's fights with champions and with the French lion recall Hereward's triumphs over Cornish giants and enchanted bears. Wallace is again like Hereward in receiving dreams and visions; and like Fulk Fitzwarin he is spoken of by renowned seers in their prophecies. But these attempts to dress him up as a hero of chivalry are for us much less interesting than those other, purely popular additions to his story which present him as an outlaw of the same stamp as Robin Hood.

In some of these latter passages Blind Harry has caught the spirit of the Greenwood story extraordinarily well. Now he speaks of the forest's freedom and its plenty:

'King Edwardis self could nocht get bettir wyn
Than thai had thar, warnage and venysonne
Off bestial in to full gret fusioun.'

Now he speaks of its hardships, of the constant changes of fortune to which those who have made it their refuge are exposed:

'Now lycht, now sadd; now blisful, now in baill;
In haist, now hurt; now soroufull, now haill;
Nowe weildand weyle; now calde weddyr, now hett;
Nowe moist, now drowth; now waverand wynd, now wet'

Now again he makes Wallace the prince of archers, like Robin Hood:

> 'No man was thar that Wallace bow mycht draw'

He pictures him, like a Sherwood outlaw, questing for venison:

> 'Eftir the sone Wallis walkit about
> Upon Teht side, whar he saw mony rout
> Of wyld bestis waverand in wode and playne;
> Sone at a schot a gret hart has he slayne'

His conduct was marked by the same generosity to the poor and needy as that of his later forest compeers:

> 'Wallace wald none, but gaiff of his *fell sys*, (many times)
> To pour and rych, upon a gudlye wis.
> Humyll he was, hardy, wis and free,
> As off rychess he held na propyrte.'

This is a man of the same kind as Robin Hood, the proud yeoman, 'comely, corteys and gode', the friend of all who are in misfortune. But, after all, this is to be expected; Wallace's task and that of Robin and all the outlaws are essentially the same, to combat tyranny, to eradicate abuse, to avenge the oppressed and to restore the dispossessed to their rightful inheritance.

There is nothing unconscious about all this. Blind Harry was fully aware of the literary conventions of outlawry. To live in and by the forest was for him to live 'in outlaw wise'. In Wallace's miscellaneous host there was room and to spare for independent spirits of this brand. Such a one was 'Cristall of Cetoun' (Seaton):

> 'In Jedwort wood for saiffgard he had beyne,
> Agayne Sotheroun full weill he couth opteyn.
> In wtlaw oys (wise) he levit thar but let.'

Another was 'Ruwayn', an outlaw of the famous Birnam wood:

> 'In wtlaw oys he had lang levyt thar
> On bestiall, whill he mycht get no mair.'

It was as a forest bandit, living free and defiant in 'outlaw wise' like these men, that Wallace's own career began and ended. This part of his story is attested in historical records as well as minstrels' fiction. It is not surprising to find that the Scottish chroniclers were the first historians to take Robin Hood seriously: men of the same stamp as he were among their own national heroes.

Robin Hood is a figure of popular imagination; Wallace's part is on the stage of history. In the end he stands closer to Hereward the Saxon than to the outlaw of Sherwood. The inspiration behind their stories is the same, a proud people's bitter indignation against the oppressions of a conqueror. Wallace's story is a violent one; sudden death continually dogs his footsteps in the pages of Blind Harry. One cannot miss the exultant note in the accounts of this bloodshed.

'Now thow sall feyll how I use to let blude!'

declares his hero. Nor is one spared any anatomical details:

'Wallace in haist be the gorget hym hynt.
On the oe'r loft cast him whar he stud,
While neyss and mowth all ruschit out of blud.'

One hears the sound of bones breaking and sees the blood spurt:
'Upon the hed ane with the steing hit he,
Till bone and frayn he gert in pecis flee'

The grim mood of the poem is set by the words which Harry puts into the mouth of his own hero:

'I lik bettir to se the Southren de (die)
Than gold or land that thai can giff to me.'

This ferocity is justified in the same way as it is in the story of Hereward, by an endless tale of the brutal and oppressive acts perpetrated by the conquerors on an innocent people. There is here the same story of murders done upon the hero's kinsmen, of the seizure of his people's lands, even the same story of the drunken soldiers of the conqueror making arrogant ridicule of the hero's race and its champions. The horrors of the description of the burning of the Barns of Ayr, with the night echoing with the cries of men dying in terror, and with the smell of burnt human flesh drifting down wind with the smoke, were for Harry and his audience only part of a just retribution on the men who had not hesitated to put Wallace's innocent Marion Bradfute to a secret death.

75

Though this recurrent theme of racial hatred reveals him as closer kin to Hereward than to Robin Hood, Wallace's story has its bearing on the stories of the later outlaws to whom we shall next have to turn. For they indisputably belong to the same family; they observe the same code, they follow the same manner of living, the same stories are even recounted of them. What this indicates most clearly is the source ˆ inspiration behind all the legends—what kind of feeling it was that prompted the popular imagination to credit this kind of story to this kind of person. For the appeal of the outlaw is always the justice of his cause: his ferocity is justified by the outrageous and tyrannical conduct of his enemies. However exaggerated or imaginary the stories may be, moreover, there can be no doubt that this tyranny was in Wallace's case real. Though Robin Hood is clearly not a hero of patriotic resistance, we shall therefore expect to find at the back of his story a similar tale of real oppression to dignify his deeds with a certain rough justice in the eyes of his admirers.

It is striking confirmation of this suggested relationship to find that in a later ballad, celebrating the deeds of another Scottish patriot, the echoes of the story of Robin Hood have become still more striking. He is the outlaw Murray of Ettrick forest, another warrior who upheld the national cause in the hour when King and Lords had forsaken it:

> 'These landes are mine, the Outlaw said,
>   I own na king in Christentie;
> Frae Soudron I this forest wan
>   When the King nor King's knights were not to see'

This poem has now acquired the traditional type of ballad opening, setting the green-wood stage:

> 'Etrick forest is a fair foreste
>   In it grows many a semlie tre;
> The hart, the hynd, the doe, the rae,
>   And of a' wylde beastis gret plentie'

The outlaws too have acquired their traditional habit:

> 'His mery men are in liverie clad
>   Of the Lincoln grene so fair to see;
> He and his ladie in purple clad,
>   O, if they live not royallie!'

The theme of the story has become that which in later stories is traditional, of how the King came to the forest and met the outlaw, and in the end admitted him and his men to his peace. The pardoned outlaw becomes the sheriff of the forest, the same outcome which rounds off the *Tale of Gamelyn*, who was in the end pardoned by the King and made chief justice of all his 'fre forest'. The appeal of the national struggle with the 'Southrons' begins to take second place to the lure of the Greenwood and the free life of the outlaw.

> 'Wha ever heard, in ony time,
>   Sicken an outlaw in his degree,
> Sic favour get before a king,
>   As did the Outlaw Murray of the forest frie?'

Later on the pure greenwood outlaw appears in Scottish ballads, such as that of Johnie Cock, the young poacher whom seven foresters hunted down and slew for shooting the King's venison. Robin Hood's features were known north of the border. 'Moray land' claimed to harbour the bones of Little John for its own. But the importance of the Scottish traditions is independent. They reveal with a clarity that is not to be found elsewhere the relationship between the stories of heroes whose part is played in history but who are also outlaws, and the later stories of men who belong to a greenwood of pure fancy. It is not just the accidental effect of indiscriminate borrowing from traditional sources that leads popular poetry to tell the same stories of men like Wallace and Hereward and of men like Robin Hood. Though their context is in many ways very different, we must therefore expect to find behind the legends of these later outlaws an inspiration which is not wholly dissimilar to that which endeared men like Wallace to the popular imagination. We shall have at the same time to account for the disappearance of the chivalrous embellishment which has been one of the hallmarks of the stories we have dealt with so far, and for the shift of scene from a definite historical setting to a country within the undefined boundaries of 'once upon a time'. If an interpretation can be found which is consistent both with this new setting and with what we have learned of the outlaws so far, it will probably be the right one.

VII

⟡⟡⟡⟡⟡⟡⟡⟡⟡⟡⟡⟡⟡⟡⟡⟡⟡⟡⟡⟡⟡⟡⟡⟡⟡⟡⟡⟡⟡⟡⟡⟡⟡⟡

The Tale of Gamelyn

⟡⟡⟡⟡⟡⟡⟡⟡⟡⟡⟡⟡⟡⟡⟡⟡⟡⟡⟡⟡⟡⟡⟡⟡⟡⟡⟡⟡⟡⟡⟡⟡⟡⟡

THE stories of Fulk Fitzwarin and Eustace the Monk were written down some time in the thirteenth century; the earliest surviving ballads of Robin Hood, the arch outlaw of English medieval legend, date from the fifteenth. We know that by then he was already a traditional figure, long famous in popular song, but the older poems about him, on which the ones we know were doubtless based, are lost. Some time between these dates, however, stands the story of another outlaw, the *Tale of Gamelyn*, written by some forgotten poet and probably about the middle of the fourteenth century. It survives in several of the older manuscripts of the *Canterbury Tales*, where it usually follows the Cook's unfinished story, which was apparently so bawdy that even the usually unblushing Chaucer found it too much for him. It was not Chaucer who wrote the story of Gamelyn, however, for it is in a rhythm that he never used; and how it came to be included among his tales is unexplained. It may be that he intended to remould it, and put a new version of it into the mouth of his Plowman or some other rustic character, and that being found among his papers it was taken for his own. But, however it came about, it is to the accident which associated the story with the name of the greatest English medieval poet that we owe its survival.

Though the *Tale of Gamelyn* is different in many respects
both from the stories of Fulk and Eustace the Monk which
precede it, and from the later ballads of Robin Hood, it is much
closer to the latter. It is not in the same form as they are, for it
is far from being a ballad; it would technically be called a
metrical romance, but there is nothing romantic about its tone
or style. It is its lack of adornment, indeed, which puts it in a
quite different category from the earlier stories, in which historical rebels are trapped out as heroes of romance. For with
the *Tale of Gamelyn* we have turned our backs once and for all
upon the world of chivalry and the courts of Kings. We shall
have no more of necromancers and dragons; there is nothing
enchanted about the forest in which Gamelyn took refuge from
justice and joined the outlaws. It is a real wood where one
stumbles and tears one's clothes, and where the wandering
fugitive feels the pinch of hunger. The reason for this is that
we have moved into a new social world, for, as anyone who has
read much medieval romance knows, chivalrous adventures with
dragons and princesses were the privilege of the nobility.
Gamelyn's father was, it is true, a knight, but he was a knight
not of the courts but of the shire, one who had increased his
heritage with his 'right hand', who prided himself not on his
prowess in battle but because his lands were his own, to give
to whom he would. We have left the world of knights, in the
romantic sense, for a world of landlords and peasants, the world
in which Robin Hood himself moved: we have come nearer to
the soil.

This new world is one which was clearly familiar to the
author of the poem, for all kinds of small details show that he
knew well the manners and customs of the countryside. We hear
of juries of the shire and of 'great moots', and of the 'dooms' pronounced therein, we hear of ploughlands and bondmen; when
Gamelyn was declared an outlaw, we hear that his 'wolves head
was cryed'; the same phrase that is found in the antique laws of
Edward the Confessor and Henry I—for the price on the head
of an outlawed man was the same as the price upon a wolf. The
world of Gamelyn is bounded by his father's shire, and its
surroundings are his natural ones. This is what makes him
different from his predecessors; for all their peasant disguises,
one would not find Hereward or Fulk Fitzwarin challenging,

like Gamelyn, the wrestling champion at a wayside fair. They belong to too different a milieu.

In their stories the similarities which showed that they belonged to the same tradition as Robin Hood were similarities of specific incident. In the case of Gamelyn it is not the incident but the tone and atmosphere which link him with Robin. This is because his story, too, is intended for a popular audience. The language and metre of the poem are popular; though they are very different from that of the ballads, it is clear that this poem also was intended for recitation, from the endlessly recurring line:

'Litheth, and Listneth, and holdeth your tonge'.

All through the poem there is a tendency to alliteration: perhaps it was based on an older, alliterative poem, in the style which seems to have developed out of the old Anglo-Saxon method of versifying, and which reached in the fourteenth century a new height in Langland's *Piers Plowman*. The story, again like the ballads, moves at speed: and it appeals to the same sentiments and tastes as they do. Perhaps it is not surprising that later generations seem to have enrolled Gamelyn among Robin Hood's own men, for it is probably his story that fathered both the Gandelyn who killed the forester Wrennock of the Dunne, and the young Gamwel who is associated with the Earl of Huntingdon in the ballad of *Robin Hood and the Stranger*.

It is clear that before going any farther the *Tale of Gamelyn* must be told. The plot is a very familiar one; it is the story of a younger son, left at his father's death in the care of a wicked elder brother who seeks to cheat him of his inheritance. The story opens at the death-bed of Sir Johan of Boundys, the old knight, who knows that his end is near, and has called to him his neighbours that he may in their presence part his lands among his three sons. He knows that his neighbours will try to cheat the young Gamelyn, who is still a child, of his share, but the old man is still determined to have his way, in spite of their wiles:

'Then seyde the knight 'I sware by Seynt Martin,
For al that ye have y-doon yit is the land myn.'

So, with his last words, he divides his all; the five ploughlands that his father left him shall go to his eldest son, five more which he added shall go to the second, and all that remains, which he has purchased of his own money, shall go to Gamelyn. The scene is set, the neighbours take their leave; a moment after Sir John lies 'stoon stille', and Gamelyn is left to the tender mercies of his eldest brother.

So much for the *mise en scène*, familiar from a hundred traditional stories. Gamelyn grew up in his brother's hall, and while his brother held his lands in ward, they were wasted and went to ruin. He grew up strong and tall, until he was on the verge of manhood, when one day as he stood in his brother's yard his mind began to turn to his wasted lands, and he determined to claim his inheritance. So he sought his brother out, and the scene that ensued was the first in their long and furious quarrel. At first his brother laughed in Gamelyn's face; he told him he was a 'gadelyng', base born, and could inherit nothing; he should be glad enough that he was given his keep. Gamelyn replied angrily to the slur on his birth that he was as well born as his brother, and the elder in rage called on his men to bind and beat the boy. But they had reckoned without the strength of this young Samson; Gamelyn seized a pestle and charged them, looking as 'a wilde lyoun'; the men fell in a heap, and Gamelyn ran past them and shut himself in the hay loft. Thence he threatened to break every bone in the body of any who came near him, unless his brother gave him back his land. For the moment the latter saw that he was beaten; in his cunning he turned all to mirth, and told Gamelyn he had only wished to try his strength. If he would live with him, Gamelyn should have his land and his kiss of peace, and more too:

> 'Thy land, that lyth laye, full wel it schal be sowe,
> And thyn houses reysed up, that ben layd so lowe'

So Gamelyn gave him the kiss of peace, and had his land, and for the moment they lived happily together.

It was not long after this that a wrestling was cried in the country, and 'there was set up a ram and a ryng', the traditional prizes for him who could overthrow the champion. Gamelyn soon decided that he would go and try his fortune, for, as he told his brother, it would bring great worship to the family if he could bring back to their hall the coveted trophies. So he set out, and as he came near the spot, he met a poor franklin weeping, who told him that the champion had just 'cast' his two sons, who had both died of their injuries. Gamelyn swore to avenge him, and leaving his horse and his shirt with him hurried to the ring.

The champion had heard some of the evil stories that Gamelyn's brother had spread about him, and when he heard his name he warned him to expect no mercy. But he had met more than his match; he tried one cast at Gamelyn, and then Gamelyn took the offensive:

> 'Of all the tornes that he couthe he showed him but one'

He cast him on his left side; his ribs were broken, and his arm gave a great crack as he fell. One champion was thus brought down, and for the moment no one seemed inclined to take up the challenge of his victor. The fair in any case was almost finished, and the wardens brought Gamelyn the ram and the ring 'for the best wrasteler that ever here came'. Flushed with his victory and with the pride of the inheritance he had so lately come into, Gamelyn thanked them, and invited all those at the fair, great and small, to accompany him home and to celebrate his triumph as his guests at the hall.

He had not, of course, reckoned on his brother's reactions. His relatives devout hope had been that a broken neck would solve the family problems, and he had no intention of entertaining half the county in his home. When he saw the 'rowte' in the distance he told his porter to bar the gate, and to let no man pass. He was not, however, like Fitzwarin, the fortunate possessor of a fortified house with drawbridge and portcullis, and the door of a manor house presented few problems to a young wrestling champion. Gamelyn drove it in with a couple of stout kicks, caught the fleeing porter, broke his neck with one blow, and in his rage threw his lifeless corpse into the well in the courtyard. In a moment this yard was clear of his brother's men; they had no desire to go the same way. Then he went to the gate, and put it wide open:

> 'He let in alle maner men that goon in wold or ryd,
> And seyde 'Ye be welcome, withouten eny greeve,
> For wee will be maistres here and aske no man leeve'

Five tuns of wine were broached, and Gamelyn swore that none should leave while a drop was left. As for any who might grumble at the waste:

> 'Who that maketh grucchyng that we here dwelle,
> He schal to the porter into the drawe well.'

Gamelyn's feast lasted seven days and nights. At the end he bade his guests farewell, and then went to fetch his brother out of the cellar where he had taken refuge. There ensued a scene which could only take place in a medieval poem which wishes to underline the spotless honour of its hero. The brother told Gamelyn that he would make him his heir, but he also told him that he had sworn before all his men to have him bound hand and foot to avenge his porter. Surely his brother now would not let him be forsworn, and dishonoured before all, but would let him bind him hand and foot, and show him thus once to his men, so that his word should be fulfilled? (The treachery contemplated here is pretty obvious, and even for its own age the episode is very naïve indeed; but the self-sacrifice of a hero, in order that a brother or companion should not be forsworn, was a favourite stock incident in medieval narrative. It is here introduced very artlessly, but the object is to show Gamelyn's honourable and trusting nature.) He let himself be bound, with the result that any one in their senses could have foreseen. He was fettered to a post in the dining-hall, where he stood for all to mock, without food, powerless, and chained hand and foot.

But Gamelyn, like all the heroes of his kind, had friends among the poor, the servants and bondmen. It was to Adam the Spencer, who had been his father's man long before, that he turned: he called him to him as he stood alone, and at last won from him a promise to loose his bonds and bring him food. Adam, however, had more to add to the plan. The brother had, he told Gamelyn, arranged a great feast on the next Sunday, and all the great churchmen from round about, abbots, priors and all would be there. Before they came, Adam promised to unlock Gamelyn's fetters. In the middle of the meal Gamelyn should appeal to them to speak for him to his brother; if they would, Gamelyn would be freed and no shadow of suspicion need fall on Adam. But if they would not, then Gamelyn should, when Adam gave the sign, cast away his fetters, and then:

> 'Thow schalt have a good staff and I wil have another,
> And Cristes curs have that oon that faileth that other.'

When the day came all worked out as had been planned. The abbots and Gamelyn's brother sat at meat, and Gamelyn stood tethered at the farthest end of the hall; his brother told them that he was mad, and to his appeals they replied only with solemn curses. Meanwhile Adam had fetched two staves and brought them to the door; suddenly the prisoner threw aside his fetters, and the guests found themselves facing two angry men, armed with stout clubs. There was no one to help them; Gamelyn had always been the champion of the servants, and they had no intention of coming to the aid of an oppressive master and his associates, churchmen though they were. Gamelyn and Adam fell on the guests, laying about them; not a man escaped unhurt:

'Thider they came rydyng jolily with swaynes,
But home agen they were y-lad in cartes and waynes.'

With one blow Gamelyn felled his brother; 'a little above the girdel the rigge bon to-brast'. Then he set him in his own fetters to 'cool his blood', while the servants brought him of all the best fare in the house.

Family quarrels were one thing, but the assault and battery of ecclesiastics was another. While Gamelyn was celebrating his release, word had been sent to the sheriff of the affair, and four-and-twenty men had formed a *posse* to come and take the offenders. The first word that Gamelyn had of their coming was when his new porter ran in with the news that there were foemen at the gate. He and Adam drove away the first group of men by a smart sally from the postern gate, but soon they saw a great rout coming with the sheriff at their head. It was no time to stay:

'Adam took by the honde yonge Gamelyn,
And everich of hem two drank a draught of wyn.
And after took her coursers and wenten her way;
Tho fond the Scherreve nest, but non ay (eggs).'

While the sheriff was searching the house and loosing Gamelyn's brother from his fetters, they were away to the forest, stumbling through the woods, Adam tearing his clothes and cursing the ill-luck that had reduced him from a comfortable servant to a hungry fugitive.

It was as they pushed their way through the forest that Gamelyn and Adam came by chance upon the outlaws. First they heard voices ahead in the thick wood; then, as they peered under the boughs, they saw the 'master outlaw' where he sat at his meal with his seven score of men about him. At first the outlaws took them for the law's spies, and seven men came out and brought them in before their 'king'. But Gamelyn's words soon assured him that these were men of his own stamp:

'Gamelyn answerde the king with his croune:
' "He most needs walk in woods, that may not walke in town.
Sire we walk not heer non harm for to do,
But if we meete a deer, to Scheete therto . . ." '

So he made them join with his men at their meal, and while they ate he heard from them their story. When it was ended, the master outlaw enrolled them in his band, and not long after he made Gamelyn master under him.

They had not been three weeks with the outlaws before the news came that their master's friends had a pardon for him from the King. So he took his leave and returned to his land, and Gamelyn was crowned King of the outlaws in his place. Meanwhile his outlawry was made public; his brother was healed of his broken back, and for the new term himself was made sheriff. Gamelyn's lands were seized, and in accordance with law, his peasants paid fine to the sheriff, as they would to a new

The outlaws in the Forest.

lord when the old died, for to the law Gamelyn was now dead. But Gamelyn was a lord whom they loved, and the new master was harsh; so his bondmen kept their faith to him, and they sent to him in the forest to tell him how things stood with him and his land. Their master heard their news and returned their greetings; bitterly he regretted that he had not killed his brother outright. For himself, he might flee, but the welfare of his peasants and their wives he could not overlook, and he swore to them he would be at the next shire court to uphold their cause. He was as good as his word.

Gamelyn went to the shire court alone. As an outlaw he had no right at law (and it is clear from the poem that its author knew the law well enough): when he strode into the 'moot hall', therefore, he put himself in the sheriff's power. He had no right to speak in his own defence, and he was allowed no chance to; he was bound and fettered and cast into the sheriff's prison to await the assize. But though he was in the sheriff's power, the law still ran for him; he had another brother, Sir Ote, the 'myddeleste' of Sir John's sons, and word now came to him of how Gamelyn was in prison. Ote was as honourable as his elder brother was treacherous: as soon as he had heard the news he saddled his horse and rode to the sheriff. The elder brother was as deaf to his pleas for family feeling as might have been expected; but he could not refuse to bail Gamelyn if his brother stood surety for him. Once more Gamelyn was released, and returned to Sir Ote's house with him.

Once again, now that he was free, his duties towards his own men took first place with Gamelyn. He was still crowned King of the outlaws; he must go to the forest, to see how things stood with them:

> 'To see how my younge men leden her lyf
> Whether they lyven in joie or elles in stryf.'

Ote tried hard to dissuade him; he was afraid that once with his men in the forest Gamelyn would never return, and as his mainpernor he himself would be bound and tried in his place. But Gamelyn swore that he would be back on the day of the assize, and so he departed to find 'his mery men under woode bough'. There he found them, and they told him of their adventures in his absence, and he told of how he had been first bound and then bailed free. Until the day of the assize he remained with his outlaws in the forest, adding to the tail of charges against him by the plunder of any rich churchmen who passed his way.

Meanwhile his elder brother had, in the business-like manner of a medieval sheriff, set about the affair of packing a jury with bribed men to hang his brother, or one of them at least:

> 'The fals knight his brother forgat he nat that,
> To hyre the men on his quest to hangen his brother;
> Though he hadde nought that oon he wolde have that other.'

At length the day of the assize arrived; the lords of the county came to the 'moot hall', the King's justice was sitting, and Sir Ote was taken and brought to court in fetters. The case was dealt with briefly; the jury delivered their verdict, and the judge of assize gave his sentence that Sir Ote should hang as an outlaw.

But Gamelyn had not failed his brother. When the verdict was delivered, Adam the Spencer was in the back of the court, and the whole band of outlaws were outside, waiting to hear his report. When Adam had slipped out and told him all, Gamelyn stationed his young men at the door, and himself strode into the hall, for, as he said, he would that day be justice himself. No one stirred as he went in; they could see the outlaws outside. First Gamelyn loosed his brother, then he crossed to the justice's seat:

> 'The justice sat still, and roose not anoon;
> And Gamelyn clevede his cheeke boon;
> Gamelyn took him in the arm, and no more spake,
> But threw him over the barre, and his arm to-brak.'

Then Gamelyn took the justice's seat, and put Sir Ote beside him; his men entered, and bound the justice and the sheriff. Next all the jury that had judged Sir Ote were bound and fettered too. Then a jury was quickly empanelled from among the outlaws: verdict and sentence were not slow to be delivered, and they were put to immediate execution:

> 'The justice and the scherreve both hanged hye,
> To weyven with ropes and with the wynd drye;
> And the twelve sisours, sorwe have that rekke!
> Alle they were hanged faste by the nekke.'

So the tables of justice were turned: the outlaws sat in judgement upon the law itself, and right triumphed.

The story now ends swiftly. Gamelyn and Ote got safe conduct to the King, and obtained his pardon: indeed, when he heard of the misdoings of his officers, he held them in good esteem. Sir Ote he made his justice, and Gamelyn, by a delightful irony of fate, was made Chief Justice of the Forest. The other outlaws were pardoned, and Gamelyn won back his land, and, what mattered as much to him, his people. So he and Sir Ote returned home, to live and die at last in prosperity. The poem is rounded off in the medieval manner with an appropriate moral reflection:

> 'They liveden togidere whil that Crist wolde,
> And sithen was Gamelyn graven under molde.
> And so schal we al, may ther no man fle:
> God bryng us to the joye that ever schal be.'

Such is the tale of Gamelyn, the first outlaw legend which has survived which is written in the English tongue. It has had a curious literary history. First it found an anomalous place among the *Canterbury Tales*, most of which are in a very different mood: neither Chaucer the satyrist nor Chaucer the writer of romance would have had much sympathy with the fierce and angry author of this poem. Later it was seen by Thomas Lodge, the Elizabethan poet and adventurer, who, while he travelled with Captain Clarke to 'the Ilands of Terceras and the Canaries' wrote it up into his renaissance romance, *Rosalynde*, 'wrote in the ocean, when everie line was wet with a surge, and every numerous passion countercheckt with a storm'. But it was a new story that he made out of the old. Gamelyn becomes the banished King of France, living as an outlaw in the Forest of Arden; his brother becomes the usurper, and with the entry of their two daughters, Aliena and Roasalynde, upon the scene, the outlaw story is changed to a tale of forest love. It was Lodge's romance that Shakespeare adapted to give the plot to *As You Like It*, introducing a further host of new characters, Jacques, Touchstone, William and Audrey. Whether Shakespeare had ever seen or heard of the older story we cannot tell: he may have, for at more than one place his play agrees more closely with the events in the tale than with those in Lodge's *Rosalynde*. But these could be mere coincidences; the story has been reshaped out of recognition, and there is nothing basic in common between old Adam and Orlando, and Gamelyn and the stout Adam the Spencer of the medieval poem.

For the latter is entirely without any of the trappings with which Shakespeare has decorated the legend. The oaks of Gamelyn's forest have no lovelorn messages in their bark; his band contains no melancholy Jacques to philosophize on the fall of a hunted stag. The appeal of the old poem does not lie in its charm, but in a certain crude vigour which is entirely its own, and in its swift moving episode. It lacks even such slight decoration as serves to freshen the ballads of Robin Hood, those pencil sketches of the charm of the greenwood, which in so many of them create an immediate atmosphere, in opening lines such as those of *Robin Hood and the Monk*:

> 'In summer when the schawes be shene
> And leaves be large and long,
> It is ful mery in fair forest
> To hear the birde's song.'

The tone of Gamelyn is, compared with the ballads, dour and angry. It is quite easily the most ferocious of the outlaw legends.

Violence and anger are, indeed, its most striking features. A certain fierce irony is the nearest its author ever gets to lightness of touch, whether it is the irony of poetic justice in the final scene where the outlaws sit in judgement upon the King's officers, or the irony of Adam's cry to Gamelyn when they are setting upon the clerics in the dining hall:

> 'Gamelyn,' sayde Adam 'do hem but good:
> They ben men of Holy Chirche, draw of hem no blood!
> Save wel the croune, and do hem none harmes
> But brek both her legges and sithen her armes'.

The descriptive passages are at their best when violence is the theme. The cracking of bones is a familiar sound to the author, and he seldom denies us the relish of anatomical details of injuries. It is with obvious satisfaction that he recalls that the well into which the ill-fated porter disappeared was seven fathoms deep. The evil champion lies with his ribs crushed, the wicked brother is 'brok-bak' for life, the churchmen are carried home with smashed limbs in 'cartes and waynes'; our parting picture is of the justice and his sisours, with the flesh drying upon their bones, swinging in the wind from the gallows. And one cannot miss the note of exultation in the poet's voice as he records these things.

As one might expect, he has made little attempt to give a softer side to the character of his central figure. Since medieval authors seldom exploited intricacies of character and tended to portray their heroes and villains as type figures rather than individuals, it is perhaps unfair to labour this point, but the Gamelyn of the tale has not, for instance, either the naïve piety or the instinctive kindness which soften the character of Robin Hood in the ballads. He is liberal enough, it is true; but it is typical of the violence which is part not only of his character but of the character of the poem as a whole, that his idea of hospitality should be to entertain half the county for seven days non-stop drinking. The most attractive side to his personality is, probably, his intense loyalty to his own people, whether it be to his brother, to his 'yong men of prys' in the forest, or to the bondmen of his manors. These characteristics, loyalty and liberality, stamp him as a man of honour and a model of good lordship; they are part of the author's type-casting of Gamelyn. They are qualities, too, which a medieval audience would hold in special respect, for they were qualities essential to the theory of the medieval social system. Apart from these Gamelyn's most striking characteristic is his physical strength. He can break a man's neck with one blow or toss him bodily into a well: with one well aimed kick he can stove in a manor door. If he has a counterpart in later literature it is Blackmore's Jan Ridd, like him the son of a yeoman-squire, who like him may lack cunning but can break the ribs of a Cornish giant in the first throw of a wrestling match and can wrench the muscle out of Carver Doone's arm with his bare hands as one would the heart of an orange. Gamelyn of course has none of the tenderness which is the reverse side of Jan Ridd's superhuman strength. As we see him he is a tough, violent man of the kind who does not hesitate to take the law into his own hands, but gifted at the same time—and this is perhaps the most essential thing of all—with an innate sense of justice.

For all the violence in the *Tale of Gamelyn* is justified, for the author and his audience, by the fact that it is done in the cause of right in the battle against injustice. The real theme of the poem is the downfall of unjust lordship. The picture is drawn with some care and does not lack verisimilitude—it is much more like real life than most of the ballad episodes. The author knew his countryside and he knew his law, and he put his knowledge to good use. He knew, for instance, that the gentry of a county would do their best to keep all Sir John's lands in one set of hands, and that they would not have much compunction in passing over the claims of a child in favour of those of someone who, if they served him, might serve them in their turn. He knew that nine out of ten guardians who held lands for a ward wasted them, and did not make much effort to make restitution, for he knew that the average medieval landlord, being less anxious about what he put into the land than about what he got out of it, would make the utmost of whatever advantages his legal position as a guardian gave him. There is subtlety as well as unscrupulousness in the elder brother's attempt to discredit Gamelyn's legitimacy; it is just the kind of plea that an unscrupulous man might put forward to justify the appropriation of another's land, trusting in the inertia of neighbours who would always favour the claim of whoever was in actual possession. As for the buying of the jury, it is again typical. The corruption of justice is one of the endlessly recurring themes of medieval satire—and indeed of medieval constitutional history. It was impossible to keep sheriffs from abusing their rights, just as it was impossible to prevent justices of the peace from becoming the retainers of great lords, so giving private individuals a controlling interest in their justice. The *Tale of Gamelyn* paints the same picture of the total corruption of justice and the law, and of the grasping and unscrupulous methods of the average landlord, as do the ballads of Robin Hood and, in a different way, Piers Plowman and a hundred other works which lament the abuse of the social and legal system in the English middle ages.

As always in the outlaw legends, the champion of justice is the master outlaw, Gamelyn, for the law can be bought by the rich, and it is only outside it that true justice can be found. His brigandage was typical in this way, for he warred for the righting of his wrong, and only the guilty had cause to fear him— and specially the guilty cleric, for the Church was notoriously the most tyrannous landlord of all.

> 'Whil Gamelyn was outlawed, had he no cors:
> There was no man for him ferde the wors,
> But abbotes and priouris, monk and chanoun'

The servants in the hall were on his side when he rounded on his brother's guests for:

> 'There was no lewede man that in the halle stood
> That wolde do Gamelyn anything but good.'

The clerks were their enemies too: 'They hadde no rewthe of men of holy cherche'. He was the champion of the poor: his peasants were as devoted to him as he was to them. Like Robin Hood, he stands for a new justice, and for a new distribution of wealth in which they shall no longer be cheated of their share; and, like Robin, he is repaid by the poor with their affection and loyalty.

The object of the poem is, therefore, through the medium of a simple and traditional story, vigorously told, to attack the abuses of the social and legal system. It is the author's assumption that knights and abbots and officers of the law are normally public enemies, and that the only champions of justice are those who are, officially, criminals. This is the assumption of all the outlaw legends, that the true relationship between law and justice has somehow, by the wickedness of men, become reversed, and in this topsy-turvy world law has become the façade of oppression and justice can only be found outside it. In the *Tale of Gamelyn* we have the most vivid expression of this idea in all the outlaw literature. For here the triumph of justice is achieved finally and only through the mockery of the law, with the justice and sheriff in the dock, with the master outlaw and a condemned prisoner sitting in the justice's seat, and with twelve forest brigands weighing their verdict as jurymen. The officers of the law are condemned and die with all the solemnity of their own legal ceremonial.

Brilliantly conceived as this scene is, however, it reveals at the same time the limited political horizons of the authors of the outlaw poems and of those who heard them. Their only answer to their problem was the same court with a different judge and a different jury. Their attack was on the corruption within the system, not on the system itself, for they could conceive of no other. Their complaint was not that the system caused destitution, but that it took from the destitute even that to which they had a just title. They did not wish to dispense with lords, for lords were indispensable. The qualities which made Gamelyn a hero of the people were not the qualities which would make him an apostle of social revolution; they were, as has been said, the qualities which would make him a just lord, his innate sense of honour, and his unswerving loyalty to his dependants. The final solution is not a new dispensation, but a change of personnel; Sir Ote shall be the King's Justice of Assize, and Gamelyn Chief Justice of all the Forest.

The outlaws' hierarchy is, indeed, a kind of parody of the normal, legal one. The outlaws have noblemen amongst them; they are 'yong men of prys', and Gamelyn and Adam know they will receive a fair reception from their chief because he is of 'gentil blood'. One incident is especially striking in this context. When Gamelyn and Adam first meet the outlaws and are hailed before their master, they ask who that master may be:

> 'Yonge men', seyde Gamelyn 'by your lewte,
>   What man is your maister that ye with be?'
> Alle they answerde withoute lesyng
> 'Our maister is i-crowned of outlawes Kyng'.

The King of the Outlaws seems a strange figure, but he is really just another mark of the fact that the outlaws accept, like everyone else, the social order with its lords and kings. The organization of the outlaw band works on the same principle as the 'feudal' system of society: to Gamelyn as king the outlaws owe the unquestioning obedience of man to lord, and as king Gamelyn has in his turn his duty as their judge and protector. The hierarchical principle was too deeply rooted in the medieval mind for men to conceive any kind of society without it. They even imposed it on substrata of their society: there were kings of minstrels and kings of jesters, and the heralds had an elaborate coronation ceremony for their Kings-of-Arms. When the peasants rose in revolt in 1381 John Lister had himself crowned their king in Norfolk: he came as near as most in English history, to being King of the Outlaws.

This mental limitation to a hierarchical scheme of things was one of the main handicaps of the socially dissatisfied throughout the middle ages. They were too conservative by instinct to think in terms of anything more than a change of masters, and in the long run, as history has shown, there is not much to choose between one family of masters and another. The *Tale of Gamelyn* also reveals the other great weakness of the oppressed. The only method by which they could envisage achieving an improvement in their lot was by violence. In a sense this was no more than the truth, for violence is the only obvious weapon to hand for those who are excluded at once by the social system and by their own incapacity (these are really only reverse sides of the same coin) from political affairs. Violence, however, when its objects were as limited as theirs were, could only be a dead-end on the road to social justice. One could put Gamelyn in the sheriff's place, but when his sons came to manhood, what guarantee was there that they would follow in the footsteps of their father rather than of their uncle? The scales, moreover, were weighted: nearly all medieval sheriffs were corrupt, and a very large number of them died in their beds. The suffering peasant must wait for a more effective saviour than the defiant, generous outlaw chief, who, albeit the hero of his dreams, was yet of the blood of his oppressors.

VIII

The Robin Hood Ballads (I)

IN its bare bones the *Tale of Gamelyn* might be just another story of Robin Hood, for in essentials their outlines are the same. Its incident belongs to the same common stock of tradition; we shall find the identical situations of the tale over and over again in the ballads of Robin, that of the knight deprived of his land by the machinations of evil men; the rescue of the captured outlawed chief from the sheriff, the final pardon obtained from the King, even the same scene at the country wrestling match, with the ram and the ring set up for a prize and the franklin lamenting the death of his sons at the hands of the champion. There is nevertheless an immense difference between the two stories, but it is a difference not of plot but of literary form. The *Tale of Gamelyn* is a metrical romance composed by an author who used popular tradition but who also understood the art of literary narrative, and whose work bears, therefore, the stamp of his individual authorship. But the poems about Robin Hood are not romances but ballads, and it is this literary form which sets them apart from the other stories we have been reviewing, and which gives them authority as genuine guides to popular tastes. Ballads which were intended for recitation to an unlettered audience did not survive if they were not popular. Since it is this literary form that gives them their special importance to the historian, it becomes necessary to discuss just what the word ballad means.

A ballad is a popular song which may be predominantly either lyric or narrative in quality. Its origins are shrouded in the oblivion of a distant past; most of the ballads which have survived are late versions of much older poems. Their authors are beyond memory, if indeed they ever had any, for they often seem not have been composed, but, as Meredith put it, to have grown 'like mushrooms from a scuffle of feet over night'. The idea that popular poetry is the creation not of individual authors, but of the folk itself, seems at first sight so curious as to be almost beyond belief. Yet this genuinely seems to be the origin of the earliest ballads. They were the songs sung at their festivals and dances by forgotten country people, and were elaborated and added to by endless subsequent generations. Some were never changed much, and that is why one may find in a version of as late as, say, the eighteenth century, a ballad whose origin clearly belongs to the middle ages. One such is the ballad of the Outlaw Murray, which was written down about the year 1700, but which in its incident carries us back to a world which is purely medieval. The oldest ballads probably did not have much more than four lines of verse, very much on the 'fee-fi-fo-fum' model, and a recurrent refrain. But from such beginnings a whole narrative tradition could spring. As the dance and song lasted, one of the singers would echo the last two lines of the first stanza after the refrain, and someone else would cap it with a second couplet, and so on, until the song and its refrain in due course contained the nutshell of a legend. Sometimes, clearly, the method was dramatic, one singer singing his verse, and another echoing its last lines and replying.

A great many ballads never got farther than this stage, painting or dramatizing a situation which might one day become a story. Folklore provided a thousand plots of this kind, for its touch has always been impersonal. In the land of 'once upon a time' there was a witch and a prince and a princess; it is the process of time and the sophistication of succeeding ages which has individualized them. It was at this stage that the popular author laid his hands on the ballad, and began to weave its plot into a narrative. He left, however, plenty of traces of the nature of his material. Sometimes he kept a refrain recurring at the end of each verse; sometimes he preserved the iteration of the last couplet of a previous stanza in the first lines of the succeeding one, so giving a sure clue to the original method of composition. In working the songs up into his story, he employed to trap it out all the assistance which the consistency of tradition afforded him; so Lincoln green becomes the livery of every outlaw, and Robin Hood will be an archer whether he draws his bow in the course of the narrative or not. So again we find half a dozen of the ballads of Robin Hood, which have otherwise nothing much in common, opening with the same description of the spring forest which has become their traditional *mise en scène*:

> 'When shawes been sheene, and shradds full fayre,
>   And leves both large and longe
> It is merye walking in the fair forest
>   To heare the small birds' song.'

The ballad maker drew on every source: history, folklore, scraps of traditional description and incident, all were called on to eke out his story. Sometimes he strung two or more stories together to make one; and his borrowings on one occasion might be less wise than on another. A long ballad like the *Geste of Robin Hood* is, therefore, likely to be a pastiche of variable quality utilizing unnumbered sources. If, for this reason, as a narrative it may sometimes lack unity, we are compensated by being brought into direct touch with the thoughts and attitudes of a vanished common people who, being unlettered, have left no other literary testament.

The ballad makers were not the only persons who drew on popular poetry and wove its situations into a story. Traditional narrative was the treasure house to which all medieval narrators had recourse for inspiration, and writers like the author of the *Tale of Gamelyn* turned to it also, for the plots of stories which would be epic or romantic as the exigences of their matter dictated. But they changed the material that they used. They wrote for audiences more sophisticated than those of the ballads, and who demanded that a story should be something more than a succession of traditional incidents. They therefore imposed on their material an internal consistency which was often absent from the original, and they filled in the gaps where a ballad strung two stories artlessly together with explanatory detail.

It would be an exaggeration to say that they understood the problems of literary construction, but they understood them better than did the popular authors. Such subtleties as the interplay of character they often failed to grasp; they overworked the possibilities of situations until their tale became repetitive, and they exaggerated the attitudes of their type-cast heroes until they became ridiculous. But given a theme, though they might be endlessly longwinded in embroidering upon it, they could usually keep the final end in view, and guide the tale to a dénouement consistent with what had gone before.

For as long as they remained recognizably ballads these literary qualities remained lacking from the popular stories, unless by some happy accident. The bare bones of a story they did possess; after all it was from borrowings from popular tradition that the finest creations of medieval narrative literature, such as the Arthurian romances, were built up. But the ballad makers did not understand these demands of literary treatment, and their popular epics, though they have developed a long way from the choruses of the dance, retain a naïveté which they owe to their origin. The situation, which was all that was given in the first place, has been elaborated until there is the skeleton of a story, but it is the skeleton only. The characters have identified themselves by name, but they remain impersonal; the incidents have found an order, but it remains haphazard. The story still lacks internal logic. The hero acts out of part, or the scene is switched, and we are not told why: we are at the mercy of what Gummere called the ballad-maker's 'seven league stride over stretches of space and time, which in regular epic would claim pages of elaborate narrative'.

The main difficulty, therefore, in the appreciation of the epic ballads, such as are those of Robin Hood, is their complete lack of those literary qualities which we have been taught to look for. There can be no true tragedy in them, because the characters are only part-formed. We have only their deeds to judge them by, and these can only tell half the story: we can know that he fought the Sheriff of Nottingham, but the real Robin Hood remains impersonal and elusive. The incidents follow one another in haphazard and unexplained sequence, and we are not told what is behind them. So Robin Hood is an outlaw, and the rest of the story is consequential thereon, but we are never, at least in the ballads, told how he became one. Episodes are thus drained of all but a very general significance. The loss of a maidenhead is just another incident in a tale which involves at least two people: a murder is a deed of blood with no overtones. Herein is the difference between the stories of Robin Hood and the *Tale of Gamelyn*. One can almost hear the author of the tale smacking his lips as the ribs of another villain crack in his hero's powerful hold; but when Much the Miller's son kills a monk's pageboy 'for ferd lest he shold tell', the incident is related with such indifference, that we are hardly even shocked at its callousness. It is as if we were viewing the whole sequence of events from an immense distance; we can see the action but we cannot identify the actors, and because they are out of earshot we can judge them only by what they do.

Most of the Robin Hood ballads belong to this class of skeletal epic. Some retain vestiges of an earlier format; so we find here and there in *Robin Hood and the Monk* the repetition of the last two lines in the opening of a succeeding stanza, and in the ballad of *Robin and Gandelyn* the beautiful refrain: 'Robin lyeth in grene wood boundyn'. But for the most part they are ballad epics of the later kind with the characteristic qualities I have described. It is these qualities which make them so difficult to retell to a modern audience, which looks to literature for something more than a traditional story. One runs the constant risk of transmuting gold into lead, of giving what is primitive the appearance of the merely quaint, what is merely impersonal the appearance of being without point. But it is a risk the historian has to take. It is always difficult to look through the eyes of a vanished past, but that is what he has always to endeavour to do. And since the outlaw ballads give us nothing but action by which to judge their significance, some of that action must be retailed before we can discuss them. The beauty of their language must inevitably evaporate as the poetry is reduced to prose, but this particular act of vandalism is for present purposes a necessary one.

There is a great host of ballads of which Robin Hood is the hero. Most of these, at least in the form in which we have them, are compositions of the sixteenth and seventeenth centuries, when Robin Hood's traditional world already belonged to a half-forgotten past. The cruel forest laws have fallen into desuetude; archery was no longer a national exercise; the abbeys whose monks the outlaws had robbed had been dissolved. Robin Hood's legend belonged, in fact, to a world so far away in time that almost anything could be believed of it, and as a result his story was sometimes changed out of recognition. So we find him becoming in tradition an outlawed Earl of Huntingdon, or a national hero, who saves besieged London from a foreign enemy. Some of the ballads have naturally changed little and are still close enough, in all probability, to medieval versions. But the fact that in some so much has been changed means that we can never rely on these later ballads as a guide to the understanding of the milieu in which the legend grew up, to help us to identify its origins or to explain its hero's first popularity. To solve these problems it will be wiser to confine our attention to the ballads which are genuinely medieval or which can be shown to be of medieval origin, for though, since they come from a less lettered age, there are fewer of them, they can tell us much more about the world in which the legend was first well known.

By far the most famous of all the ballads is the *Littel Geste of Robyn Hode and his Meiny*, and by good luck it is also one of the oldest. The date of the earliest black-letter version is disputed, but it is only just later than the end of the fifteenth century. The language, however, is full of antique forms which show that it has not been greatly altered from a far older original, and it is possible that the poem as it stands could have been put together as early as 1400. It is an epic ballad, the work of an author who has strung together parts of at least four earlier ballads. That he was drawing on stories which were already traditional he himself confesses:

> 'He wente hym forth full mery syngynge,
>   As men have told in tale.'

In linking his stories together into a single epic he sometimes showed considerable skill. But on occasion the change of scene or mood is too sudden and here we can detect him and see how he worked. We can also see him at work in another way, for some of his stories survive elsewhere in individual versions which, though they are not older than his, show that there was a common original which both he and others of his kind used.

There seem, as has been said, to have been at least four ballads which the writer of the *Geste* worked into his story, the ballad of *Robin Hood and the Knight*; the ballad of *Robin Hood, Little John and the Sheriff*; the ballad of *Robin Hood and the King*; and the ballad of *Robin Hood's Death*. The first two of these have been fairly skilfully worked into one another; the last two remain stories in their own right, unconnected with the preceding history except by the identity of their hero.

The curtain rises in the *Geste* to reveal Robin leaning against a tree in his forest of Barnesdale, where he is already famous as an outlaw. Like the witch in the fairy story, he has no antecedent history:

> 'Robyn was a proud outlaw
> Whyles he walkede on ground.'

His men, Little John, Scarlock, Much the Miller's son and the rest of them, are gathered about him, and he is telling them how an outlaw should bear himself. It is to them now that he gives his famous advice, which we must treasure as a statement from the lips of the master outlaw himself as to what the outlaw's code was. To the poor they shall be all courtesy:

> 'Loke ye do no husbonde no harm,
> That tylleth with his plough;
> No more ye schal no good yeman,
> That walketh by grenewode shawe.'

But to the rich and unjust no mercy is to be shown:

> 'These bishoppes and these archebishoppes,
> Ye shall them bete and binde;
> The hye Sheriff of Notyngham,
> Hym holde you in your mynde.'

This is to be the law of the outlaws. Having told them what their life is to be, and so foreshadowed the rest of the story, Robin declares he will not dine till he has a guest to dinner. So Scarlock, Much and Little John go up 'the Sayles' to Watling Street, to see whom they may waylay and bring to dine with their master.

So the ballad maker has set his scene. He has told us what kind of men it is of whose doings we are to hear, and plunged us already into the middle of their story with the dispatch of the three outlaws to fetch in the first 'guest' that shall pass this way. The tale is fairly started, for Little John and his companions had not been long at their watch before they saw a knight, coming by Barnesdale by a little dark road, a 'derne strete'. This was no warrior in polished armour; he was a man who carried about his person the marks of misfortune: 'all dreri was his semblaunce', and he rode a sorry mount in simple array, his head bowed and his feet swinging free of his stirrups. When they accosted him, however, and hailed him before their master his answer was courteous. Robin's fame was known to him already as the friend of all with whom the world had dealt harshly, and with him it had dealt harshly enough.

Just to what extremities his misfortunes had reduced him was revealed later when, as he rose after dinner to take his leave, Robin demanded of Sir Richard atte Lee—for that was his name—the price of his meal. His guests of noble blood did not dine free at Robin's table, but this knight was so poor he had not the wherewithal to pay, for he had lost all his estate. Little John had searched his bags in secret, after the usual custom of the outlaws, but there was no more in them than the ten shillings which he had told them he carried with him. Robin was amazed; he was at a loss to explain how this knight had come to travel in such reduced circumstances:

> 'Tell me one worde' sayde Robin,
> 'And counsel it shal be;
> I trowe the werte made a knyght of force
> Or ellys of yemanry.

> 'Or ellys thou hast been a sori husbonde,
> And lyved in stroke and stryf
> An okerour, or ellis a lechoure' sayde Robyn,
> 'With wrong hast led thy lyfe'

But it was none of these things. Sir Richard's fortune had fallen into the hands of hard men; his son had killed a knight of Lancashire, and to buy his pardon his father's land were 'sette and solde', for they were in pledge to the Abbot of St. Mary's York for four hundred pounds he had lent to Sir Richard to redeem his heir. His friends of fairer times had deserted him with his fortunes, and now he must go to the abbot to beg a delay in which to make repayment; otherwise he was a ruined man, and there would be nothing left for him, having lost his inheritance, but to cross the seas, and to seek a new life in the land where Christ died.

It was in order to help just such victims of the injustice of the law that Robin Hood plundered the rich. Who would the knight give as his pledge, he asked? The knight had no friends; he could only pledge his own word by the honour of Our Lady. But that was enough:

> 'By dere worthy God', sayde Robin,
> 'To seeke all Englonde thorowe,
> Yet fonde I never to my pay
> A moche better borowe.'

So Robin Hood opened his coffers and four hundred pounds were told over to the knight, and with it Robin made him a present of new cloth to mend his apparel, and a horse and harness worthy of his estate. Lastly he gave him a pair of gilt spurs, which were the sign of knighthood, and Little John for his esquire. So the knight took his leave, promising he would be back 'this twelve month day' to repay the outlaw and to redeem his pledge.

John and Sir Richard now rode on for York, for the day when he must repay his loan to the abbot was due. It was on the day itself, indeed, that he rode into the abbey, where his enemies were already gathered to seize his lands and divide them. There was the abbot there, and the crooked justice who was in his pay:

> 'The hye justice and many mo
> Had take into theyr honde
> Holy all the knight's debt,
> To put that knight to wronge.'

Only the Prior of the abbey warned them that it would do them no good thus to despoil a knight wrongfully of his lands. When Sir Richard came into the abbot's hall they already looked on the land as their own:

> 'The day is broke' sayde the justice
> 'Lond gettest thou none!'

For a moment they were allowed to relish their triumph. Sir Richard was going to assay them to the full; from the abbot he turned to the justice to beg a longer day, and from the justice back to the abbot; he painted vividly his woes, and the fate that he must face if he had no further delay. But these were stony hearted men; they had come for a purpose, to take his inheritance from him, and they did not intend to spare him. Their hard answers were fresh from their lips when Sir Richard at last pulled out his bag, and flung down Robin's four hundred pounds upon the table.

An unpleasing scene followed. Baulked of his prey, the abbot now wanted to get back what he had laid out to take it; he turned on the justice and demanded his bribes back again. He was refused even a penny. He could hardly now ask for a 'favour' of Sir Richard for the service he had done him (the usual way in which interest would be charged in an age which condemned profit as usury); all his scheming had been brought to nought and to his shame. All that Sir Richard left him were the rags he had come in, for as he left he put on the new robes which Robin had measured out for him in the forest. So he took his way home to 'Verysdale' where his lady met him at the gate.

There remained only one task to be accomplished, the repayment of his loan to Robin Hood. It was a different knight who rode out from his home towards Barnsdale a year after this, clothed all 'in red and white', with a 'launsgay' in his hand and a hundred bowmen in his retinue. They were to find at least one adventure in their way, however. As they passed by a bridge he and his men came upon a country fair; there there was a wrestling match, and a white bull, a courser and a pipe of wine had been set up for a prize. But the wardens here were not seeing fair play; the trophies had been won by a yeoman who was a stranger in those parts, and all had rounded upon him and were about to slay him. Sir Richard and his retainers were not going to stand by and see this done; they had taken a lesson in pity for those in misfortune from Robin Hood, and the sight of them with their bows as they came onto the fairground stopped the riot. Sir Richard had space cleared for him, and in presence of them all he made over the prizes to the yeoman. He was, however, too generous a man to bear any grudge against the foolish company of people there. With his own money he bought the wine from the victor and ordered that it should be broached on the spot. It is with this act, so well in character with that of another wronged knight, Gamelyn, that the ballad maker leaves Sir Richard for a moment to talk of other things.

We have in fact reached a break in the first ballad which forms part of the *Geste*. The second ballad is, however, worked into the story with very considerable skill. We last saw Little John doing service as his squire to Sir Richard at the gate of St. Mary's abbey. When and how he took leave of the knight we are never told; when we meet him again he is still Sir Richard's man, but is without employ for he is now going with the young men to shoot in the sheriff's contest for archery at Nottingham. Now Little John could shoot an arrow as straight as Robin Hood himself: there was no one else at the gathering who shot to the mark so often. The sheriff was amazed, and was eager to take him into his service. Little John explained that he was retained by Sir Richard, but if the sheriff could get his master's leave, he would serve him. It was thus that John found himself in service to the Sheriff of Nottingham for a twelve month. He had called himself for the time being Reynold Greenlefe of Holderness, and in that name he had board and fee of his master.

One day while the sheriff was out hunting, Little John had a tremendous quarrel with his cook, who refused to serve him. They fell to blows, and after three hours of sword play the upshot was—as it always is in the outlaw legends—that John was so filled with respect for his opponent that he begged him to be his friend and to come with him to join Robin Hood in the forest. That same night they stole away together, carrying with them the sheriff's silver spoons and three hundred pounds in good coin.

All this time the sheriff was still away hunting; Little John knew he could as yet have no news of what had happened, and that he must be hunting in this same forest, not five miles away. A stratagem immediately occurred to him. He took his leave of Robin, and knowing his way well enough, soon came up with the sheriff. Where had he been, the sheriff demanded of him:

> 'I have be in this forest:
> A faire syght I can se;
> It was one of the fayrest syghtes
> That ever yet sawe I me.

'Yonder I sawe a ryght fayre harte,
    His colour is of grene:
Seven score of dere upon a herd
    Be with him at bydene.'

It is the same old tale with which Fulk Fitzwarin lured John
into his hands, and the Sheriff of Nottingham was no more wily
than the King. He found himself betrayed by his man into the
outlaws' lair; he was face to face with his arch enemy, Robin
Hood, where he sat at supper in the forest with all his outlaws
round him.

There follows the famous scene in which the unhappy sheriff
has to sit down to a dinner of poached venison, served on his
own plate, with the outlaw chief and his band. But the joke is
here played to the full. After the dinner Robin Hood and his men
took away the sheriff's furred mantle and his rich coat and
clothed him in their own livery of Lincoln green; he was not
to be allowed to depart until he had passed a night with the
outlaws, and tried for himself the hardships to which the law
condemned their order. It was a rough night he spent in the
forest; he would as soon have had his head 'smyte off' than
spent another with them:

'This is harder order' sayde the Sherif
    'Than any ankir [anchorite] or frere;
For al the golde in Mery Englonde
    I wolde not long dwell her.'

Before he left, Robin made him take his oath that he would
never harm him, 'by water ne by londe'; then he went away
heavily, for he had lost much, with all the stolen plate and the
three hundred pounds which had been the price of his dinner in
the forest.

We go back here to the beginning of the story again, on the
eve of the dénouement of this part of the poem. The sheriff has
ridden home: Robin has sent Little John, Much and Scarlock up
again under the Sayles to Watling Street to watch for a guest
whom they may bring in to his dinner. It was not long before
they saw two black monks who were riding by Barnesdale, the
high cellarer of St Mary's and another monk with him. They
were soon led in before Robin Hood, and while they were talking with him the outlaws were searching their bags. How much

had they with them, asked Robin? But twenty marks, was the answer. But when their money was counted out there was eight hundred pounds in their coffers, all the money, declared the outlaws, for which Our Lady had stood pledge, and the interest therewith: it was but to be expected of her that she would send it with a monk of her own abbey, St. Mary's. Robin took all there was with glee, and since he could not stay to dine, he bid the Cellarer good speed:

> 'Grete well your abbot' sayd Robin
> 'And your pryour, I you prey,
> And byd hym send me such a monk
> To dinner every day.'

When Sir Richard appeared moments after at the head of his men he therefore found his debt already paid. To him Robin gave the four hundred pounds of interest which St Mary had sent him; and so the knight lost nothing at the last in all his adventures. He took his leave of the outlaw chief, and he too went his way.

So far the ballad maker seems to have used two basic sources, a story of Robin Hood and Sir Richard and the monks of St Mary's, and a story of Little John and the sheriff which he has inserted quite cleverly into it, grafting the second story into the first by fitting it in before the other has reached its final scene. We now come to a real break in the story. Some appearance of continuity has it is true been given, because the *dramatis personae* are still for the moment the same; the monks of St Mary's have left the stage, it is true, but Sir Richard is still about—and the sheriff is in Nottingham, plotting his revenge. But the parts they are to play now will be different to those of the first part of the ballad, for the mood of the poem has significantly changed. So far it has been almost gay: now it takes on a more sombre note. Sir Richard is no longer the knight of misfortunes; he is a stalwart and vigorous ally of the outlaws who is ready at the pinch to raise his drawbridge against the sheriff and stand siege in his castle. The sheriff is no longer the rueful figure, whom we saw a few stanzas back riding from the forest, his heart:

> '. . . as ful of grenë wode
> As ever was hepe of stone.'

107

He has become a hard fierce man, bent on vengeance, and prepared to lead his men in force into the forest in quest of it. Most
significant of all, the outlaws themselves have become less
gentle. In the whole of the first part of the ballad not a drop of
blood has been shed, by them or any other; in this coming part
of the story they will have to shed plenty of it before they are
out of their troubles.

Once again we are introduced to a new part of the story by
a scene which is really a repetition of one we have already witnessed earlier in the poem. The interlude of Little John's adventures with the sheriff opened with a shooting match, and
now once again we meet the outlaws travelling to the sheriff's
contest at Nottingham. There they excelled all in their prowess
at archery. In the verse here we at once notice something new:
Little John and Reynold Grenelefe have become distinct characters:

> 'Lyttell John and good Scathelock
>   Were Archers good and free:
> Lytell Much and good Reynold
>   The worst wolde they not be.'

Robin Hood, nevertheless, was of course, the best archer of them
all:

> 'Thryes Robyn shot about,
>   And always slist the wand.'

It was to him that the sheriff's men brought the prize of the
'gode arowe' for the best archer that ever there was.

Even in the hour of his victory, however, treachery was afoot.
Robin Hood was known: hardly was the prize delivered before
there was a great blowing of horns, the sheriff's men started
from their ambush, and the fight began:

> 'Ful many a bowe there was bent,
>   And arowes let they glyde;
> Many a kyrtell there was rent,
>   And hurt many a side.
>
> 'The outlaws' shot was so stronge
>   That no man might them dryve,
> And the proud sheriffës men
>   They fled away ful blythe.'

As the sheriff's men ran for cover under the hail of arrows, the outlaws made a break for the forest. But they could not move fast: Little John was wounded and had to be helped along by his master. So they made for the castle 'double dyched' of Sir Richard atte the Lee, which lay but 'a lytell within the wood'. As they ran in pursued, the drawbridge was raised, and Sir Richard's men made ready to man the walls against the sheriff.

When the sheriff and his men came up Sir Richard addressed them from his walls. He would not surrender the outlaws, he declared, and he would take full responsibility before the King for his actions. Let the King be judge between them. The sheriff had insufficient force to besiege him, and so he assented, but he meant nevertheless to do all in his power against him. He was the first to come before the King and refer to him his complaint; Edward promised he would soon be with him and that he himself would take both Robin Hood and the knight who had defied his officer. Back in Nottingham, the sheriff began to raise men, and meanwhile he set an ambush for Sir Richard. Hawking by the river, the knight was suddenly surprised by his men, and was hurried away bound to the city. The sheriff had no intention of letting him put his case. When the King came to Nottingham he would find as evidence of the knight's crimes the body of a dead traitor, who could no longer account for his actions. There were to be no accidents this time; preparations were made directly to put the knight who had been brought in a prisoner to execution.

The north, however, was a stormy country and even in Nottingham the sheriff was not safe. Already the outlaws, warned by the knight's wife, had mustered and were marching in force upon the town. As Sir Richard was being taken to the gallows they were filing through the streets: then they sighted their enemies. Robin drew his bow upon the sheriff: he fell, pierced by the outlaw's arrow. Then Robin's men drew their swords and charged. The outlaw chief himself struck off the sheriff's head; many of the sheriff's men were soon down, and the rest took to flight. Robin hurried to Sir Richard: his bonds were cut, and a bow pressed into his hand. The raid had achieved its object: it was now time to make a getaway. Robin's men left Nottingham with the same speed which they had come, hastening back now to the fastness of the woods:

'Leve thy hors the behynde,
And lerne the for to rene
Thou shalt with me to grenë wode
Through myre, morre and fen!'

The sheriff was left where he had been struck down; his men were still in flight, and Sir Richard and the outlaws gained their forest lair in safety.

Meanwhile, however, more powerful forces were mustering against them. King Edward was coming north; already he had put Sir Richard outside the law and taken the knight's land into his own hands. Once he had arrived in the north country, he soon saw what havoc the outlaws had caused in his forests; from Nottingham to the pass of Lancashire his venison had been poached freely, and he swore a great oath that Robin Hood should be taken, and should lose his head. Things progressed little, however, despite the King's promise of all Sir Richard's lands to him who brought in the knight, dead or alive. No one, as his councillors told him, was likely to enjoy Sir Richard's lands in peace while the outlaws were at large. If he were to take Robin, he must work by guile and not by naked force. It was one of his foresters, a man who knew the ways of the wood and the outlaws, who at last put him in the way by which he

The King rides to Nottingham to pursue the outlaws.

should be brought face to face with his elusive enemies. He had only, he told the King, to put on the guise of a rich monk and to ride by the forest in a small company, and he would lay a hundred pounds that he would meet Robin Hood before his journey's end.

When the King, disguised as a rich abbot, came riding past the wood's edge, the outlaws were as ever on the watch, and like so many before him, he fell straight into their ambush. It was very soon clear, however, that they had to do this time with a very unusual abbot, for Edward remained kingly and liberal even in the clothes of a skinflint churchman. The outlaws had only to ask for alms, and forty pounds, all the soi-disant abbot had with him, were theirs freely and for charity. But there was more largesse at hand; from under his habit the abbot now produced the King's writ, sealed with his great seal, ordering Robin to come to him and dine with him at Nottingham. It was this which gave Robin his chance to reveal himself unconsciously to the King in his true guise as a faithful and generous, though wronged, liegeman. As he looked at the seal he gave an exclamation; it was the true seal of his own lord, the King, whom, he declared, he loved more than all the world. Turning to the abbot, he insisted that as the bearer of such a welcome message, he must dine with him there and then in the forest, before he returned.

A splendid meal was laid before the abbot. Afterwards the outlaws proposed they should show him their prowess in archery, and two wands with rose garlands on them for a target were set up. The abbot was amazed at the distance at which they proposed to stand to shoot; it was fifty paces longer than was normal. They decided to shoot for forfeits; whoever missed the mark should lose his tackle and receive a buffet from his master. There was a good deal of horse-play: at last Robin himself failed of the mark, and it was his turn to take a buffet. But he had no master there. Turning to the abbot, therefore, Robin delivered him up his arrow, and begged him to 'serve him' with a buffet in his turn. For a moment the King demurred; then he rolled up his abbatial sleeve, and delivered Robin a terrific blow with his warrior's right arm.

As Robin picked himself up again ruefully, he looked hard and 'wystly' at the abbot. Then suddenly he recognized the familiar features under the hood, and he went down upon his knees before him:

> 'My lord the King of Englonde,
> Now I know you wele'

he murmured. Sir Richard and the 'wylde outlaws' went down on their knees beside him, and Robin begged humbly pardon for them all. Edward was as gracious as he had been from the moment he had met them. All were taken back into his favour and he made but two conditions, that the outlaws should leave the green wood, and that Robin should enter his own service. The terms were agreed and the King paid Robin the highest honour that he could, for he put aside his 'monk's weeds' and donned himself the green livery of an outlaw. Then in a great rout they all left the forest. The men who were watching from Nottingham saw them in the distance, an army of green-clad bowmen coming over the fields, and they feared the King was slain. But Edward was at their head with Robin, and when they came to Nottingham it was to feast and celebrate their reconciliation. Sir Richard was forgiven, the outlaws were dispersed, and Robin Hood went away from Nottingham in the King's court as his servant.

In the natural course of events this would be the end of the story. The legends of Hereward and Fulk Fitzwarin end with the return of their heroes to royal favour, as do the *Tale of Gamelyn* and the ballad of *Adam Bell*, the outlaw of Inglewood forest. The ballad of *Robin Hood and the Monk* ends with the outlaws enjoying the King's peace, albeit by a stratagem. Our author, however, has tacked on to the rest of his narrative the story of Robin Hood's death at Kirklees. He has done it, as always, with no little skill, for he has given us warning that the tale is not yet ended in Robin Hood's aside as he follows the King out of the forest:

'But me lyke well your service,
  I wyll come agayn full sone,
And shote at the donnë deer,
  As I am wonte to done.'

He will be true, therefore, to his assertion that Robin remained an outlaw 'the whyles he walkede on grounde', and will give us a picture of Robin languishing at the King's court for his greenwood life, until at last he takes his leave and returns to the forest. But the survival of two other ballads, which seem to be of individual origin and tell the same story of the death of the outlaw chief, prove that this is another tale tacked on artificially as a finale. The version I shall give will be based on these as well as that in the *Geste*, as one at least of them appears also to be old, and to retail them individually would involve wearisome repetition. And they are much fuller, for the *Geste* dismisses the whole final interlude in six stanzas.

For two and twenty years after he had left the King, says the *Geste*, Robin Hood remained as an outlaw in Barnesdale, for he was no sooner back in his former haunts than he took to his old habits again. At the last he became sick, and he resolved to go to his kinswoman, the Prioress of Kirklees Abbey, to be bled. Here, suddenly and inexplicably, a sense of impending doom settles over the story.. From the moment he announced his intention, his men were doubtful of Robin's wisdom. Will Scarlett told him he should not go without half a hundred bow-men to guard him against treachery, but he did not listen to their warnings, and took with him only Little John. As these two took their way to the Abbey, those whom they passed seem to have known Robin Hood was going to his death. After a while they came to a 'black water' with a single plank across it for a bridge: by it an old woman, doubtless a witch, was kneeling, and 'banning' Robin Hood. Robin turned to ask her why she was laying a curse upon him—but, alas, in the manuscript from which this incident is taken, the answer has been torn away and with it eight stanzas. When we catch up with the story Robin is talking to a group of people, doubtless also women, who are weeping for:

> '. . . his deare body
> That this day must be let bloode.'

They have a parting gift with them for him, but we do not know what it was, as this also was explained in the lost stanzas.

Robin, however, passed on to Kirklees, and there his kins-woman the Prioress let him in, leaving Little John without. Still Robin suspected nothing, though there was a menace in the nun's words as she produced the bleeding irons:

> 'I hold him but an unwise man
> That will noe warning leeve.'

Robin stripped his arm, and the irons were applied. It was only then he realized he was betrayed:

> 'And first it bled the thicke, thicke blood
> And afterwards the thinne;
> And wel then wist good Robin Hood
> Treason there was within.'

At this tantalizing moment there are another nine stanzas missing in the fullest of the ballads. When the story is resumed, Robin, weak from loss of blood, is fighting one Red Roger. The third of the ballads has left this whole incident out, but from the brief account in the *Geste* it seems that this Red Roger is Sir Roger of Doncaster, and the prioress's paramour, but why they fought is never told at all in any surviving ballad. Robin seems to have tried to escape by the window, but Roger wounded him as he made towards it. Summoning all his strength, Robin hit back and dealt him his death blow, but he had lost too much blood, and when Little John burst in, having heard the noise of the fight, his master lay dying on the floor of the chamber where he had been bled. John could do nothing more, unless it was to avenge him, but the dying outlaw forbad him to do as he wished and burn Kirklees Abbey to the ground.

> 'I never hurt fair maid in all my time,
>   Nor at my end shall it be;
> But give me my bent bow in my hande,
>   And a broad arrow I'll let flee;
> And where this arrow is taken up
>   There shall my grave digged be.'

So Robin Hood was buried within a bow's shot of the abbey where he had been betrayed and died, and there tradition centuries later still showed his grave. Of all the stories of him, this of his end is the most mysterious. The tragedy is that the answer to its riddle remains lost with the stanzas which were already torn from the ballad manuscript when Percy, seeking the *Reliques of Ancient Poetry*, first acquired it.

It is significant that we are not in the least assisted in unravelling the web of events which surround Robin Hood's end by the foregoing narrative. It tells us something about the ballad maker's method. His attempts to establish a connexion between the various sequences which he had strung together into one story were really very superficial. He made no real effort to give his tale any unity. He borrowed wherever he found material, and questions of relevance or literary suitability did not affect him. He made no effort to harmonize the gay mood of the first part of his story with the more sombre one which succeeded; because his sources were traditional he saw no need

114

to change them. He did not bother to explain the feud of Robin and Red Roger, or seek to prepare his audience for the final scene by introducing the latter into the earlier parts of the poem (which would have made the whole dramatically comprehensible); and once again, the reason was that he saw no need to alter tradition. Red Roger was traditionally the agent of Robin's betrayal at the last, and he did not have a part to play in the other known stories of the outlaw; there was therefore nothing incongruous about introducing a main character within six stanzas of the end of the poem. What mattered, clearly, was the popularity of the story, not its artistic unity, and the author therefore made no attempt to unify it and so set upon it the stamp of his own personality. So, when we come to look at other ballads we need not worry much about confusions which might arise from the individual interpretations which different authors might put upon the same tale. The ballad makers borrowed widely, but they did not adapt, and whatever story they tell us, we can be sure that it retains at least as much as they could understand of its traditional quality.

IX

The Robin Hood Ballads (II)

ONE of the most striking features of the *Geste*, which results
from its method of composition, is its wide variation of mood.
The scene is set with delightful description of the greenwood
and its charms, which comes from the traditional spring song;
but charming as this opening is, one cannot help feeling that it
would be more appropriate as the introduction to a tale of love
than to the story of rough men and fierce deeds in waste places,
to which it is in fact the preamble. Yet again it is hard to reconcile the violent tone of these later passages with the gay levity
of others. It is hard to believe that the sheriff who is discomfited
by the good-humoured guile of Little John is the same hard,
revengeful man who expiated his crimes in his own blood in the
fierce fight in the market place of Nottingham. One important
fact that we shall learn by looking now at the other early ballads
of Robin is that these apparently incompatible attitudes are
only the reflection of the infinite variety of mood in popular song.
They are all equally traditional, and so are equally characteristic
of the traditional Robin Hood myth.

There are three ballads over and above the *Geste* which are
of proven early origin and so demand attention. The first is the
Story of Robin Hood and the Potter, which has something of the
same light tone of the earlier parts of the *Geste*. The other two,

the ballads of *Robin Hood and Guy of Gisborne* and of *Robin Hood and the Monk*, though they open with the traditional picture of the gaiety of woods in spring, are more tumultuous stories, with their complement of daring rescue scenes, fierce fights with foresters, and murders callously performed where the occasion demands it. Some brief account of their plots seems to be needed in order to give a firmer basis for generalization about the characteristics of the Robin Hood story. Traditional as its stories are, the *Geste* after all represents the eclectic preferences of one author, and we must therefore examine these other poems to make sure we are getting a true and inclusive impression of the original tradition.

The ballad of *Robin Hood and the Potter* has echoes of the story of Little John and the sheriff in the *Geste*, and it recurs in many later versions, in which the role of the potter is played by a butcher, a jolly pinder of Wakefield, and so on. Many writers have regarded it as of later origin than the stories in the *Geste* cycle, and they may be right in so doing, but the version which survives is old, probably belonging to the beginning of the sixteenth century. The story has the traditional forest opening, and the outlaws are discussing the deeds of a 'prowd potter' who often passes their way, but pays no 'pavage' to them for going by unmolested. Little John once attempted to stop him, but the potter gave him 'thre strokes' so stout that he swore never to lay hands on him again. Robin Hood now decides he will try his luck, and goes out to accost him in the way.

Robin Hood fared no better than Little John. The potter knocked his sword clean out of his hands, and he would have handled him more harshly if Robin's men had not rushed out to save him. The potter, too, might now have fared worse, but both men were generous adversaries. Robin held out his hand to the man who had worsted him; henceforth they should be in fellowship. While the potter was taken to dine with the out-laws, Robin begged him to lend him his clothes and his wares and to let him go to Nottingham to try his luck in selling them. There he set up his stall in the market, and soon had attracted buyers by the knock-me-down prices for which he was offering his pots. The sheriff's wife was attracted, and to her he made a present of the last of them and in gratitude she asked him in to dine at the sheriff's table. There everyone was talking of a shooting match which was to be held that day, and the potter declared he would be there to see it. Of course, when he was on the green, Robin could not resist taking a bow and, naturally again, he carried away the prize, to the amazement of all present, who wondered how it was a potter could ever have come to be such a bowman.

It was from Robin Hood himself, the potter declared to the sheriff, that he had learnt his skill. 'Would that I were standing by that outlaw now,' muttered the sheriff, musing many un-avenged injuries, and unconscious of the irony of his words; 'I wish that you could show him to me.' 'That is easily accomplished,' replied the potter. 'You have but to follow me to the woods.' So they went off together, and soon they were in the forest, 'under the leffes grene'. But when they had gone a little way, Robin took out his horn:

> 'Roben set hes horne to hes mowthe
> And blew a blast that was god;
> That herde his men that there stode,
> Ffer down yn the wodde.'

In a moment outlaws were about them on every side, with Little John at their head, laughing and demanding of his master how he had fared as a potter in Nottingham.

The rest of the story is little different from that of Little John and the sheriff in the *Geste*. The sheriff had ruefully to dismount, muttering that, if he had known who the potter was earlier, Robin should not have come back to the 'ffeyr fforest' 'this thowsande year'. He was forced to surrender his horse, and all that he had with him. In return Robin gave him a white palfrey, which he sent as a present to his good wife, and to the potter he gave ten pounds, three and more times as much as his pots had been worth. So Robin Hood had all his goods and the sheriff went back to his wife in Nottingham who laughed long and loud at the means by which Robin had got payment for the pots he had given her.

The next ballad, that of *Guy of Gisborne*, is, as it stands, not so early as that of *Robin Hood and the Potter*, but in origin it is older, for a fragment of a play about Robin and Guy, which seems to have been a dramatization of the same story, survives among the papers of Sir John Paston, its date being about the year 1475. Essentially this is just another variation on the now familiar theme of the rescue of a captured outlaw from the hands of the sheriff, but it is highly individual both in its tone and in its details. The opening of the story is incomplete; it seems to have told of a dream Robin had sleeping in the forest of two yeomen who set upon him and did him injury, one of whom, clearly, was Guy of Gisborne. Little John told him not to trouble himself over it:

> 'Sweavenes [dreams] are swift, master,' quoth John
> 'As the wind that blows ore a hill.'

But Robin was sure this dream had meaning for him, and was a warning, and he bid John follow him to seek the two yeomen of his fancy in the forest. Just as they caught sight of what seemed to be one of them, however, they began to quarrel, and Robin Hood went forward alone to meet him.

Little John started on his way home, but he had not gone far when in a glade he stumbled on the dead bodies of two of his companions, who had been slain within the hour. Going on up the rise he caught sight an instant later of the sheriff's men, hotly pursuing Will Scarlett. Quickly he drew his bow and fired a bolt; the arrow found its mark, indeed, and one of the sheriff's men fell, but the bow snapped in John's hand in the same moment, and he was left defenceless. The sheriff's men now rounded on him, and he was taken a prisoner. Summary justice was all that the sheriff showed to an outlaw; he told John he would hang him upon a hill, and then he bid his men bind him to a tree and to continue the pursuit of the other outlaws. It was at this moment that they heard in the distance the horn of Sir Guy of Gisborne, which he had promised he would sound if he caught up with Robin Hood and killed him.

Robin had meanwhile come up with the man he and John had spotted, who proved to be a yeoman clad in leather and with a bow in his hand. They fell to talking and so walked on together; and as they went they agreed to have a shooting match by the way. Robin's superb aim, as always, awoke the admiration of his fellow. 'Tell me your name,' exclaimed Sir Guy, 'for you are a man who would outshoot Robin Hood.' But Robin would not tell him his name till he told his own, and when Guy gave it he knew it for that of a forester who was his old enemy. But he still stood to his part of the bargain: 'I am Robin Hood of Barnesdale,' he said, 'and I am ready to fight you here and now.' So the two drew their swords and fought: Robin was wounded in the left side, but he caught Sir Guy a moment later off his

Robin Hood's fight with Guy of Gisborne.

guard and killed him. Then he cut off Sir Guy's head and stuck it on the dead man's bow's end, and he cut it in the face so that no man born of woman could know whose it was. After this he took off his green coat and put it on the body, and himself put on Guy's leather jacket and pulled its hood about his head. Then he put the dead man's horn to his lips and blew a blast upon it.

It was this blast that the sheriff heard and he rejoiced in his heart at the thought of Robin Hood dead. Soon he and his men saw, as they thought, Sir Guy coming towards them. They hurried to greet him, and the sheriff offered to him any boon that he might care to ask. But the boon that was asked by Sir Guy was a strange one: it was that the outlaw now bound to the tree should die here and now, and by his hand. It was nevertheless granted. Guy drew his knife, and bid them all stand back; then he walked towards Little John. But instead of striking when he came up to him he slit the bonds with a single cut, and thrust Sir Guy's bow which he was still carrying into John's hands. Then the two of them turned on the sheriff's men —but they were already in flight. Not fast enough, however, for as they ran a shaft from Little John's bow caught the fleeing sheriff in the back and pierced his heart.

The verse of *Robin Hood and Guy of Gisborne* is bright and vivid and suits the sharp violent mood and scenery of the poem. It cannot however be said that its author was much of a story-teller. Too many loose ends are left when he has finished his story. We are never told what the significance of Robin's dream was; we are told nothing of how the sheriff surprised Will Scarlett and his two companions who were killed; we are never told the antecedent history of Robin and Guy, though it is clear that theirs was an old quarrel. The same criticism cannot however be levelled at the other early ballad of Robin Hood, that of *Robin Hood and the Monk*. This is in many ways similar; it too is a variation on the theme of the rescue of an outlaw; it again highlights violence, and it is also written vividly. But it is at the same time a well told tale; the incident is managed with greater skill, and there are no unexplained problems left at the end for the reader to solve on his own.

The opening is very similar to that of the story of Sir Guy. Robin had upon a day resolved to go to Nottingham to hear a mass, and he took with him Little John for a companion. As they went on their way they began to quarrel, and John left Robin to go on alone. Arrived in the town he went into the church of St. Mary and there kneeled down to pray, but while he was thus occupied he was recognized by a 'great-hedid munke' who was standing by. Though it was the middle of the service, the monk ran out to inform the sheriff and to raise the town, and even as Robin was praying they came down to the church with a great rout of people to take him. They burst in at the doors waving their clubs; Robin drew his sword and rushed on them. Twelve were slain before he was overpowered by sheer numbers. He was led away a captive, but not before, as always, an unnoticed friend had slipped away to take the news of his capture to the outlaws in the forest.

So it befell that, when the monk who had given the alarm was sent himself to carry the news of the capture to the King, the outlaws had already laid their plans. As he came near to the edge of the wood he fell in with two yeomen, who insisted on accompanying him, for, they told him, if he went on alone with his page he was sure to fall into the hands of Robin Hood and his men. But as soon as they were in a lonely place, Little John and Much, for it was they disguised, turned on him: they knew he was their man for he had already boasted to them of his part in the betrayal:

'He was my maister' seid Litull John
   'That thow hast brought in bale:
Shall thou never come at our King
   For to tell him tale.'

'John smote off the munke's head,
   No longer wolde he dwell:
So did Much the littull page,
   Ffor ferd lest he wolde tell.'

John and Much rifled the dead bodies and hid them; then with the letters about them they set out for the court. Arrived in London they delivered their letters to the King, who was delighted to hear the outlaw was at last taken. Much and John he rewarded, and retained them as yeomen of his own household; then he gave them letters to carry back to the sheriff, bidding him bring his prisoner bound before the King in person, for he had a great desire to see him.

When the two outlaws reached Nottingham again they found the gates barred, for there had been more than one attempt to rescue Robin. The King's seal was a good enough pass, however, and they were soon brought before the sheriff to deliver their letters: they had come in place of the monk, they said, since the King had rewarded him for his part in the affair with the Abbey of Westminster. The sheriff gave them a warm welcome; he bade them to dinner and gave them quarters in his own house. All drank deeply that evening, and the house was sound asleep when John and Much rose and went to find the porter. They killed him as he rose, and took his keys; then they hurried to the jail and let out the captive Robin. By the morning all three were far away and when the alarm bell began to ring:

'Robin was in mery Scherwode,
   As light as lef on lynde.'

It was a sorry tale that the sheriff had to tell the King of how he had been tricked and the outlaw chief was at large once more.

He might have died for his negligence, had not the King been tricked too, for he had given John and Much his peace himself:

> 'I made hem yemen of my crown,
>   And gaf hem fee with my hand:
> I gaf hem grith' seid oure kyng,
>   'Throwought all mery Ingland.'

A king's word, once given, was not lightly to be revoked; the poem ends with the King's rueful comment 'little John has begayled us all'. It was not often that anyone ultimately outwitted the elusive outlaws.

Before this chapter is closed, there are two more ballads which demand attention. The first is the beautiful little ballad of *Robin and Gandelyn*. It is of much the same date as the ballad of *Robin Hood and the Monk*, the manuscript of which is from about 1450, but in form it is older. It is little more, indeed, than a ballad of situation, for though the characters in it have got names they do not even aspire to such individuality as antecedent history or a known locale might give them. Robin is no more than a name for a green-wood poacher; he is not yet Robin Hood, the outlaw *par excellence* and the head of a famous band. Wrennock is a forester; but we know nothing of where his forest is or who is his master. The skeleton of a story there is, but no more; the ballad recounts an incident but does not explain it. It has still a long way to go before it will become a true narrative.

It is a story which the singer heard in the forest itself, he says:

> 'I herde a carpying of a clerk
>   Al at a wodes ende.'

Robin and Gandelyn, two outlaws, had gone to the greenwood to shoot venison; they were a pair of bold archers:

> 'Stronge thevys were tho chylderin non,
>   But bowmen gode and hende,'

and they had gone a little way only when Robin brought down a deer. But as he bent over it, there came an arrow out of the west and pierced him. Gandelyn looked about and he saw towards the sun the forester Wrennock and they drew their bows against each other:

'Wher at sal our marke be?'
    Seyde Gandelyn.
'Everich at otheris herte'
    Seyde Wrennock again.'

It was Wrennock that fired first, but his bolt passed between
Gandelyn's legs; Gandelyn's shot was true to its aim, and the
forester fell where he stood. So Robin was avenged: the poem
finishes with Gandelyn's cry of triumph:

'Now salt thu never yelpe, Wrennock
    At ale ne at wyn
That thu hast slawe goode Robin
    And his knave Gandelyn.'

So the poem ends, and we are left only with the echo of the chorus:

'Robin lyth in grene wode bowndyn.'

The other ballad of which something must be said is the tale
of the three outlaws of Inglewood, Adam Bell, Clym of the
Clough, and William of Cloudisley. This is a full-blooded narrative poem, rough and violent; but it too is early, dating from,
at latest, the beginning of the sixteenth century, though its
origin is doubtless far older. It is so like many of the stories of
Robin Hood that there is little need to enter into its detail. It is
really no more than a pastiche of two traditional stories, the
tale of the rescue of the captured outlaw and the tale of how the
outlaws won the King's forgiveness. Of the three outlaws, two
were single, but the third, William, had a wife in 'mery Carlisle'
and he languished for her in the forest. So he went to visit her,
and in the town he was betrayed by the old woman that lodged
with them. Though his wife held the door against the sheriff's
men with an axe while he shot from the window, his home at
last was fired; he was driven from his retreat and taken a
prisoner. Next day he was to be executed, but already his
friends had been warned by the swineherd's boy whom he had
befriended in the wood, and they were hurrying to Carlisle. In
the traditional midnight scene at the gate the porter was murdered, and they took his keys:

'Now I am porter' sayd Adam Bell,
    'Broder, the keys have we here;
The worste porter to mery Carlell
    That ye had this hundred year.'

They were in wait next day when William was led to execution. They had marked their men: at the crucial moment two arrows were let fly, and the justice and sheriff fell in the market place. Before their men had rallied the townsmen had loosed William, and in a terrific battle which followed the three outlaws held the men of the law at bay and made their break for the woods.

Carlisle was left in confusion, but they knew the crimes they had that day committed could never be forgotten. Before the news came to him, they must hurry to the King and stake all on what must surely be their last chance of pardon. Even so it was a slender one, and the King would have hanged them for the deeds that were already known of them, if the Queen had not pleaded for their lives. She was only just in time to save them; for hard upon their heels came the news of their new crimes in the north. The sheriff and justice had been slain, the constables of the town put to confusion, and there was more to their account too:

> 'The baylyes and the bedylls both,
>   And the sergeauntes of the lawe,
> And forty fosters of the fee,
>   These outlaws had y-slawe;
>
> 'And broken his parkes, and slain his dere;
>   Over al they chose the best;
> Such perelous outlaws as they were
>   Walked not by east nor west.'

But the King's word once given could not be revoked, and they were now in his peace. Indeed, he was to be glad of it, for he had gained to his own service the three finest archers of all England. In a scene which echoes the familiar story of William Tell, Cloudisley, in the King's presence, cleft an apple set upon his son's head from sixty paces. It was after this that he and his fellows took the King's 'cloth and fee' and became his men; they were to serve him faithfully from then to their lives' end.

There is something to be learnt from these last two poems. In *Robin and Gandelyn* is preserved the embryo of an outlaw ballad; here we have the brief, depersonalized outline of an incident which may one day be worked up into a story, or into an episode in a longer poem. Its two outlaws have acquired traditional names, but they have no history; the poem is not a miniature, but a preliminary sketch, and the figures cannot yet be identified, because the artist has not yet given them features. In the tale of Adam Bell we see a story developed as far as, in the world of balladry, it is ever likely to be. The incidental material has been worked up into a full-blooded popular epic. By comparing the two we can see how far the limitations of the original source material still survive in the finished product, and this will help us to see what we can and what we cannot expect to learn from the ballads.

The Joly Robyn of the first of the two ballads is the prototype of the later Robin Hood. It obviously makes not the slightest difference, however, whether the hero of the later version is called Robin or Adam Bell, for in essential there is no difference between the ballad of Adam Bell and one of the long Robin Hood ballads. The scene is the same, the forest where outlaws roam with 'bows and arrows keen'; the story of the rescue of the outlaw chief and the winning of the King's pardon are the same at heart; traditional incidents, such as the wrestling match scene or the shooting of the apple from the child's head, are woven into the web of the story in the same way. The locale and the detail of incidents are of course different; but the mood is constant, and the heroes, who are type-characters, are different in name only. Adam and his companions are forest outlaws living on the King's venison, their enemies are the sheriff and the justice, their friends the poor and neglected, they are superb archers and endowed with superhuman strength. They are no different in these respects from Robin Hood and Little John and Much the Miller's son. Ultimately the one story is so like the other that there is very little to differentiate them. What we must therefore remember is that we are not dealing with a host of different stories, but with a host of versions of the same story, and that what is significant is the similarity of tone, the forest setting, the animus against the law and its officers, the callous indifference to bloodshed, and not the differences of detail. At the same time we must remember that we are not dealing with a series of individual characters, but with a type-hero, the outlaw, who, though he may appear under more than one alias, remains essentially the same, and that what is significant about him is not his name or his individual acts, but his conventional attitudes. We are still moving in a primitive world where the sequence of cause and event and the intricate, intimate clashes of personality are not understood. Narrative is a chain of accidents whose links constitute the episodic life-story of a conventional figure, whose attitudes are known in advance and remain ultimately unaffected by events. This is not a sophisticated approach to the problem of telling a story, but it makes the interpretation of the narrator's views easier, because they are the only views which the story bothers to express.

X

The Historical Background
of the Robin Hood Ballads

T HE thrill of the outlaw legends comes from the fact that they
celebrate the deeds of those who were 'agin' the law', but this
thrill does not derive from the glamour of theft in a romantic
setting. Robin Hood was no Captain Kidd, not even a Dick
Turpin; he was the enemy of the existing order, not a parasite
on it. Herein lies the historical significance of the outlaw stories.
What is striking about them is that they reveal that, in an age
when the Rule of Law was respected as the foundation of good
government, those who put themselves outside and against the
law became nevertheless popular heroes. There can be only one
reason for this, that the existing order was generally regarded
as tyrannical. Tyranny was to this age the definition of the
abuse of law, for under its rule law was founded in the wills of
wicked men and not in reason, and acts of tyranny, therefore,
though they might be legal, could not be legitimate. Since law
itself was ultimately unassailable, protest against abuse must be
to some extent specific. What the outlaws can tell the historian,
therefore, is what it was that contemporaries regarded as
abusive in the existing order of things, and this is a manner more
vivid and expressive than that of his usual witnesses, the minor
clerks of courts and councils who recorded official acts in a style
whose aridity and bombast they thought appropriate thereto.

The interpretation in this sense of the stories retailed in the earlier part of this book is not difficult, because they record the struggles of known men against known oppressors. King John and William the Conqueror are figures from history, who lived and died in the historian's world of *anno Domini,* and whose tyrannical acts are recorded in contemporary annals. Their enemies, Fulk Fitzwarin and Hereward, were known men and remembered in the same sources, so the very lack of historicity about their legends becomes historically significant; it shows that oppression was real and that there was widespread popular sympathy for those who set themselves against it. The authors of the lost poems about these men worked into their stories traditional material in order to present their principal characters as heroes, because they regarded the stand that they had made against tyranny as in itself heroic. They wove legend into the web of history in order to make its moral clearer. The tales they told are as a result at once vivid and delightful, and instructive about specific periods of history.

The stories of Robin Hood are not so easy to interpret. In the first place their origins are different—at least if the experts are right in their diagnosis; their authors did not borrow from the storehouse of tradition, for the stories grew out of tradition itself. There is nothing in them to pin down their heroes to a particular point in history: references to Robin Hood in the chronicles indeed exist, but they are not contemporary; there is no one who will say that it was in his time that Robin Hood lived as an outlaw, and enrich his story with personal reminiscence. This does not of course mean that there never was a Robin Hood; it means only that if there was, he was not a man of sufficient standing to catch the eye of contemporaries. One way out of the difficulty may be to pinpoint this forgotten character by identifying either the name or the detailed incidents of his story with known persons or events, and if this can be done, we can obviously say a great deal more about him. Alternatively, it may be possible to identify the particular cause for which he stood in legend with some cause known independently, either by the nature of the incident or by its traditional trappings. Both these approaches have been tried, but as they introduce new comparative evidence it will be well to see first what sort of information the ballads themselves can furnish

129

and what the traditional characteristics of the story are.

Whatever their origins may have been, the ballads as we have them have grown to the stature of true narrative, which means that they recount specific events in the lives of named persons. Hence, though for reasons already stated it may be unwise to make too much of them, we had better start by seeing what there is to be said generally about these incidents and characters.

The first thing that strikes one about the incident is that it is traditional. This is indicated clearly by its endless recurrence; the several stories of the rescue of a captured outlaw are not ultimately individual, but are a series of varying embroideries upon a single situation. It is the same with the stories of the King's ultimate reconciliation with the outlaws. Kings did, it is true, frequently pardon those whom they had placed under their ban, as John did Fulk Fitzwarin, and William Hereward the Wake, but this does not mean that Gamelyn and Adam Bell and Robin Hood obtained pardons either because individual historical characters on whom they were ultimately modelled did so, or because the internal logic of their stories demanded that they should. Rather the ballad makers took advantage of a situation which had verisimilitude and which seemed, for reasons which will be explained in due course, to be appropriate to the stories of their heroes. The same applies to the story of the knight cheated of his inheritance; it is not necessarily true, but it is true to life, and that is all that matters. One must not, of course, assume that because an incident or situation is recurrent it is unhistorical; the opposite could easily be argued and this must be borne in mind, since some have seen behind the incidents of ballads actual historical events which have lost their individuality by attrition. Endless iteration in song which is becoming traditional has, they say, rendered these events all but unrecognizable. It is, however, clearly wise to regard with suspicion the historicity of an incident, albeit probable enough, which recurs again and again in essentially similar stories, unless there are very strong grounds indeed for its identification with some actual event.

Suspicion is clearly justified still more fully where not only the general outline of a situation but the actual detail is recurrent. Where this is the case the incident clearly belongs to a common stock of traditions and has nothing to do with any one particular individual rather than another. The story of the outlaw who disguised himself as a potter and so went to spy on his enemies is told first of Hereward the Wake, then of Eustace the Monk, then of Robin Hood; it is also told of the Scotsman William Wallace. Medieval authors had a passion for disguises; the irony of the situation in which enemies or lovers met incognito seems to have endlessly delighted them. So one will find Hind Horn coming to the presence of his beloved Rimenhild in the guise of an old woman, to see if her heart is with him still, and Ippomedon tourneying before his lady in a series of disguises, each time winning the prize and filling her with intrigued admiration for this mysterious victor. The outlaw ballads use the convention repeatedly; Little John appears as Reynold Grenelefe and takes the sheriff's fee, the King disguises himself under the habit of a monk and so comes to visit Robin Hood in the forest, Robin Hood dresses himself in the leather jacket of Guy of Gisborne and rescues Little John. But the disguise of a potter seems to belong to these stories particularly; it is the outlaw's favourite ruse and its repetition strongly suggests that the story is traditional rather than historical.

It is the same with the story of the abbot who was robbed because he would not tell the truth about the sum of money which he had with him. In the poem on *Eustace the Monk* he is the Abbot of Jumièges, in the *Geste of Robin Hood* he is the Abbot of St. Mary's, but this is no more than the author's acknowledgement of the demands imposed on him by his locale; the incident is clearly the same. It happens to be particularly appropriate to a story of this genre, because it shows that the outlaws regarded themselves as bound by a moral code of their own making. The story of how Fulk Fitzwarin took the merchants' cloth when he learned that it was King John's and that they would not lose thereby is no more than a variant on the same theme. Poetic justice is the subject of the outlaw ballad, and so it borrows a traditional scene in which this is achieved. Because it is appropriate such an incident can be worked into the story with ease, so that it seems to fall out naturally; the borrowing from tradition is clearer still where a scene has no special appropriateness to the narrative. There is no reason at all, for instance, why Sir Richard atte Lee and his men should stumble on a country wrestling match on their way to visit Robin Hood. The same incident does not really do much to further progress in the *Tale of Gamelyn*, beyond giving the hero yet another opportunity of displaying his muscular prowess, though here the author, a man of greater literary perception than the ballad maker, has worked it into his story with greater skill. The sole reason for the inclusion of the incident in both cases was that the story was at once traditional and colourful, and that is why it found its way by a roundabout route from the song and gossip of the medieval fairground to the drama of Shakespeare's *As You Like It*. Another striking example of an incident borrowed from the common stock of tradition is that in which William of Cloudisley at sixty paces shoots the apple set upon his own son's head. The same story is told of William Tell, and it recurs elsewhere in Norse and Germanic legend, in the stories of Weland the Smith and Dietrich von Bern. Its origin is probably in pagan myth, but it is not to be supposed for a moment that the English ballad-maker was aware of this. If he had thought it was a story of the sun-god he would prob-ably have eschewed it with pious disapproval; for him it was no more than a traditional tale of superb archery, and he worked it into a story to which it had no relevance because he wished to show that his hero was a superb archer.

The fact that many of the episodes in a tale can be shown to belong to a stock of popular legends, which do not attach to any one story or even to any one cycle of stories in particular, does not of course imply that its hero must be legendary as well. In an age when oral tradition was vigorous, historical reputation acted as a natural magnet to myth, and as we have seen the stories of outlaws who undoubtedly existed include a great deal of what is undoubtedly traditional fiction. But the traditional ballad heroes fall into a different category to these figures in older stories. They are, as we have seen, type cast, and are not identifiable, at least on the evidence of the ballads themselves, with known historical characters. We shall do best therefore to start by considering them within their own literary limitation as typical figures.

This limitation is in fact one which is to be expected of the principals of any medieval narrative. The age did not take readily to our idea of human beings as individualized by infinitely varying personality; they distinguished rather between different types of men identifiable by conventional characteristics. They recognized kings and saints and conquerors, but they did not see much to choose between one conqueror and another, between, say, Henry V and Alexander. This is why the great figures of the middle ages are so elusive and impersonal; their revealing, human individuality escapes us because in the contemporary world it went unnoticed. Attempts to get beyond this mere classification usually stopped short at special emphasis of one or more conventional characteristics. So for instance in Malory's *Morte d'Arthur*, Lancelot and Galahad are both type-cast as chivalrous knights, but Lancelot is *par excellence* the courtly lover and Galahad the soldier of Christendom. Outlaws similarly constituted a type, and the heroes of the more sophisticated outlaw stories achieved a similar degree of personality. So Gamelyn is the strong man of the outlaw world and Eustace the Monk its master of disguise. The heroes of the ballads, however, remain little more than type characters with names. Before asking whether there is any further evidence which may justify our considering them as individual persons, it will therefore be proper to consider just what their conventional qualities are, for this can at least tell us what kind of man it was that the ballad audiences wished to hear about.

The stock characteristics of the outlaw hero are to some extent those typical of any medieval hero. He is courteous, brave, and, yeoman that he is, he bears himself with a certain dignity. He is strong and resourceful, skilled in the ways of the wood and in the use of his weapons; above all he is an archer. He is loyal to the King and he is conventionally pious. In these respects there is little to distinguish Robin Hood from Little John or Adam Bell. If Robin has an individual characteristic it is his special devotion to the cult of the Virgin Mary, but in the context of his age such an attitude can hardly be said to individualize him. Besides these traits there are of course those physical features which inevitably accompany outlawry, a forest lair, a feud with the law and its officers, an existence by poaching and robbery. But these again are features of outlaws in general, and can hardly be said to have much to do with the personality of any one individual.

The depersonalized character of their heroes is in one sense

133

a limitation on the outlaw ballads. But in another sense it is of prime importance, because it is the type characteristics of the actors that dictates the mood of the poems. They impose on them what literary consistency they can boast, for they stamp traditional source material as appropriate or otherwise. The qualities of their enemies are significantly the exact antitheses of those of the outlaws: they are grasping where Robin Hood is generous, deceitful where he is frank, oppressive where he is compassionate. Similarly the traditional incident is chosen and interpreted so as to bring out the typical qualities of the heroes. What is inappropriate is excluded. This is why in the early ballads we hear nothing of figures traditionally associated with Robin Hood like Maid Marian and Friar Tuck. They only come in later, at a stage when various traditions were becoming confused and overlaid, because the circumstances from which the older situations drew inspiration were ceasing to exist. They were, no doubt, genuine figures of popular legend, but the type of person that they represented had no part to play in the situations of the outlaw world. The Robin Hood of the original legend did not naturally have a forest love, nor was the renegade friar naturally an outlaw. It is for this reason that in the genuinely early stories Tuck and Marian do not appear at all.

From this initial analysis of their character and incident there thus appears some sort of picture of what, stripped of inessentials, an outlaw ballad is. It is a story in which stock characters of a certain kind are placed in traditional situations which evoke stock responses. This suggests that if we are seeking further illumination, we shall be wise to concentrate on what can be deduced from the general features of the stories, and not for the moment to attach too much importance to the individual detail of variants of traditional stories.

Let us look first at the scenery which forms the backcloth of the outlaws' drama. This can clearly tell us a great deal about the kind of world in which the outlaws lived, and some of this information is fairly definite. We observe immediately that it is a purely medieval world, one which by the early sixteenth century would be beginning to look antique. The scene is set in the King's forest, and the savage forest laws which visited crimes against his venison with arbitrary penalties are still in full vigour. The classical enemy of the outlaw in all the legends (not just those of Robin Hood) is the sheriff, and by the end of the middle ages the power and importance of the sheriff, at least as an officer responsible for the enforcement of the law, was already in decline. We do not hear in the ballads anything of the men who were taking his place in local government, those justices of the peace whose position was to become a cornerstone of the Tudor monarchy. The other constant enemies of the outlaws are the abbots and monks of the great monasteries, which disappeared from the English landscape in Henry VIII's day. We know in any case that by that time the name of Robin Hood was famous in popular legend all up and down England. Most of our early ballads seem to bear a date between about 1450 and 1500, but the world of which they sing sounds older. There is not much apparent notice taken of the changing conditions of the end of the fifteenth century.

The signs are clear that this medievalism of the outlaw legends was not a conscious attempt on the part of authors to locate their narratives in the hallowed setting of time past. The manners and customs of a medieval world were, for the ballad makers, the familiar background of their everyday existence. They knew its laws and their abuses. Robin Hood's remark to Sir Richard atte Lee when he learned of his reduced circumstances,

> 'I trow thou wert made a knight of force
> Or ellis of yemanry',

is a clear reference to the medieval practise of distraining those who had lands sufficient to support the rank to undertake the obligations of knighthood. The maker of the Cloudisley ballad knew the penalty for poaching under the forest law, and he knew the technical term for it, offence against venison:

> 'They were outlawed for venysoun
> These three yemen everichone'.

The maker of the *Geste* knew that a man who had become the retainer of one lord could not take the fee of another and so be retained by him; so Little John had to get the leave of Sir Richard in order to enter the sheriff's service in the guise of Reynold Grenelefe. These are all technical points, and it seems unlikely that anyone but a genuine contemporary would have made much of them.

135

The last is an especially striking instance. It brings up the questions of livery and maintenance, which were the besetting abuses of English society in the later middle ages, and which were belaboured endlessly in popular social satire. The point was roughly this. When a lord retained a man to serve him he gave him a fee by which he was retained, and a livery with his personal signs or badges to wear; and he agreed to maintain him in all his causes, which meant he was bound to help him at law with all the influence and favour his position could afford. The theory of this contract was noble enough; a man bound himself by the intimate ties of personal loyalty to serve another, who in turn granted him his good lordship and undertook to comfort, succour and supply him. In practice, however, it obviously laid the way open for all the abuses of bribery, corruption, and influence upon justice; the retainers of a lord who was sufficiently powerful could get away with murder. So we find Langland wringing his hands in the poem he addressed to *Richard the Redeless* in 1399 over the tyrannies and misdeeds of retainers:

'They plucked the plomayle from the pore skynnes,
    And shewede her signes ffor men shulde drede
To axe ony mendis ffor her mysdedis:
    Thus leverez over loked youre liegis ichonne'.

His was no voice in the wilderness. The satirists of the age echoed his words again and again; 'jurors bear peyntyd slevys'; 'now mayntenerys be made justys', these and such like phrases are their constant refrain.

It is therefore significant that the ballads of Robin Hood are full of references to livery, maintenance and their abuses. The justice in the *Geste* is maintaining the abbot's cause against Sir Richard:

'I am hold of the Abbot,' seyde the justice
    'Both by cloth and fee'.

Sir Richard himself had his retainers, clothed and fee'd, the same bowmen whom he led forth to visit Robin in the forest and who held his castle against the sheriff. William of Cloudisley and his two fellows became the queen's retainers:

'William, I make the gentleman
    Of Clothynge and of fee;
And thy two brethren yeman of my chambre,
    For they are so semely to see'.

136

So again in the *Geste* Robin Hood became the King's man, retained at his fee and at the price of a new cloth each year against the 'time of Yole'.

In the context of this world peopled by lords and their re-tainers, Lincoln Green became simply the livery of Robin Hood's or some other outlaw's company. So we hear in the song of the Outlaw Murray:

> 'His merrie men are in liverie clad
> Of the Lincoln green so fair to see,'

and in later ballads we hear of Robin giving his cloth to Little John, to an unknown ranger who has fought with him, to young Gamwel and others. When in the *Geste* the King left Sherwood forest, he put on Robin s green livery and rode clad in it at the head of the outlaws:

> 'All the people of Notyngham
> They stode and behelde;
> They saw nothing but mantels of grene,
> That covered all the Felde.'

To wear another man's badge or his livery was the highest compliment a lord or ruler could pay to him. When the Em-peror Sigismund in 1416 on his visit to England wore Henry of Lancaster's collar of the letters SS it was at once superb diplomatic tact and a sign of their close alliance. The author of the *Geste* was clearly aware of this significance of wearing Robin's livery, and just how high in royal favour it placed Robin Hood. This shows that he lived at a time when liveries and personal badges were in everyday use, and when the point of some special usage, like this one, would be readily understood by his audience.

Livery and maintenance continued to cause trouble in Tudor times, though they had ceased by then to be the universal grievance they had once been. They do not seem to have at-tracted much notice as a problem before the latter years of the thirteenth century when they were first mentioned as an abuse[1]. We are beginning to be able to pin down the world of the out-law ballads to a specific period in the middle ages, for their

---

[1] Though there are earlier references in legal records, as one to a Yorkshire bandit in 1218 whose men were said to wear his cloth. But literary references are very rare before the fourteenth century.

constant references to liveries and retaining seem thus to be appropriate to the fourteenth and fifteenth centuries rather than any others. A large number of other features stamp them as of this period, and features at that which are so characteristic that if they were taken away, the stories would be left barely recognizable. Anyone therefore who wants to place a historical Robin Hood in some earlier temporal context, is going to have profited himself little, for it can be answered to him that even if such a man did exist, it would scarcely affect our judgements on the hero of the ballads. He is too much caught up in situations which belong to one time and one time only to preserve any longer recognizable traits of a historical ancestor in another period.

Of these features which link Robin Hood indissolubly with the last two centuries of English medieval history the most striking is archery. Again and again situations in the ballads resolve about the outlaw's skill and accuracy with the bow and arrow. The bow in question is Adam Bell's 'bow of yew', the longbow whose use and design the English perfected and which could shoot farther and more accurately than any other. It was in the great wars with France that this bow first became famous; it won England the battles of Crecy and Poictiers and Agincourt, and made English archers famous from one end of Europe to the other. Its first victory was the battle of Halidon Hill, fought against the Scots in 1333, where Edward III's army is said to have been half recruited from the poachers of Sherwood; the first great victory of gunpowder in any English war was Chastillon in 1453 where the French artillerymen mowed down the English cavalry of the veteran Talbot. These dates give some sort of termini, though they are very rough ones, for the longbow continued in general use many years after 1453. It would however be generally accurate to ascribe the golden age of archery in England to the fourteenth and fifteenth centuries: it was then that the longbow won its famous victories and that archery became a national pastime.

One great advantage of the longbow was that to wield it required neither great technical skill nor professional training. It was the weapon of the common man, of the English yeoman, and he had acquired his experience in its use not on foreign fields but in years of practise shooting at his village butts. The finest archers of all were the Welshmen, for it was in the wars upon their marches that the longbow was first developed; the men of Sherwood were significantly also remembered as among the best marksmen of England. But the use of the weapon was general, for by Edward I's Statute of Winchester every man in England must have his own arms and be ready for service in an emergency, and where the knight had to keep hauberk, helmet and sword against such a day, the simple peasant had his bow. The English kings understood clearly the advantage to themselves of having a nation of archers at their beck and so they gave royal patronage to the sport of archery. Both in towns and villages, by a famous ordinance of Edward III, contests in archery were commanded to be organized on festivals and holidays for the encouragement of the art. There is surely an echo of these ordinances in the recurrent scene in the ballads, in which the disguised outlaws carry away the prizes at the sheriff's contest at Nottingham.

The prowess as archers of the ballads' outlaws stamps them as of the period when skill with his bow was the accomplishment *par excellence* of the proud yeoman. It is significant that in the *Tale of Gamelyn*, written on the basis of a traditional story probably some hundred years before the ballads as we know them, there is no mention of archery. Another difference between the tale and the ballads which is striking is again a matter of date. Robin Hood was essentially a good yeoman; Gamelyn was a knight's son, and his peasants were 'bonde men', that is to say, villeins. The word yeoman does not occur in the tale; there is not any mention of unfree peasants in the ballads. For all they tell us, the whole manorial system might have passed out of existence. This seems to reflect the great change which was taking place in English agrarian society from the second half of the fourteenth century onwards.

It is always unwise to generalize about conditions of the rustic world, because they vary so much from place to place as well as from time to time. But in general it may be said that whereas the average peasant of the thirteenth and early fourteenth century was an unfree tenant bound by the age-old custom of his manor to work two or three days in every week of the year on his lord's demesne and farming for himself a strip among the village holdings of perhaps thirty or forty acres, by the beginning of the fifteenth century the pattern of peasant existence was changing. Due to new economic trends it was becoming less and less profitable for a lord to farm his lands himself, and demesnes or home-farms were being rented out to tenants. Many of these tenants were wealthy peasants, the descendants of the same men who had once been bound to labour on the lord's land in return for their own ....ll holdings, and they were employing as paid labourers the descendants of other peasants whose lot had been less fortunate. These peasants might still be villeins at law, but it is clear that they were much freer men than their villein forefathers had been. Many unfree bondmen were becoming yeomen, and acquiring a new pride and independence in the process. Robin Hood's 'good yeomanry', the equivalent in a different stratum of society of good lordship, is therefore significant; it shows that his story belongs to the age in which the countryman was ceasing to be bound to the soil of his own manor, which was the same as that when a new, prouder kind of countryman was winning the King's battles for him with his longbow in France.

The treatment of the forest and its laws in the ballads seems to confirm this setting of the ballad outlaws' world in the last century and a half of medieval history. As was explained much earlier, the forest included in the middle ages very extensive areas which included cultivated areas as well as wood and waste, and in which, for the sake of the preservation of game, special laws ran. These laws were extremely harsh, and they were also arbitrary, for those who lived within the forest had no right to appeal to the common law against the judgement of the forest courts. Offences against the forest law were of two kinds, offences against 'vert', that is to say against the trees and game-covers, and offences against the 'venison', the game itself. In the thirteenth century and before it there was widespread agitation against the forest laws, which was led by the barons and knights who regarded them as detrimental to their interests. This agitation concerned mainly the extent of the forests and the harsh punishments arbitrarily imposed on those who had offended against the King's vert by making clearings in the wood. But by the middle of the fourteenth century the boundaries of the forests were to all intents settled, and from Edward III's time onward offences against the vert were treated with far greater leniency than before. All the rigours of an arbitrary law could, however, and still often were invoked against those who committed offences against the venison. What this meant was that though the forest laws remained anything but a dead letter, interests in their enforcement had shifted. On the one hand were now the kings and knights and barons who owned woods and warrens; on the other stood the peasants and yeomen, who cast envious eyes at the plentiful head of game in these places. For them the right to hunt meant the right to keep down beasts which were damaging their crops and opportunities to supplement both their diet and their income. These were quite different interests from those of the men who had wrung the Charter of the Forest from the King's guardians in 1217 and wrangled with the King for the last ten years of Edward I's reign about the perambulation of the forest boundaries and their right to clear trees in order to cultivate the soil.

There is not a suggestion in the outlaw ballads that those who sung them had ever heard of such a thing as an offence against the vert. There is not a woodman in all the variants of the Robin Hood legend: the peace of the forest is undisturbed by the sound of the axe. Its boundaries, moreover, are assumed as known; neither the Sheriff of Nottingham nor anyone else claims as forest what is not forest by right. On the other hand the outlaws are all poachers, and their offences as such are significantly regarded as venial:

> 'Sire we walk not here non harm for to do
> But if we see a dere, to shete therto'.

So says Gamelyn to the master outlaw, and Robin Hood echoes him:

> 'We be yemen of this forest,
>   Under the grene-wode tree;
> We lyve by our kyngis dere,
>   Other shift have not we.'

The last word is with the clerk who sang of Robin and Gandelyn 'al at yon wodes ende':

> 'Stronge thevys were tho childerin none,
>   But bowmen gode and hende;
> He wenten to wode to getyne him fleych,
>   If God wold it hem sende.'

The ballads are tuned, in fact, to the mood of peasants hankering after the venison which is preserved for their masters. The other earlier abuses have been overlooked, which is significant, for they affected the peasant as much as the more vociferous land-lord. Since the ballad makers were not in the habit of ignoring widespread complaint, this seems further to identify the world of the ballads with the England of the later fourteenth and fifteenth centuries.

This seems to be the period to which all the familiar char-acteristics of the ballads point as that of their first popularity (at least in the form in which we know them). A context in the last quarter of the thirteenth century would, it is true, just fit their background. It is in Edward I's reign that we first hear serious complaints of the abuses of livery and maintenance. It was Edward I, similarly, who in his Welsh wars first made exten-sive use of archers, though his men were not armed with the longbow. The thirteenth century heard also complaints against preserved hunting rights in parks and warrens. Signs of the decay of the manorial system, once dated to the period after the Black Death, are now seen at least as early as the beginning of the fourteenth century on many estates. But at this stage the trends are only incipient. Though there were archers in his armies, it is absurd, as Morris says, to picture the soldiers of Simon de Montfort drawing the longbow. When in the 1270s the men of Exmoor and other western forests sent in a long petition against the tyranny of forest officials, they were still harping on the excessive penalties and rigorous prosecution of crimes against the vert. It is still on the woes of an unfree peasantry, tied to the manorial soil, that men like Robert Manning of Brunne and the unknown author of the *Song of the Husbandman*, a bitter tirade on the sufferings of the rustic written in Edward I's time, complain. A date forty years or so after the end of the thirteenth century, when the evils which were then first apparent had grown and attracted wider atten-tion, would fit the background of the outlaw ballads better. The hundred years between 1350 and 1450 seem to be the most suitable context in which the ballads as we know them could have achieved such popularity as to stereotype their form and background for the rest of time.

One would very much like to pin down their date between

limits even more narrow, but the evidence is wanting. If any of the names could be identified, it would make the task simpler; but Robin Hood and his men are not easy to track down, and his enemies, such as the Sheriff of Nottingham and the Abbot of St. Mary's, are known by their roles and not their names. In the *Geste* the King is indeed named; he is comely King Edward, but there are four King Edwards known to English medieval history. Edward III, who reigned from 1327 to 1377, would seem to fill the part best; but both the warrior King Edward I, who died in 1307, and Edward IV, who came to the throne in 1461 and was known in his day as the handsomest monarch of Europe, could just fit. In any case the King's name does not tell us much. In later ballads the King is Henry; clearly the ballad makers simply chose the name of a king who was known to them, perhaps that of the current sovereign, and did not thereby imply a reference to any particular period. There were anyway other popular ballads of a King Edward appearing among his humbler subjects in disguise, and the choice of name really tells us nothing.

The choice of locale on the other hand does. Robin Hood had two traditional haunts, Barnesdale forest in Yorkshire and Sherwood in Nottingham. Those who told his story had clearly some knowledge of the country; all the spots they name belong to the same areas; Kirklees and Doncaster and York and Nottingham are none of them so far apart, and some of the lesser place-names such as the Sayles and Plumpton Park would be only known to a local. As these places are all muddled higgledy-piggledy in the scenes of the outlaw ballads, however, it is clear that it was the authors of older versions, and not the ones that survive, who knew them so well. The fact that Robin Hood was well known across the border in Scotland further attaches him to the north; indeed, the Scottish chroniclers of the fifteenth century were the first historians to remark his deeds. Significantly it is in the north, and in particular in Yorkshire, that most of the landmarks with which his name is connected are situated; there it is we find Robin Hood's Bay, his well, even his grave. Though by the end of the fourteenth century his legend seems to have been known all over England, its origin is clearly in North Country tradition.

These facts about the date of the outlaw ballads, the social

143

status of their heroes and their place of origin are about as much in the way of definite information as can be gleaned from a study of the ballads. We must confess that there are severe limits on the knowledge thus acquired. The detail of their background connects them with the general social situation of a given period, but not with any known event. Nearly all the famous outlaws whose careers can be traced in history were put outside the law in times of political upheaval. There were plenty of political upheavals between 1350 and 1450, but the ballads do not connect Robin Hood with any of them. So far our information concerning him remains unparticular. The connexion with the north advances us a little, but it is hard to see what conclusions are to be drawn from it; though his story started there it was soon popular universally. It is only the place names that attach it to a particular area; the incidents could have occurred anywhere, for there were forests and sheriffs and yeomen all over England. It remains to be seen whether further evidence can be found which will link Robin Hood's story either with some particular event or series of events, or with some known cause for which men struggled in his day.

XI

◇◇

The Outlaw Ballad as an
Expression of Peasant Discontent

◇◇

The characteristic plot of the Robin Hood ballads, and indeed of all the later outlaw stories, is very simple. It is a tale in which wicked men meet a merited downfall, and the innocent and the unfortunate are relieved and rewarded. As the wicked are always the rich and powerful and the innocent the victims of poverty and misfortune, they may be said to be in essence stories of social justice. Though an occasional episode may have nothing to do with this theme, this is only the result of uneclectic borrowing by authors who only half understood the demands of their material. In fact the general drift of nearly all the stories is the same; clearly it was not only their traditional source which was shared by the ballad makers, the circumstances which inspired them were common to them also.

Their theme is the righting of wrongs inflicted by a harsh system and unjust men. It is this that raises the stature of Robin Hood above that of the common thieves who lurked about every highway in a lawless age; he was no ordinary robber:

> 'Strong thievys were tho childerin none
> But bowmen good and hende.'

He stole from the rich only to feed the poor. It is this that gives point to his ferocity; he was dreaded only by those whose

145

wealth was undeserved. It is also this that gives point to his liberality; there is more in it than the traditional medieval loyalty of master to man, for he was open-handed also to all those in real need, the victims of misfortune and the oppressed poor. For he was essentially the people's hero. His friends were to be found among the pindars and potters of the world, or with knights whom fraud or mischance had reduced to penury; he belonged to a different social world to exiled nobles like Hereward and Fulk Fitzwarin, whose companions were high born like themselves. The lowly people whom he befriended responded to his championship of their cause; always in the ballads and stories they are the outlaws' staunchest allies. Richard atte the Lee lowered his drawbridge to let in Robin Hood's men as they fled from the sheriff, though by his act he risked his life and lands; it was the swineherd's boy whom they had helped who slipped away to the forest to warn Adam Bell and Clym of the Clough that Cloudisley was a prisoner in Carlisle. So it was too with Gamelyn; the simple folk stood steadfastly by him:

> 'There was no lewde man in the hall that stod
> That wolde do Gamelyn anything but good'.

It was people such as these that were embraced in Robin Hood's 'good yeomanry', and their rewards were tangible. The potter went away paid for his wares three times over; Sir Richard had again not only his four hundred pounds but the interest thereon that doubled it. Alan-a-Dale in another ballad had back his bride who had been 'chosen to be an old knights delight'; the widow in the ballad of *Robin Hood and the Three Squires* not only saw her sons who had been condemned to die for poaching free once more, but also avenged upon their enemies. Robin Hood was true to his own maxim, 'Look ye do non housbonde no harme'; he was the man to right the wrongs of the poor:

> 'What man that helpeth a gode yeman
> His frende then will I be,'

he declared. Where he acted, moreover, justice was not only done but was seen to be done.

Martin Parker, who compounded his *True Tale of Robin Hood* out of old ballads, was near enough to the mark when he sketched the character of his hero:

146

'The widow and the fatherlesse
    He woulde send means unto,
And those whom famine did oppresse
    Found him a friendly foe.'

But the poor man of Robin Hood's story is not the traditional toiling, suffering peasant of so much medieval literature, whose cry of woe, unheard on earth, goes up to heaven where his reward is prepared for him. There is hardly a hint of pathos in the ballad-makers' treatment of those victims of want and injustice whom the outlaw helped in need. The peasant people with whom Robin Hood mingled were yeomen, independent and with a pride in themselves and their free status, who would brook interference from no man. Robin himself was a yeoman 'corteys and free'; Little John when he first met his master was a young giant, 'brisk' and 'lusty', already famed far and wide for his strength; Alan-a-Dale was a bold youth clad in a scarlet cloak and with a bow in his hand. When in the ballad of *Robin Hood and the Tinker* the outlaw asked the man what knave he was, the answer was proud and defiant:

'No knave, no knave', the tinker said,
    'And that you soon shall know;
Whether of us hath done most wrong
    My crab tree staff shall show'.

It was his independence of speech, his demand that he be not

Robin Hood and the Bold Tinker

147

trifled with, that won the potter Robin Hood's friendship and
the freedom of his and the outlaws' society:

> 'By my trowet, thou says soth' sayde Roben
> 'Thou says goode yemanrey.'

There is nothing menial about the bearing of Adam the Spencer
in *Gamelyn*; Adam Bell and Clym of the Clough 'had dread for
no man', even in the King's hall. Their independence of spirit
is an essential part of the atmosphere of the outlaw ballads; the
whole theme of the 'free forest' revolves around it. The life of
those who dwell in the woods may be harder than that of hermit
or friar, as the *Geste* declares, but at least it is free; the men of
the forest choose their own law and live untrammelled. With
their bows in their hands and the waste of woodland about them,
these are the freest spirits in the land; they are not bound to any
soil or to the whim of any master:

> 'Mery it was in grene forest,
>   A'mong the leves grene,
> Where that men walke bothe east and west,
>   Wyth bowes and arrows keen.'

They belong to a society of their own, and in their own terri-
tory they speak on equal terms with whoever comes, be he
bishop or baron. There is nothing humble about the yeomen of
the ballads; poor they may be, but they hold themselves erect
and proud, 'comely, corteys and good'.

On the one side in the ballads stands Robin Hood and the
great brotherhood of good yeomen, independent and defiant.
Against them on the other side are ranged all those who use
their rank and possessions to cheat and oppress, to hold down
the poor in unwilling thraldom. Two classes of men in particular earn the undying enmity of the outlaws, the officers of the
law and the rich churchmen. The retribution which always overtakes them in the end reveals their incorrigible villainy. It is in
the ferocious verse of the *Tale of Gamelyn* that the bitterness of
the hatred in which these men were held finds its fiercest expression; in it we can almost hear the groans of the maimed clergy
who were carried home from Gamelyn's hall in 'carts and
waynes', and the rattle of the bones of the sheriff and justice

upon their windy gallows. But the same theme runs consistently through all the outlaw poems.

It is strange to find in the guardians of the law the villains in a poetic cycle whose undercurrent theme is the triumph of justice. Yet it is consistently so: the sheriff, the King's justice, and the foresters who enforce the arbitrary precepts of the law of the King's forest, are the men who are singled out to be the victims of an exemplary retribution. It is significant, therefore, that the ballad makers are always careful to particularize the abuse which these men have made of their position. The sheriff is a man in whose word no one can put the slightest trust; no trickery or injustice is too despicable for him to stomach. Though the case between them is *sub judice* and Sir Richard atte the Lee has sworn to answer for his conduct before the King, the sheriff will have him ambushed when he is hawking alone by the river, and do his damnedest to see him hanged before any questions can be asked. If he takes an outlaw in the wood, there will not even be the mockery of a trial; Guy of Gisborne or the first-comer may crave his death for a boon and will be satisfied. The sheriff in *Gamelyn* does not shrink from shedding the innocent blood of his own brother:

'If he have not that oon, he will have the other.'

It is the same with the justice. His judgements have been bought almost before a tale begins. What hope had Sir Richard of obtaining a delay at the law when his judge was already the abbot's man?

'I am holde with the abbot' sayde the Justice
'Both with cloth and fee.'

Judge and jury alike in *Gamelyn* had been hired to hang Sir Ote; the process in their court provided not justice but a legal travesty thereof. These men have earned the fate that overtakes them in long careers of crime, and when the end comes no pity is wasted on them, for only by their death will men ultimately be free from their oppression. So when finally in the ballad of *Robin Hood and the Three Squires*, the Sheriff of Nottingham is hanged on his own gallows 'in the glen', we may speak justifiably of the poem having a happy ending. The tale of his misdeeds has already revealed him to be incorrigible in wickedness.

This care to particularize the crimes of sheriff and justice explains the curious attitude of the outlaw poems towards the law's officers. They are not hated because of the law which they administer, but because their administration of it is corrupt. Before justice's guardians are attacked it is made clear that their justice is a mockery. There is no animus against the law itself; did not Sir Ote in the *Tale of Gamelyn* himself end his days as the King's justice? Significantly in the case of the foresters the treatment is not the same. They are slain indifferently; Adam Bell and his companions had forty dead foresters to account for, and Robin Hood is said to have killed fifteen of them single-handed as he went to Nottingham:

> 'You have found mee an archer' saith Robin Hood
> 'Which will make your wives for to wring'.

There are no tears shed over Guy of Gisborne or Wrennock of the Dunne, though the story of their crimes remains untold. The reason is not far to seek, and it lies in the nature of the law the foresters administered. The forest law was arbitrary and tyrannical; it threw men into prison on suspicion to await trial at the convenience of the forest justices. It knew no equity, and those who lived on lands where it ran had no recourse to common law to protect them from its injuries. For the venial sin of poaching the penalty could be death. It was not for any real crimes committed, the widow told Robin Hood, that her three sons were condemned to die; it was:

> '. . . for slaying of the King's fallow deer,
> Bearing their long bows with thee.'

It was because they enforced without mercy a merciless law which had its foundation not in custom nor equity but in arbitrary will that the foresters were hated, as the dying words of the Scots outlaw, Johnnie Cock, whom they shot as he hunted in the woods, tell us:

> 'Woe be to you, foresters,
>   And an ill death may you die!
> For there would not a wolf in a' the wood
>   Have done the like to me.'

Here it is the law itself which is resented, because there was no shadow of justice in it. The crimes of sheriffs and men of law are retailed because in the ballad-makers' ideal world the sheriffs and justices would be better men; those of the foresters are not because their calling itself is unjust and in an ideal world they would be out of work.

The case of Robin Hood's other traditional enemies, the rich churchmen, is very similar to that of the men of law. Once again their misdeeds are particularized. Their greed, their frauds and their lying have been proven to the hilt before they come to grief. Indeed there is not much of the priest about them in the ballads. They are hard, pitiless men, who in their covetousness have forgotten the Christian quality of mercy. To the pleas of Gamelyn, chained to the post of his brother's hall, they were deaf as the post itself; Sir Richard atte the Lee begged in vain to the Abbot of St. Mary's for a delay to pay his debt:

'The abbot sware a full grete othe;
 'By God that dyed on tree,
Get the londe where thou may,
 For thou getest none of me'.

It was no wonder that Robin Hood gave his famous bidding to his men:

'These bishoppes and these arche bishoppes
 Ye schal hem bete and bynde.'

Their conduct deprived them of any claim which their religious calling might make on his mercy, or that of any other of their fellow Christians. But once again, as in the case of the men of law, it is noticeable that Robin Hood's animus is against particular churchmen and not the Church itself. When the King came to Sherwood disguised as an abbot, Robin would only take half the alms that he offered him, and his conduct was courtesy itself; he took the abbot 'full fayre by the hond' and spread a royal feast before him 'under his trystel-tree'. He himself was always the model of conventional piety. His own sorrow in the forest was his enforced absence from the mass:

'Yea, on thyng greves me' seid Robin,
 'And does my hert mych woo;
That I may not no solemn day
 To mass or Matyns go.'

According to the *Geste*, he built a chapel in Barnesdale dedicated to the Magdalene. Our Lady was his patron saint; when

Guy of Gisborne wounded him, his prayer to her 'that was both
mother and may' gave him strength for the riposte. It was not
against religion that he fought, as the mythologists who see in
him a devotee of the witch religion,[1] would have it; it was
against the rich cleric whose insatiable hunger for land would
not stop short at fraud. It is as landlords, not as priests, that
abbots and monks play a part in the outlaw ballads, and it is as
unjust and ungenerous landlords that they are robbed, beaten
and bound.

It is the churchmen of rank whom the outlaws persecute, the
bishops and archbishops, the abbots and the officers of the great
monasteries. Against the lesser clergy they have no animus,
and in the friars, significantly, they find their friends. Though
he does not come into any of the early outlaw ballads, Friar
Tuck seems to have been long associated with the outlaws. In
the fragment of a play of Robin Hood among the Paston papers,
which dates from 1475, he has a part to play, and before that in
the reign of Henry V, there was a real outlaw, Richard Stafford,
who went under the alias of 'Frere Tuk'. The friars were just
the kind of persons whom one might expect to be the outlaws'
friends. They were vowed to poverty, and their rule made them
the natural critics of the monks who could enjoy privately the
profits of their wide estates in the seclusion of their cloisters.
As mendicant preachers they mingled with the poor, and many
of them shared the same humble origins with the people of the
countryside. Whether or not he was really the same man as
Tuck, it need not surprise us that the *Ballad of Robin Hood and
the Curtal Friar of Fountains Abbey* should end with the latter
bound for the greenwood in the company of Robin's merry
men.

Though it is among those who have riches and high rank
that Robin's enemies, both in the religious and in the secular
worlds, are to be found, it is important to note that the poems
about him reveal no animus against wealth or rank as such. The
poems do not just divide the world into rich and poor, and
describe the struggle of their champions. To hereditary rank
Robin Hood payed the respect which his age regarded as appropriate. Richard atte the Lee was justly proud that he was a
knight, and what the ballad maker is anxious that we should

[1] See Appendix 1.

know is that he enjoyed that rank by a right of birth which he does not attempt to question:

> 'A hundred wynter here before
> Myn auncestres knyghtes hath be.'

For him there was something essentially wrong about the idea that the son of an old family should lose his inheritances, and the attempt to wring it from him is contributory to the injustice of the abbot's part. Robin Hood and Little John by contrast honoured Sir Richard as was due:

> 'It were great shame' sayde Robin
> 'A knight alone to ryde'

and for just that reason he gave him Little John to be his knave and go with him. Knights and lords seemed to the ballad makers to be an essential part of the social system, and they did not question their right to a high social status. They even reproduced in the ranks of the outlaw's own society a graded hierarchy; Gamelyn was 'King of the Outlaws', and the crown that he is said to have borne shows that this was not an empty euphemism for the leadership of a robber band, but a title which set him apart, giving him duties towards his men as well as the right to their obedience. As soon as he was free of prison he must hurry back to his subjects in the wood, to see how they went about their business and to judge their quarrels:

> 'To see how my yonge men ledyn her lif
> Whether thy live in joye or ellys in stryf.'

Gamelyn, like Sir Richard, belonged to the hereditary knightly class, and he too was proud of his breeding. His brother's slurs on his legitimacy roused him to the quick: he was no 'gadelyng',

> 'But born of a lady and gotten of a knyght.'

It was only meet that the king of the outlaws should be a man of high birth. In some stories Robin Hood himself is made out to be a noble, though he is more usually a proud yeoman. One tradition makes him an outlawed Earl of Huntingdon; another makes him the child of 'Earl Richard's daughter', born in the greenwood, out of wedlock it is true, but of a father who was also of gentle blood:

> 'O Willie's large O'lith and limb
> And come o' high degree'

The object of the ballad maker here is quite clearly to increase the stature of his hero, and like others of his age he took it that nobility of blood gave a man a right to special status and consideration. The middle ages were profoundly respectful to hereditary rank and they did not question its title to homage. They did on the other hand question the right of those whose actions belied any nobility of mind to the enjoyment of the privileges of noble status. They were not indignant against an unjust social system, but they were indignant against unjust social superiors. The ballad makers accepted this contemporary attitude and echoed it in their poems.

This explains why the ballads have nothing to say of the economic exploitation of the poor, of the tyranny of lords of manors whose bondmen were tied to the soil and bound by immemorial custom to till their land for him. For we might expect, from what we know of the social system of the country-side in the middle ages, to find Robin, as the champion of the poor, freeing serfs from bondage, harbouring runaway villeins in his band, and punishing the stewards of estates whose conduct was every whit as harsh and unjust as that of the officers of the law. But the middle ages did not view social injustice, as we do, in terms of the exploitation of one class by another; they admired the class system as the co-operation for the common well-being of the different estates of men. They recognized three different classes in their society; the knights and lords, whose business it was to protect Christendom in arms, the clerks who had charge of its spiritual well-being and whose duty was prayer, and the common men whose business it was to till the soil. Each rank had its obligation to discharge its proper duties without complaint, and, in the case particularly of the first two classes, not to abuse the privileges which its function gave it. That they were made to 'swink and toil' gave the peasants no ground for complaint; their occupation, as one preacher quaintly put it, lay in 'grobbynge about the erthe, as erynge and dungynge and sowynge and harwying' and 'this schuld be do justlie and for a good ende, withoute feyntise or falshede or gruechynge of hire estaat'. But those who failed to discharge their duties and abused their position had no right to a place in the system, nor to the profits of association. 'They neither labour with the rustics . . . nor fight with the knights, nor pray and chant with the clergy; therefore,' says the great Dominican, Bromyard, of such men 'they shall go with their own abbot, of whose Order they are, namely the Devil, where no Order exists but horror eternal.'

The law's object is ultimately to uphold social justice, and to the middle ages social justice meant a hierarchical social system. The trouble came when those who belonged to a high class used the wealth, which was given them to uphold their proper rank, to corrupt the law and abuse it for their own profit. Their ultimate sin was the use of their originally rightful riches to purchase more than was their due. For this reason, those who were shocked by flagrant injustice into attacking the accepted system criticized not the economic oppression which it almost automatically implied, but the corruption of evil men whose personal greed destroyed the social harmony of what they regarded as the ideal system. The method which these men employed was to buy the law, and to control by their position its application. It is for this reason that the outlaw ballads, whose heroes are the champions of the poor, are silent about the multitudinous economic miseries of the medieval peasant, and are concerned only or at least chiefly with an endless feud against the corrupt representatives of the law. Contemporary opinion diagnosed the disease which was gnawing at society as the personal corruption of those in high rank; that such disease was the inevitable accompaniment of their hierarchic system they simply could not see. This is why the animus in the outlaw ballads is against oppression by those who own the law, not against exploitation by those who own the land.

The cast of contemporary thought also explains the immunity from criticism of one particular lord in the outlaw ballads, that is, the King. Because they accepted that the law, with all its hierarchical implications, was ultimately just, and confined their attacks to those who administered it to wrong ends, men had to accept the justice of the law's ultimate fountain head, the King. Reverence for the King stood upon a basis even firmer than respect for high rank in medieval thought. He stood apart from the social system, in it but not born of it like the baronage, hallowed and anointed but not of the hated race of clerks, God's minister in the land, made sacred by the mysteries both of religion and tradition. He was its guardian, God's vicar in whose hand was placed the sword of temporal power, and from whose court no appeal lay in this world. We are trespassing here upon the edge of one of the great unsolved problems of medieval thinking, that of the powers of the King who in person is human, but the authority of whose office is divine. Whether as the Roman law declared the laws were in the King's mouth, or whether, as ancient custom implied, he was but the guardian of a law to which he and his people alike owed obedience, was a question over which the subtle doctors of the schools were themselves divided. The fiction of the King's two bodies, the corporal body which was mortal, the phenomenal shell of regality, and the mystic body which was undying, explained the problem posed by his office but did not solve it. About the answer a thousand problems revolved, as the question of tyrannicide and the right to depose an erring monarch, and the question of prerogative and the force of the King's arbitrary will; but these were problems far beyond the understanding of the humble minstrels who sang the outlaw ballads and of the simple men who heard them. They only knew that the King was the ultimate repository of a law whose justice they acknowledged, and they saw treason against him as a betrayal of their allegiance to God himself. If they could only get past his corrupt officers, whose abuse of the trust reposed in them amounted to treason in itself, and bring their case before the King, they believed that right would be done. Their unshakeable faith in the King's own justice was the most tragic of the misconceptions of the medieval peasantry, and the ballad makers and their audiences shared it to the full.

Thus it is that just as the outlaws love the God whose servants they persecute, so they honour as truly as any of his subjects the King against whose officers they war:

'I love no man in all the worlde
So well as I do my King'

declares Robin in the *Littel Geste*. In that ballad, indeed, comely

King Edward is treated as almost as much a hero as Robin Hood himself. There is another ballad on this same theme where it is 'King Henry' who comes to the forest in disguise and is made welcome by the outlaws. All sorts of variant stories of the King's mixing in disguise with poachers of the forest and being entertained by them were once known, and several survive. There is one which tells of how Edward IV met with a tanner when he was out hunting, which has significantly opening lines very similar to the traditional summer setting of the scene in the ballads of Robin Hood; another tells of the King's clandestine feasting on poached meats with a shepherd in Windsor forest, in which the King adopts the name of Joly Robyn; another, which is incomplete, of his meeting a friar in Sherwood who combined the roles of hermit and forest archer. All these men are ultimately forgiven for their offences by the King and admitted to his intimacy. So also, when they finally come to him, the King always sees the justice of the outlaws' case and pardons them. He took Robin Hood with him to serve at his court; he pardoned, at his Queen's entreaty, Adam Bell and his companions; he forgave Gamelyn. Over the deaths of his servants he seldom shed any false tears. To Sir Richard he returned his lands which were confiscated; Ote and Gamelyn became his justices; Robin Hood and Adam Bell became his yeomen and exchanged their Lincoln green for the King's livery. The King is the *Deus ex machina* of the outlaw stories; by his authority the righting of wrongs done which has been the theme of the poems is stablished fast, and those who have served him loyally, if illegally, are rewarded. Occasionally, as in the ballad of *Adam Bell*, pardon is wrung from him unwillingly, but one knows that his word, unlike the sheriff's, cannot be broken when it is once given. Robin Hood in the ballads is the arbiter of an unofficial justice which accords with the unrecognized moral law; the King is authority, which ultimately endorses the moral law and makes its justice official.

The concept of justice is one which has held different meanings for different ages, and we should not, because it is said to be based in the moral law, read too modern an interpretation into it. The medieval picture of the day of judgement, with its vivid, hideous detail of the suffering of damned souls in a nether world of bestial demons, stands to remind us that for this age justice was retributive. It is this that explains the callousness, amounting almost to brutality, of some of the outlaw stories. Medieval man saw nothing tragic in the downfall of the wicked; awful and exemplary it might be, but not poignant. Justice, moreover, was in no way impaired by the fact that it could only be achieved by violent means, for the resort to force was ultimately nothing less than an appeal to the judgement of God, which does not err. The levying of war in a just cause was a duty, not a last resource forced on one by dire necessity. The shedding of innocent blood was of small moment provided the cause had absolute justice; had not God himself been forced by the exigences of nature, when he visited his wrath on the sins of Sodom and Gomorrah, to consume three other cities in the same storm of fire, although their inhabitants had not run up a more than average debit balance of sin?[1] After all, the innocent had their reward laid up for them in heaven. If through mischance their fate was caught up on this earth in the retribution which overwhelmed the wicked, it was not a matter for undue regret, since death to them was but the gate to a better world. For an age of faith such as was the medieval period, there was nothing incongruous about justice and violence going hand in hand: they were familiar bedfellows.

The wildness of their life and the violence of their deeds cannot therefore be made a reproach to the outlaws. In taking the law into their own hands they were only falling back upon the ancient right of those who could not obtain justice to use force, and to use that force in the cause of others could only be altruism. When they shed the blood of their enemies, they were performing meritorious acts of retributive justice. Hence the endless tale of death and bloodshed which runs through the ballads. There are few holocausts so dramatic as the bloodbath with which the *Tale of Gamelyn* is rounded off; but it will not do to forget the forty foresters of the fee killed by Adam Bell, or the bloody mutilated head of Guy of Gisborne which Robin set on his bow's end, or the rotting corpses of the monk and his 'little page', hidden in the moss by the wayside in Barnsdale in *Robin Hood and the Monk*. Nor should one forget Gandelyn's words of triumph over the body of Wrennock of

---

[1] This incident is quoted by Honoré Bonet, who in his *Tree of Battles* wrote a lengthy justification of war.

the Dunne, or Robin Hood's exultant cry in the *Geste*, as he stands over the sheriff's body in the square of Nottingham:

> 'Lye thou there, thou proude sheriffe,
>   Evyll mote thou cheve!
> There myght no man to thee truste
>   The whyles thou were alyve.'

Face to face with their enemies, one will find the outlaws pitiless enough, for one cannot spare thought for pity in the cause of justice.

This streak of violence does not, of course, run through all the ballads. There are some, like that of *Robin Hood and the Potter*, which preserve the gay mood of their opening lines throughout. But it is important not to overlook it in other ballads, because it is so much taken for granted that it can quite easily pass unnoticed. There are the exultant moments which strike one, as those quoted above, but there are plenty of deaths which are recorded without comment. The monk and his page are assassinated and quickly forgotten; the sheriff in *Guy of Gisborne* is shot down running and his death is dismissed in a line; in the ballad of *Robin Hood and the Three Squires* the drama of the sheriff's execution is quite undeveloped (by contrast, for instance, with the same scene in *Gamelyn*). This might be taken for callousness, but it is hardly even that. It is simply the recognition of the fact that in the cause of justice, blood must most probably be shed; indeed, that it ought to be. This is the second tragic misconception of the common man of the middle ages, that because his cause was just and force was an appeal to the judgement of God, his ends would be served by recourse to violence.

Behind the matter of the later outlaw stories, therefore, there seems to lie the common man's demand for social justice. This is the only consistent theme which runs through most of the poems. We have seen that the manner of its presentation accords well with what we might expect to be the prevalent attitudes of the times. What we have still to see is whether history will bear out this interpretation and show that in the fourteenth and fifteenth centuries, the period which seems from their background to be the setting of the ballads, there was a real demand from the common people for social justice. If there was, we must further examine whether or not it was framed in terms which accord with the recurrent grievances urged in the ballads.

By and large, the earlier middle ages seem to have been a period of oriental passivity among the common people. We know a great deal about the terms of their bondage, about the number of days in a week on which a villein had to work on his lord's land and about the fines and reliefs which he had to pay; we know plenty too about the economic organization of manors, the methods of tilling the soil, the function of lords' officers such as bailiffs and reeves and haywards. But of the peasants' attitude to all this we know very little. We can imagine that he grumbled, for the burdens put upon him seem to us to have been almost intolerable, but history has left no witness to his complaining of his hard fate. Once in a while we hear of the angry tenants of some specially tyrannical lord suddenly breaking into revolt and assassinating their master or burning his house; or of some body of peasants withdrawing their services from their lord in protest against some particularly harsh innovation. But these revolts and protests are confined to one estate at a time, and one and all seem to fizzle out in failure. They are not part of any great movement. The average peasant does not seem to have had much to say to the conditions which bound him to poverty and ancestral thraldom, and in the history of the age he plays his passive role in sullen silence.

But in the last centuries of the middle ages the giant who strides through modern times, the labouring man, collective and impersonal, seems to be stirring for the first time in his sleep. He is only half awake as yet, and with only glimmerings of political consciousness his efforts are doomed to failure. But from all over Europe comes the same story. Suddenly the passive peasant is in arms, and his wrath breaks upon his oppressors like a thunderstorm. In 1358 it was the peasants of France who rose in revolt in the hour of national disaster, when the King was a prisoner in England and the country was riven with civil war, and for a moment they caught their masters off their guard. The quelling of this rebellion of the *Jacquerie* was the one good deed for France of Charles the Bad, King of Navarre. In 1381 it was the peasantry of England who rose in the great Peasants' Revolt, and marched with Wat Tyler and John Ball to London. Their rising too, was relentlessly put down. In 1525 it was the peasants of Germany who took to arms, inspired by the preaching of Luther, only to be betrayed when their hero, horrified at the effect of his words, threw in his hand with the princes. In England at the end of the middle ages there seems to have been a permanent subcurrent of popular discontent, 1381 was the first occasion when it flamed up into widespread revolt, but there had been rumblings of the coming storm for years before that, and there had been scattered outbreaks of violence up and down the land. Stories were abroad of gatherings or recalcitrants in the woods at night, and of men banding together to support one another in a struggle for justice. In the very year after 1381 there were rumours of revolt in the West Country; there was open revolt in Cheshire in the 1390s, and there were many scattered local outbreaks over the succeeding years. Jack Cade's revolt in 1450 saw peasants marching on London once more, though there were others too, of higher rank, among the rebels. In Robin of Redesdale's revolt in the North in 1469 poor men again had their part. Down to the time of the Pilgrimage of Grace in 1536 and Kets rebellion in 1549 there seems to be a constant simmering of popular discontent just below the surface. But the same tragic sequel of repression follows all these outbreaks. They are bursts of sleepy-eyed wrath; half-blind, the peasant does not quite know what it is he is fighting for, except for a world in which his lot shall be less harsh. There is no realism about the aims he professes, and his leaders have not the understanding of politics to make realistic plans for the event of success. But though these risings were doomed to failure before they started, they do reveal just that background of widespread popular unrest which would make men listen, and admire the stories of an outlaw whose defiance of the law was more successful than their own.

Modern historians who have examined the causes of these revolts have diagnosed them in economic terms. But because the rebels were medieval men living in an age which tended to see everything in terms of law their demands were largely legal, which is what we would expect from the outlaw poems with their persistent bitterness against the men of law. Let us take the example of 1381. The revolt began when the Essex men rose against the King's officers and put Chief Justice Bealknap, who was sitting at Brentwood, to flight. At Bury, where there was a fierce outbreak, Chief Justice Cavendish was among the first to be assassinated. When the rebels reached London, they broke into the Temple and burned all the books of the lawyers that they could lay hands on. When Wat Tyler presented the demands of the rebels to the King at Smithfield they were couched in legal terms. This is the account of them which is given in the *Anonimalle Chronicle*:

> 'And the said Wat then listed the matters which were in question, and he demanded that there should be no law but the law of Winchester, and that sentence of outlawry should not be pronounced in any case at law henceforth, and that no lord should have seigneurial jurisdiction . . . but that all should be in the King's lordship . . . and that there should be no bondmen in England, and no serfdom, but that all should be free and of one condition.'

What a bondman meant was a villein, and villeinage was a legal status, not an economic one. The lord's rights over his villeins were again legal, for he could tax them at his will; they were his justiceables and against him, and him only, they had no recourse to common law. To be sure he could and did use his legal advantages for the purpose of economic exploitation, but what the peasant felt and hated were the legal disabilities of his position, and his first demand was that they should be abolished.

What the rebels of 1381 demanded was in effect not a review of the whole system but reform on particular points in it which bore harshly on them. Once satisfied of this and issued with new charters, most of them were content to return to their estates. Their aims were bounded by local horizons, and this was in part the reason for their downfall. The rebels of St. Albans, for instance, were not particularly concerned to aid a general movement; they were concerned to get Wat Tyler's aid in wringing from their abbot the concessions which he had consistently denied them, the right to use handmills in their own homes, the right to hunt in the chases and warrens of the liberty, and the right to govern their borough through their own corporation. Significantly, the rebels put their case in terms of the restoration of old liberties of which they had been illegally defrauded by tyrannous masters in the past. Rumours were running about of ancient charters which had been conveniently lost; at Bury it was the terms of a charter of Canute which the rebels demanded, at St. Albans they set the abbot hunting his muniments for a long charter written in golden letters and said to have been granted by King Offa in the eighth century, six hundred years previously. Significantly again, the peasants were careful by their conduct to prove the justice of their cause: they would not demean it by indiscriminate looting. When they set light to John of Gaunt's vast palace in London, the Savoy, its priceless treasures were carried away and cast into the Thames; those who were caught thieving were thrown into the flames and were consumed with the house. They ravaged and burned but they did not steal, for they were God's avengers of injustice, and what they did, they did in the name of the Father, Son and Holy Ghost, and King Richard. All this is just what we might expect from the tone of the outlaw ballads.

Besides the men of law, Robin Hood's other traditional enemies were the rich clerks, and they were the other enemies also of the peasants of 1381. If ever anyone followed to the letter Robin Hood's advice to his men:

> 'These bishoppes and these arche bishoppes,
> Ye schal hem bete and bynde,'

it was Wat Tyler's men who beheaded Simon of Sudbury, the Archbishop of Canterbury, on Tower Hill. He was not the only cleric to suffer at the hands of the rebels: John of Cambridge, Prior of Bury, was killed in Suffolk along with Sir John Cavendish, and so was the Abbey's steward, John de Lakingheth. All up and down the areas affected, monasteries were attacked, and the court rolls and manorial extents which recorded the terms of their tenants' services solemnly burnt; at Canterbury in Kent, at St. Albans in Hertford, at Bury in Suffolk, at St. Benet's Holm and Benham and Carrow in Norfolk. The peasants had good cause to hate the possessionate clergy. A corporate land-lord always tends to be harsher than a personal one, because its officer cannot, as an individual owner can, take account of cases of special hardship, because his duty is to the corporation, not the tenant. The medieval church was no exception to this rule. They had besides the reputation of being particularly conserva-tive landlords; where for instance a borough lay within an abbey's liberty, the monastery often clung to its rights of jurisdiction over the affairs of the inhabitants long after all the neighbouring towns had obtained royal charters giving rights of self-government.

Deep resentment of the Church's vast wealth and especially that of the monasteries, was in any case a widespread feeling in this period and shared by many of higher rank than the peasants. In the later middle ages the monasteries were ceasing to play the prominent part which had once been theirs in the religious and intellectual life of the kingdom. Comparatively few bishops of the fourteenth and fifteenth centuries were monks, and intellectual leadership had switched by then to the rising universities. More and more the monasteries' public role seemed to be limited to that of influential landlords; it was as landlords that their abbots' voices had weight in the parliaments and councils of the realm, while their work of prayer was carried out unseen in the cloister—if indeed it was carried out. The habits of many monks were becoming lax, and their outlook more secular; Chaucer's monk was known better as a huntsman than a man of God. Of course, there were exceptions by the legion, and the monasteries still doubtless housed many men of saintly life and thinking; but men were already beginning to wonder whether these multitudinous religious houses were really serving sufficient religious purpose to justify the vast estates which they were constantly and carefully extending. They were the butt of a great troop of satirists; Wycliffe castigated their unmerited riches in his fierce rhetoric. In the Parliament of 1371 a move was made to seize the land of monasteries, and there were many even among the great who were ready to support it. Rumblings of the storm which broke upon the English monasteries in Henry VIII's time could be heard nearly two hundred years before. We need not be surprised to find Robin Hood's preying on the rich clergy regarded as an act of elemental justice.

Among the lower clergy the discontented peasants found many sympathizers. John Ball, the mad priest of Kent, was one of their leaders; John Wrawe, leader of the Suffolk rebels, was the Chaplain of Ringsfield. In particular the friars were accused of being in league with them; their insurrectionary sermons were said by many to be at the back of the revolt. William Langland, writing his *Vision of Piers Plowman* only a few years before, had complained of the social anarchy which they preached:

'They preche men by Plato and proven it by Seneca,
That alle thinges under hevene ought to be in comune.'

One can see in the ecclesiastical demands of the peasants the
influence of the ideas of the medicant orders, with their doctrine
of evangelical poverty for the Church. This is what Wat Tyler
asked for in this matter: 'That the goods of Holy Church be no
longer left in the hands of men of religion . . . and that there
shall be no bishop or prelate in England save one, and that their
goods and lands and all their possessions be divided among the
Commons, saving to Churchmen enough to live on.' Jack
Cade's rebels in 1450 showed the same animus against the rich
clergy, but Sir Thomas More exaggerated when he wrote that
they intended 'to kyll up the clergie, and sel priestes heddes as
gode chepe as shepes heddes, thre for a peni, bie who would'.
The peasant rebels had their friends among the clergy, in the
poorer of the friars and parsons and the hedge-priests like John
Ball; it was rich clerks who abused their wealth and oppressed
the poor that they hated.

It will not do to overlook the deep undercurrent of religious
feeling in the minds of the peasants; 'We are men formed in
Christ's likeness and they handle us as beasts.' Echoes of the
sermons of the great homilists run all through the sayings
attributed to the rebels. Even John Ball's famous catch

'When Adam delved and Eve span,
Who was then the gentleman?'

was not new; the same rhyme is found in a poem written on the
hermit's life by an English anchorite in the early fourteenth
century. John Ball's letter to the peasants opens with a call to
them to stand together in Christ:

'John Balle seynt Marye prist gretes wele alle maner men and
byddes hem in the name of the Trinite, Fader and Sone and
Holy Ghost, Stande manlyche togedyr and in trewthe, and
helpeth trewthe, and trewthe shall helpe you.'

The *Continuator of Knighton's Chronicle* collected a series of
other 'letters' of this kind which were said to have circulated,
curious little pastiches of catch phrases, and nearly all have a
religious tinge. 'John Mylner asketh helpe to turne his mylne
aright. He hath grounden smal smal; the King's son of Heven

he schal pay for alle.' Rygt and mygt, wylle and skylle; God
spede every dele.' 'God do bote, for now is time.' Behind these
snatches culled largely from contemporary pulpit literature,
one sees the same conventional, trusting piety that is a feature
of the Robin Hood ballads, and which here is combined with
strong anti-clericalism.

Even in matters of detail, the themes of the outlaw ballads
accord well with the historical attitude of popular discontent.
The Forest Law is not usually looked on as a major item in the
demands of the peasants of 1381, but where it was brought up
it appeared in the form in which we should expect it, in insistence on the right to hunt freely in parks and warrens. *Knighton's
Chronicle* mentions as one of Tyler's demands the request that
'all warrens, as well in fisheries as in parks and woods, should
be common to all; so that throughout the realm, in the waters,
ponds, fisheries, woods and forests, poor as well as rich might
take the venison and hunt the hare in the fields.' The rebels at
St. Albans carried before them a rabbit tied to the end of a lance
which was supposed to symbolize their claim to the right to
take game in the abbot's chases. The intimate connexion between discontent over the forest's game-laws and peasant unrest in this period is brought out in a petition to the Parliament
of 1390, passed as a statute a mere nine years after the Revolt.
It was then complained that 'artificers and labourers . . . keep
greyhounds and other dogs, and on festivals, at times when
good Christians are in Church hearing divine service, they go
hunting in the parks, rabbit preserves and warrens of lords and
others and ruin them utterly'. It was such hunts, the petition
declared, that gave these people an opportunity for holding 'at
these times their meetings for debate, covin and conspiracy, in
order to stir up riot and sedition against Your Majesty and the
laws'. In all ways these peasants seem to be behaving in a
manner remarkably similar to that of the ballad outlaw. But
this point need not be laboured; we have seen already that the
outlook towards this matter of the forest in the ballads conforms
exactly with that of the rustic population of the later middle ages.

Again as regards the King, the attitude is just what the
stories of the outlaws would lead us to expect. The rebels'
implicit trust in the boy King Richard II, who even if he had
wished to would not have been able to help them, was one of

the most tragic and pathetic features of the revolt of 1381. 'The commons,' says the *Anonimalle Chronicle,* 'had among them a watchword in the English tongue: "With whom haldes yow?" And the reply was "Wyth King Richard and the trew communes"'. Their aim as they proclaimed it, was to free the King of his evil councillors. When, in the moment of crisis in Smithfield when Wat Tyler was struck down, Richard rode forward with incredible courage to put himself at their head with the cry 'I am your King', they followed him in quiet obedience from the field. By a tragic irony, it was the time which their immediate response to his appeal to their allegiance obtained which gave the authorities their chance to collect

Execution of the 1381 rebels.

sufficient men to surround and quell them. But the lesson of 1381 taught them nothing; Jack Cade's rebellion in 1450 was premature and failed to cash in on potential Yorkist support, and the reason was that it aimed not to depose the King but to disempower evil councillors, the party 'that surrounds the King and fills him with such ideas as that our Sovereign Lord is above his laws . . . and may make them and break them as him list'. Popular rebels and outlaws alike believed that in order to usher in a new reign of justice they had but to free the King from the influence of the evil men who for the moment surrounded him.

The shocked imagination of the upper classes credited the rebels of 1381 with all kinds of extravagant aims, such as to divide the kingdom into provinces with rulers of their own appointment and to put every member of the aristocracy to the sword. To judge by their actions, this picture is quite misleading. As we have seen they had implicit faith in their King; their foremost demand was that their new charters of liberties should have the authority of his seal. Of such prominent men as lost their lives at their hands, almost all were tainted more or less directly with responsibility for maladministration and oppressive measures. When the rebels burst into the Tower they made no attempt to harm the King's mother, the aged and popular Princess of Wales: Sir Robert Hales and Simon of Sudbury, who were led out to execution, were the men who, on account of their offices, were held to be responsible for the hated poll tax. Others who died were tainted in similar ways: John Legge, Sergeant-at-Law, was said to have advised the King to re-levy the tax because there had been mass evasions; Sir John Cavendish as a Justice had administered the oppressive Statute of Labourers which held down wages to a minimum; others were killed because they were associated either with oppressive measures or with men who were supposed to be guilty either of their framing or their enforcement, such as John of Gaunt. These men were for the peasants 'traitors', for it was their evil counsel which was misguiding the King and ruining the country, and they demanded their heads with insistence. But they did not demand the heads of the whole aristocracy. Nor did Cade's rebels in 1450: 'We blame not all the lords, nor all that is about the King's person,' they declared, 'nor all gentlemen, nor yeomen, nor all men of law, nor all bishops, nor all priests; and we will not rob nor reve, nor steal; in order that these defaults be amended, and then we will go home.' As in the outlaw ballads the villains are named individuals, the Sheriff of Nottingham and the Abbot of St. Mary's, not the wealthy as a class, so the leaders of 1381 and 1450 made their attack on particular men who were guilty of oppression, and not on the social system as a whole.

Such general demands as the peasants made were, as we have

seen, couched in legal terms. This was because the law was the most subtle and burdensome of the instruments in the hands of the oppressor. By comparison direct economic exploitation was of secondary importance. In the fourteenth century the direct cultivation of large home farms, which could be carried out cheaply with villeins, who were bound by the custom of the manor to perform free labour services for their lords, was not nearly as profitable as it had once been. As what the landlord of the fourteenth century wanted was cash which would enable him to live in style in a world in which cultivated luxuries were becoming increasingly accessible and where a man's status was judged by the ostentation of his living, his reaction to the situation was to rent out his lands and to extract all that he could from the legal advantages of his position. A great deal of the demesne land which was thus rented out was taken up by one-time peasants, many of whom in course of time accumulated large holdings, which they farmed with hired labour. These men were beginning to constitute a new class, the yeoman farmer, a man who might have quite considerable means at his disposal. He was a man of very different status and outlook from his ancestor of a hundred years before, who farmed perhaps 15–20 acres as a villein holding and worked three days a week on his lord's land. Even his paid labourer was likely to be more independent than his villein forbears, for the hired man is always more free than the serf.

Chaucer and Langland, the great contemporary satirists, both complain of the pride and the new airs which the peasant of their day was giving himself, while one of the chroniclers attributes the Peasants' Revolt to the 'grassesse', the 'fatness', of the common people of England. There is more than some truth in his diagnosis. For even though he became a farmer in his own right, the peasant remained at law a villein. The disadvantages of this status were inevitably the more irksome as he who bore them became more independent. For all his prosperity, the villein still owed the lord tiresome customary dues; he had to pay arbitrary taxes—'tallages'—at his lord's will; he must pay him merchet when his daughters married; if any of his women-folk strayed from the path and produced a child out of wedlock he could be made to pay a fine, 'leyrwite'. He was still bound to appear in the lord's manor court, and could be fined if he absented himself; he still had no redress against his lord at common law, though as regarding every other man he had its full protection. He could neither buy nor sell land without his lord's licence, and if he did, the lord was legally entitled to confiscate it. So one finds, for instance, the Abbey of the Holy Cross at Waltham in 1366 entering onto thirty acres of land which had been acquired in fee simple by one of their bondmen, 'as it was lawful for them to do'. This rule was bound to be particularly irksome for the prosperous peasant farmer. It is no coincidence that among the many demands which the tenants of St. Albans presented to the abbot in 1381 was one for the freedom to alienate their land to whom they would. Meanwhile the hired man was hit by such measures as the Statute of Labourers, introduced to keep down wages in the period when labour was scarce after the Black Death of 1349. It hit the peasant farmer too, for in a world where justice was open to influence, he was much less likely to get away with paying his men more than the legal wage than was his social superior, and he might therefore be left with no labour at all. The Statute of Labourers was justly and deeply resented. Sir John Cavendish was not the first to suffer for his part in enforcing it. Long before there had been attacks with violence on the Justices of Labourers: in 1352 there were riots at their sessions both in Northamptonshire and Lincoln, and in 1351 at Tottenham they were driven from their seat of judgement by armed peasants and the prisoners whom they had condemned were released.

So it was against the tyrant law that the peasants railed most, for it was on his account that they suffered most bitterly. Above all they demanded their freedom: and for them freedom meant equality before the law. They demanded that there should be no bondmen throughout England. Everywhere that they went they seized and burnt the records of manorial courts; their ancestors would never have done this, for the immemorial custom of the manor afforded them their only flimsy protection against new and arbitrary demands for service from their lords. But the peasants of 1381 were not so much interested in services and for them these rolls merely preserved the lords' legal title to hold them in bondage. They demanded that the law of Winchester should run throughout the land. Historians have sometimes been puzzled as to what this can have meant, but there seems to be a ready answer; what the peasants were demanding was the law of the great 'Book of Winchester', *Domesday Book*.[1] It was an old tried law that those villeins who lived on lands which were of the ancient demesne land of the Crown were 'sokemen'; that is to say that they were to all intents and purposes free. They could not be arbitrarily taxed; their services could not be increased; they could seek redress at common law against their lord, if the King had granted away the land. The method of proving that one's manor belonged to ancient demesne was by reference to Domesday; if it had been the King's land in the time of William the Conqueror the rights of those who dwelt on it were assured. This matter was one which was in the minds of the peasants in this period; a petition in Parliament in 1377 complained that 'in many lordships and localities in this Kingdom England, the villeins and those who hold in villeinage . . . are refusing their customs and services due to their lords. . . . for by colour of certain exemplifications out of *Domesday Book*, and by the misinterpretation of these, they claim they are quit and utterly discharged of all manner of serfdom.' The demand that the law of Winchester be universal was just part of the demands of a new, more independent type of peasant, whose pride in himself observers like Chaucer noted with disapproval, for equality before the law. It was the natural reaction of a conservatively-minded age to base demands for new rights on supposititious liberties of time past; the reference back to Domesday is of a piece with the peasants' other claims based on antique rights, on the conditions of Henry I's time, for example, or on the terms of charters of Anglo-Saxon Kings such as Canute or Offa. The basis of their case was that the true law of ancient days had been illegally altered by their oppressors in succeeding ages. The freedom they demanded was theirs lawfully, and they showed by their actions that they, like the outlaws, were prepared to fight for their right.

The attitude of the peasants toward the law of the land explains two marked features of the outlaw ballads. It explains the independent attitude of the yeoman of the poems. Robin Hood is the ideal hero of the new countryman of the fourteenth and fifteenth centuries, whose free, proud spirit was impatient of restraint. For though the Peasants' Revolt was a tragic

[1] This explanation was suggested to me by Mr J. O. Prestwich.

failure, its foremost aim was realized over the succeeding years; it was impossible in the long run to deny to the peasant the legal rights of a free man when he was already free in all but name. Gradually during the fifteenth century the villein faded from the English social landscape: by Tudor times his status was an antique anomaly. Robin Hood, the good yeoman 'comely, courteys & free' is just the kind of man to command the admiration of the men who in 1381 were demanding a freedom which, they declared, had only been lost in the abuse of time past.

The attitude of the peasants toward the law also explains the manner of presentation of the outlaw ballads. Since in the hands of evil men the law had become a tyrant and the pillar of injustice, who could better represent the cause of right than the man who had set himself against it? Law was a mockery; justice was only to be sought outside it. A Latin poem of the early fourteenth century puts the situation in its real terms: 'the lawful man shall be put in prison; the thief who ever does wrong shall escape'. 'Yiff he goth to the law,' says a preacher of the poor man, 'there is no helpe; for trewly lawe goys as lordship biddeth him'. Behind the propaganda of the Peasants' Revolt lies the conviction that the social system and the law which supports it has been warped into the machine of monstrous corruption. 'Jack Trewman doth yow know that falsness and gyle havith regned to long, and trewth hath ben sette under a lokke, and falseness regneth in everylk flokke. No man may come trewthe to, but he sing "dedero" [i.e. offer a bribe]'. It was upon the head of the poor man that all the injuries of this corrupt system ultimately descended.

'From Scotland into Kent
This preaching was bysprent,
And from the Easte frount
Unto Saynte Myghelles mount
This sayeng did surmount,
Abroed to all mens eares,
And to your graces peeres—
That from pillar unto post
The powr man he was tost;
I meane the labouring man,
I meane the husbandman,
I meane the ploughman,
I meane the playne true man.'

Little wonder that, smarting in his damaged pride, the 'playne true man' listened to the stories of Robin Hood and revelled in the deeds of one who had set the law at defiance with more success than himself.

It is probably no accident that our first certain reference to Robin Hood comes from the years just previous to the Peasants' Revolt. William Langland, writing his new version of *Piers Plowman* four years before in 1377, pictured his chaplain priest Sloth sitting by the way and saying:

'I can not my pater noster as the prest hit saith,
But I can rymes of Robyn Hoode and Randle Erle of Chester.'

In the very age of the revolt itself the ballads of Robin Hood were being heard by discontented countrymen up and down the land, and the awful events of 1381 showed that they had listened with attention. But it should not be deduced from this or from the close attention paid in this chapter to the Peasants' Revolt that Robin Hood's legend has any direct connexion therewith. The Peasants' Revolt has been examined in detail because its event supplies the most dramatic presentation of the causes of popular discontent. But one must remember that the embers of that discontent were smouldering all through the last two centuries of English medieval history. In 1381 these embers flashed into flame. The tragedy was in the recourse to violence; violence could achieve nothing for the peasant, for he had no leaders with political insight and in any case the corruption which he was fighting was the inevitable accompaniment of the hierarchical system which he accepted. But since the law was in the hands of his enemies he could obtain no redress, and force was the only way left open to him. His case was hopeless. It was only in the imaginary England of the ballad makers that an ideal hero could emerge triumphant from his defiance of the injustice of the system, and, by rounding off the careers of a few corrupt officials in a splendid victory for retributive justice, usher in a new dispensation in which the poor man obtained his due from the harsh world.

XII

The Historicity of Robin Hood

ONCE the ballads are set in their historical context of the wide-spread popular unrest of the later middle ages, a great many of the problems which they pose disappear. We can see now why it is that they remained the literary property of the popular audience; it was impossible to adapt to the demands of aristocratic readers stories which were so directly inspired by contentious social thinking. This was not the case with, for instance, the stories of Fulk Fitzwarin who was the ideal of an independent baronage, and for that reason his tale is full of that kind of chivalrous adventure which appealed to an upper class public. We can also now account for the violent mood of the outlaw legends in terms of the very real bitterness of common people against the corruptions of the system, and for the presentation of that bitterness through the medium of stories centring about the deeds of a hero who was agin the law, because the law appeared as the corrupt instrument of aristocratic tyranny. Certain questions, however, still remain for the historian. Firstly, can he track down the mysterious personality of the hero of the ballads? Is the legend of Robin Hood based ultimately, if remotely, on the life of some historical person, or is he an ideal creation, a figure of the popular imagination, about whom traditional stories once credited to older heroes have collected, adapted by singers of a new generation to the changed attitudes of a later period? And secondly, what verisimilitude is there in the story of Robin Hood? Is the type-cast outlaw chief of the ballads a projection of the wishful thinking of the common man, or is he drawn, with some excusable romantic distortion, from the life?

The second question should not need to be put if we can succeed in conjuring from history a real figure on whose life story the ballads are ultimately based. Conjuring there will certainly have to be, for the historian's inquest has not yet brought forward any reliable witness who will testify that Robin Hood lived and died in his own times. We have, however, at least some indication of where we should look for evidence. Langland's reference to 'rymes of Robyn Hode' in *Piers Plowman* gives us a *terminus ante quem*. It is clear that this is no accidental allusion to an obscure local figure: by the end of the fourteenth century Robin's fame was already universal. His name was becoming proverbial. Writing about the year 1410 the severe author of the treatise *Dives and Pauper* knew him as a traditional figure of popular song and admonished those who 'gon levir to heryn a tale or a song of Robyn Hode or of sum rubaudry than to heryn masse or matynes'. The poet who somewhere about 1400 wrote the *Reply of Friar Daw Topias to Jack Upland* also knew him as a popular hero and the prince of archers:

'On Old Englis it is said
"Unkissid is unknown",
And many men speke of Robyn Hode
That shotte never in his bowe.'

It was probably of him, again, that Chaucer was thinking thirty years before when he wrote in his *Troilus and Criseyde* of 'hazellwood there Jolly Robin plaied'. This is probably not earlier than the *Piers Plowman* reference, and it does not actually speak of Robin *Hood* specifically; 1377 stands therefore as a first firm date. We must however leave time for the legend to circulate and proliferate; if there was a Robin Hood, he must probably have lived thirty or forty years earlier at least. At the same time, since it is only at the very end of the fourteenth century that he appears as a universally known figure, the possible period for his life cannot be pushed back indefinitely. Considering the silence of chroniclers and poets alike before that time, it would seem very unlikely that he could have lived earlier than, say, the first quarter of the thirteenth century. The hundred and sixty odd years which divide the reign of John from that of Richard II is the likeliest hunting ground for a historical Robin Hood.

Significantly it is between these rough dates that most of those who have attempted to treat Robin Hood as a real historical character have located him. These people may be divided into three groups. In the first are a series of medieval Scottish chroniclers, whom such Tudor historians as mention the outlaw seem mostly to have followed. In the second come the various antiquaries who, at various times in the sixteenth, seventeenth and eighteenth centuries wrote about Robin Hood; among these must be counted also the Tudor chronicler Grafton. Lastly there are the various historians of the nineteenth and twentieth centuries, both professional and amateur, who have sought to find a historical basis for the legend. Let us begin by considering what the first of these groups have to tell us.

Of the three Scottish chroniclers who are the first historians to mention Robin Hood, two belong to the fifteenth century and the third to the beginning of the sixteenth. All of them treat him without question as being a historical figure; and they all wrote long after the latest possible date at which he might actually have been alive. In fact they all assign him to the thirteenth century or the years just before it, the period in which we would expect to find him. The first of them is Andrew of Wyntoun, whose *Metrical Chronicle* was written about the year 1420; he was then an old man and his memory would have taken him back to the middle of the fourteenth century. Under the year 1283 he writes these four lines:

> 'Lytel Jhon and Robyne Hude
> Waythmen were commended gude:
> In Yngilwode and Barnysdale
> They oysyd all this time thare travail.'

This, alas, is all he has to say of them. No known ballad associated Robin with Inglewood in Cumberland: probably Wyntoun was confusing his story with that of Adam Bell and his three companions. Robin Hood is next referred to in Fordun's *Scotichronicon*, which is much older than Wyntoun's work, but the passage in question, which occurs only in a single manuscript, turns out to be one of several added to the chronicle by

Walter Bower about 1450. He assigns Robin Hood to the years immediately following the revolt of Simon de Montfort, that is to say about 1266. This is a very reasonable conjecture; many of the great Earl of Leicester's followers remained in arms long after his defeat and death at Evesham in 1265, and some of them, as we shall see in due course, seemed to have lived in much the same manner as the legendary outlaws. 'At this time' writes Bower, 'the famous robber Robin Hood, together with Little John and their companions, rose to prominence among those who had been disinherited and banished on account of the revolt. These men the stolid commons remember, at times in the gay mood of comedy, at others in the more solemn tragic vein, and love besides to sing of their deeds in all kinds of romances mimes and snatches.' Once again, there is no hint as to how the chronicler arrived at his date. He recounts only one incident of Robin Hood's life—how he was one day surprised by the sheriff at mass in a chapel in the secluded forest, where a terrific struggle took place, ending in the triumph of the outlaws. This is clearly based on some variant of the traditional story found in the ballad of *Robin Hood and the Monk*; Bower therefore knew the ballads, and it may have been some now lost passage in one of them which suggested the date to him. But it may equally well have been hearsay or an intelligent guess, and one cannot make very much of it.

The third Scottish chronicler who wrote about Robin Hood is John Major. His *History* was published in 1521, and his story preserves a quite independent tradition. 'About the time of King Richard I, according to my estimate,' he writes, 'the famous English robbers Robert Hood and Little John were lurking in their woods, preying only on the goods of the wealthy. . . . This Robert retained with him a hundred well armed men, whom a force of four hundred would have hesitated to attempt to dislodge. His deeds are sung all over England'. Major has little to add besides comment on the courtesy of Robin Hood's conduct; 'he was the prince of robbers, and the most humane'. He gives no hint of the nature of his sources, but what he was probably going on was some version of the tradition, which was widely accepted in the sixteenth century, that Robin Hood was a claimant to the earldom of Huntingdon who had flourished between an approximate date of 1160 and the year 1247. This life span would include the reign of John, a not unreasonable period since it was one in which, as we see from the story of Fulk Fitzwarin, there actually were outlaws at large.

By antiquaries of the sixteenth and succeeding centuries this tradition seems to have been accepted as based in fact. Its description of Robin Hood as a nobleman however renders it immediately suspect, for this is clean contrary to all the evidence of the earliest ballads, which positively labour his yeoman extraction. Leland, however, who was an almost exact contemporary of Major, bears out this point of the story: 'there', he says of the grave at Kirklees, 'the nobleman-outlaw Robin Hood lies buried.' Thereafter there is a cloud of witness. The famous annalist Stow simply follows Major word for word. Grafton, who claimed to obtain his information from an 'olde and aunciente pamphlet', also placed Robin Hood's career in the last years of the twelfth and the first years of the thirteenth centuries, and the anonymous life of the outlaw, which was found, among the Sloane manuscripts and seems to have been written late in the sixteenth century, gives an identical account, with a good deal of minute detail which there is nothing to confirm. By the seventeenth century the idea had become virtually accepted, and it was in this historical context that men like Anthony Mundy and Martin Parker set their plays and poems of Robin Hood.

An Earl of Huntingdon should not be too difficult to track down, and the antiquary Stukeley believed that he had done so. He identified Robin Hood with a Robert Fitzooth who was descended from Richard Fitzgilbert, one of the Conqueror's companions, and who lived in the time of Henry III. Richard's son Robert had married Alice, daughter of Waltheof and Judith, the Conqueror's niece, whose elder sister Maud had brought the Earldom of Huntingdon to her successive husbands, Simon of Senlis and David of Scotland. The title has passed to their descendants, but as the direct line had failed in 1237, in Stukeley's opinion Robert Fitzooth might have laid a claim in right of his descent from Alice four generations back. As there were descendants in the female line much closer than he, and as evidence suggests that, even if there had not been other claimants, he had no right to the title on the terms of peerage law as it was then known, this does not amount to much. When one adds to this that the derivation of Hood from Fitzooth is a philological impossibility, and that the early ballads have nothing to say of Robert's ancestry or his spurious claim to the Earldom of Huntingdon, there does not seem to be much value in the theory. It is scarcely credible that the rebellion of a nobleman with a claim to an ancient title would have gone unnoticed by the chroniclers, but they say nothing of it. In any case, a date for Robin Hood's outlawry in the reign of Richard I or John (for all the authorities who support this theory ascribe this part of his career to 'the wild and extravagant disposition' of his youth), would imply an uncomfortably long period of gestation for his legend.

There might be rather more to say about this theory if we had any clue as to how the tradition of Robin Hood's noble birth originated. Grafton's 'olde and aunciente pamphlet' has long since disappeared, and we have no idea of its date. The information it gave seems however to have been very similar to that given in the Sloane manuscript life of Robin Hood; it may have even been its source as well as that of Grafton. As a great deal of the material in all this life is taken direct from the ballads, it is unlikely that its author had any more reliable authority at his disposal. Its mention of Marian and the Pindar of Wakefield shows that late and unreliable ballads were used as well as old ones. The whole story, with all its minute detail of Robin Hood's birth in Henry II's time, his outlawry for debt and the confiscation of his lands (Grafton claimed that this was recorded in the Exchequer rolls), is nothing more than a mushroom growth of fiction in the rich soil of tradition.

One of the attractions of the identification of Robin Hood suggested by Stukeley was that it appeared to accord reasonably with the date of his death given in an old epitaph believed to have been inscribed on his grave. The quaint verses in question were found among the papers of the antiquary Gale:

'Hear undernead dis laitl stean
Laiz robert earl of Huntingtun
Near arcir ver az hie sa geud
An pipl kauld im robin heud
Sick utlawz az hi an iz men
Vil england nivr si agen.
   obiit 24 kal dekembris 1247.'

This epitaph is clearly spurious. During all the chequered history of the English tongue, neither its spelling nor its pronunciation were ever so hideously mauled as here. The verses do not seem to have been inscribed on any known tombstone of Robin Hood. But a grave and a stone which may have borne an inscription there really were at Kirklees, and since Leland mentions this in his *Collectanea* the tradition which grew up concerning them must have already been old at the beginning of the sixteenth century. Graves and epitaphs were just the kind of evidence to impress the antiquaries, and they took the tomb at Kirklees as a sure sign that Robin Hood was a genuine figure from history.

Unfortunately endless confusion surrounds this matter of Robin Hood's grave. Grafton speaks of a stone set up after his death by the Prioress of Kirklees which was still shown: 'The prioresse of the same place caused him to be buried by the highway side, where he had used to rob and spoyle those that passed that way. And upon his grave the sayde prioresse did lay a very fayre stone, wherein the names of Robert Hood, William of Goldesborough, and others were graven. And the cause why she buryed him there was, for that the common strangers and travailers, knowyng and seeyng him there buryed, might more safely and without feare take their jorneys that way, which they durst not do in the life of the sayd outlawes. And at either end of the sayde tombe was erected a crosse of stone, which is to be seen there at this present.' This account agrees reasonably with that given in the Sloane life, and it appears that the same tomb was actually drawn in the seventeenth century by the antiquary Nathaniel Johnstone.

Early in the next century the inscription was no longer legible; 'near unto Kirklees' wrote Thoresby, the historian of Leeds, 'the noted Robin Hood lies buried under a grave stone that yet remains in the park, but the inscription scarce legible'. So far accounts more or less tally, though since the inscription could no longer be read in Thoresby's time one cannot be quite sure that the same stone is intended. The inscription includes no date, and it is therefore impossible to say when it was written. It is unfortunate that Leland, the earliest authority, does not mention it, and perhaps, since he was by habit a careful antiquary, it is just a little suspicious.

These suspicions could be justly called unreasonable but for further conflicting evidence. Other accounts of the tomb do not tally, and raise grave doubts as to whether it was ever clear what it looked like. Grafton, as we have seen, spoke of a stone with an inscription and with a cross set up at either end. Thomas Gent, writing in 1730, spoke of a tombstone with an effigy upon it. Gough, in his *Sepulchral Monuments*, illustrated what is clearly a different tombstone, a plain stone with a cross 'fleuree' thereon 'now broken and much defaced'. Sir Samuel Armitage, the owner of Kirklees Park in the early eighteenth century, had this grave excavated; but as the ground under it to a depth of six feet was quite undisturbed, it was concluded that it was 'brought from some other place, and by vulgar tradition ascribed to Robin Hood'. Whether Gent's story that the tombstone was moved by a knight who placed it at the hearth of his great hall is a distorted version of this story of the excavation it is hard to say. But we seem by now to have at least three different tombs: there is one, Grafton's, with a cross at either end and an inscription; there is one, Gough's, with a simple cross (whose design incidentally suggests that it was not meant to bear any inscription); and there is one, Gent's, with an effigy. We have still moreover got to account for the provenance of Gale's inscription, spurious though it is, for it looks as if it may really have been written on some stone or other at an antique period. The cavalier poet Martin Parker appended this note to his *True Tale of Robin Hood*. 'The Epitaph which the prioresse of the Monastery of Kirkes Lay in Yorke shire set over Robin Hood, which . . . was to bee reade within these hundreth yeares', though in old broken English, (was) much to the same sense and meaning (as follows):

'Decembris quarto die, 1198, anno Richardii primi 9.
    Robert Earle of Huntington
    Lies underneath this little stone.
    No archer was like him so good:
    His wildnesse named him Robbin Hood.
    Full thirteene yeares, and something more
    These northerne parts he vexed full sore.
    Such outlawes as he and his men
    May England never know agen.'

The original in 'old broken English' was no doubt the epitaph found in Gale's papers. It looks unhappily as if we may have a fourth stone to account for.

The evidence of graves is in fact thoroughly unsatisfactory. Little John had three graves, in two of which bones were actually said to have been found. There was one in Ireland, where he was said by some to have been executed: there was one at Hathersage in Derbyshire and another in Scotland. The one at Hathersage was opened in 1784, and a thigh bone 29½ inches long is said to have been found, which the clerk of the parish put in his window with a label on it; it was conveniently stolen by Sir George Strickland, an aristocrat with an eye for curiosities, and subsequently seems to have disappeared. Hargrove in his *Anecdotes of Archery*, printed in York in 1792, described this grave thus: it 'is distinguished by a large stone placed at the head, and another at the feet, on each which are yet some remains of the letters J.L.' Apart from the letters, this has a suspicious echo of Grafton's description of Robin Hood's grave. The matter is confused further when we find there were bones in Scotland too. 'In Murray Land,' writes the sixteenth-century chronicler Hector Boece (*c.* 1540) 'is the Kirke of Pette, quhare the banis of Lytill Johne remains in gret admirationn of pepill. He has bene fourtene fut of hycht with square membris effering thairto. VI yeris afore the cumyng of this werk to lycht we saw his hanche bane, als mekill as the haill bane of ane man; for we schot our arme in the mouth thairof. Be quhilk apperis how strang and square pepill grew in our region afore they were made effeminat with lust and intemperance of mouth'. Faced with eye-witness accounts as conflicting—and as incredible—as these, one is not inclined to pay too much attention to the evidence of other supposed graves. One recalls the strong tradition of a stone with an inscription which marked the grave of King Arthur, and that in that instance, though it is probable that the grave existed, it is quite impossible to believe that the historical leader of the Britons who may have lived in the sixth century could have been buried beneath it. One of the eternal problems of the medieval historian is that medieval writers seldom had much hesitation about falsifying the evidence.

The possibility that the grave described by Grafton and others with its inscription may have commemorated a genuine

Robin Hood has however been taken by modern historians who wish to make him out to be a historical character as affording some corroboratory evidence of their theories. As the inscription is undated this still allows them a fairly free hand, and various suggestions have therefore been put forward. One or two have agreed with the nineteenth-century Frenchman Thierry that he was one of the Anglo-Saxon leaders just after the Norman Conquest, basing their case on the similarity between his legend and that of Hereward. This seems highly unlikely: Robin is originally a French name and it seems impossible to believe it could have been borne by an Englishman of the Conquest period; it is difficult to explain, if he lived at this period, why he is not heard of at all for the next three hundred years: in addition, while plenty of unpleasant things are said about members of the ruling class in the ballads, the one reproach which is never held against them is French extraction. Other historians, with the testimony of Fordun and a certain intrinsic probability on their side, have made Robin Hood an outlawed follower of Simon de Montfort. But by far the most consistent effort has been to identify the outlaw with a certain Robert Hood, who was a tenant of Wakefield manor in Edward II's reign and may have been involved in the rising of Thomas, Earl of Lancaster, in 1322.

This theory, which is based on some quite striking circumstantial evidence, has been worked out in detail by three historians; the nineteenth century antiquary Joseph Hunter, Dr. E. Walker of the Yorkshire Archaeological Society, and Mr. Valentine Harris. The basis of their case is that a Robert Hood appears in the Wakefield Court Rolls, whose career can be squared with that attributed to Robin Hood in the early ballads. The first reference to this man is from 1316 when Robert Hood and his wife Matilda bought a plot of land in Bickhill; that they held it for some period is indicated by a subsequent entry in 1358 which mentions 'a tenement on Bickhill, formerly in the tenure of Robert Hood'. In the year 1322 the North Country was shaken by the revolt against Edward II of Earl Thomas of Lancaster, and after his defeat at Boroughbridge his followers were outlawed and their lands confiscated. In the 'Contrariants roll' for Wakefield listing forfeited properties there is mentioned 'a building of new construction on

Bickhill'. The supporters of the Wakefield theory identify this with the tenement of Robin Hood, and suggest therefore that he was a follower of Lancaster and outlawed for his part in the rebellion. In the next year, 1323, Edward II was in the North, and he spent some time at the end of the year at Nottingham. From April 1324 onwards commence a series of payments made to one Robert Hood, a valet de chambre at his court. This individual they identify with the Wakefield tenant. He was absent from his place of service for several months in 1324, and after the end of that year payments made to him ceased altogether.

If one is prepared to identify the Wakefield Robert Hood and the valet de chambre, and to take it that the confiscated tenement at Bickhill really was his, it is suggested that his career would tally exactly with that given to Robin Hood in the *Geste*. The *Geste* conveniently never explains how he became an outlaw, so there is nothing there to contradict the idea that he he was a follower of Lancaster. After Lancaster's defeat he was outlawed, and for a little over a year he remained so. During this time some of the various incidents in the *Geste* would have taken place. In 1323 when Edward was in the North, Robert is taken to have come to him at Nottingham, where the King genuinely was, and as he did in the *Geste*. As in the *Geste*, the King pardoned him and took him into his service. After about a year in his service ('twelve moneths and thre' according to the *Geste*, rather less by historical calculation), he left the court. Thereafter, it is supposed, he returned, as the ballad says he did, to the life of an outlaw, and died ultimately at Kirklees.

A certain amount of corroboratory evidence is quoted in favour of this theory. The locality seems to be right, for Wakefield is close enough to Barnesdale, the traditional site of Robin Hood's activities in the earliest ballads. Names which occur in them, like the Sayles, a tiny tenancy of the manor of Pontefract, would, it is pointed out, be known only to a local man. Barnesdale at the time in question seems to have been known as a dangerous area: Hunter quotes a statement which records that in 1306 three Scottish churchmen, the Bishops of St. Andrews and Glasgow and the Abbot of Scone, who were coming south on an embassy, had their bodyguard increased from a force of eight to one of twenty archers between Pontefract and Tickhill 'on account of Barnesdale'. Edward II, who was famous for his good looks, would fit well the part of 'comely King Edward' in the *Geste*, it is said. The Kirklees part of the story is also declared to have historical probability. Roger of Doncaster, the villain of the death ballad, is said there to have been the prioress' paramour. Extracts from the Archbishop of York's register show that there was moral disorder at Kirklees round about the right period: in 1315 he had heard 'scandalous reports in circulation about the nuns, . . . that they admit both clergy and laymen too often into secret places of the monastery and have private talks with them, from which there arises suspicion of sin'. This would tally well with the story of Robin Hood knocking 'upon a pin' and the prioress letting him in alone, and with the tale that she was the mistress of a knight.

Mr. Harris has gone farther and attempted to identify various members of Robin Hood's band with persons mentioned in the Wakefield Court Rolls. He finds an Adam Schackelock who could belong to the same family as Will Scathelock of the ballads; a John le Nailer in 1329, who could be Little John, as it is traditional that his real surname was Nailer; and a family of Withehondes from whose name that of Gilbert of the White Hand may have been derived. He also finds a Richard of the Lee who appeared at a Wakefield manor court in 1317, and a Roger de Doncaster, to whose father, William, John le Nailer demised land. But though the coincidences are striking, these names are not easy to square with the legend. Neither the Richard of the Lee nor the Roger de Doncaster of the Court Rolls look much like their ballad counterparts: it is not easy to distort a Wakefield tenant of 1317 into a knight whose ancestors had held their free inheritance for more than 'a hundred winter'. Mr. Harris identifies his Roger de Doncaster with a chaplain of the same name who witnessed a legal deed in Yorkshire in 1301; there is nothing particularly likely about this, but if he was a chaplain he could hardly be squared with the knight of the ballad. And if he was not the same man, and there were two Rogers de Doncaster, why not more? The Court Rolls of Wakefield in the early fourteenth century prove the existence of at least three Robert Hoods, and if the central character was multiple, why not the others? All the names involved are fairly common. There are other serious difficulties too; the derivation of 'of the

White Hand' from Withehonde is not easy,[1] and the further identification of a Wakefield man whose *surname* was Reynold with Reynold Grenelefe is quite unacceptable.

In fact the whole series of coincidences on which the Wakefield theory is based is a great deal less striking on examination than it is at first sight. There is no clear evidence that the confiscated tenement on Bickhill was Robert Hood's, and the 1358 entry in the Court Rolls rather suggests it was not. It would hardly be natural to identify a plot of land by the name of a man who had lost his title rather than by that of a subsequent owner. There is absolutely no evidence that the Robert Hood of Bickhill or either of the other Wakefield Robert Hoods was ever outlawed or went to Nottingham to obtain a pardon. There is nothing whatever to suggest that the valet de chambre of Edward II came from Wakefield, and the idea that he ceased to receive payments because he had returned to Barnesdale is absurd, because an entry in the King's Household accounts made on 25 November 1324, makes it clear that he was retired on account of old age. 'To Robyn Hod, formerly one of our porters' it reads 'a grant of five shillings by royal command, because he can no longer work'. The corroboratory evidence is equally unsatisfactory. Edward II is a peculiarly unfortunate choice for the King Edward of the ballads as he was universally unpopular, and his great enemy, Thomas of Lancaster, was in fact regarded by common people in the North Country as a saint. The immorality rife at Kirklees in the early fourteenth century is no sort of coincidence: the same old trouble of incontinence was still a smirch on the priory's fair name in 1337, and in any case the Yorkshire nunneries were never famous for high moral tone. In the first sixty years of the fourteenth century, according to Eileen Power, 'nineteen out of the twenty-seven houses came before the Archbishop of York's notice at one time or another in connexion with cases of immorality or apostasy'. It begins to look as if the circumstantial evidence quoted to favour Robin Hood's origin in Wakefield will not bear scrutiny.

One attraction of the Wakefield Robin Hood has been that, if one allows a certain period for the development of the legend, the date of his supposed activities will fit fairly well with a first reference to Robin Hood as a famous outlaw in 1377 (in

[1] It is sometimes spelt 'With-the-hounde'.

the B. version of *Piers Plowman*) and with a first reference to
a place named after Robin Hood in 1422 (the reference to
Robin Hood's stone, near enough to the site later called Robin
Hood's well, in the Monkbretton cartulary). If the Wakefield
candidate is to be discounted, therefore, it looks as if we shall
be wise to look for a more convincing historical Robin earlier
rather than later. The thirteenth century is in fact the period
with which the earliest chronicle references all associate the
outlaw. Besides, there are details in the ballads (such as
references to distraint of knighthood and to ecclesiastical usury)
which may suggest a thirteenth-century context for the original
Robin Hood—even though the general background of the
ballad stories has a later flavour. He could be reasonably
made into a follower of de Montfort who remained in arms
after the Earl's death; for we know that many of them did
continue their resistance and were consequently outlawed.
Though Simon's revolt had nothing to do with the grievances
of the common people and was an affair of the knights and
barons, yet there is no doubt that subsequent legend turned
him into a popular hero. Miracles were reported at his tomb
and songs sung of his fame; surely one of his men could have
become a popular hero whose renown in due course of time
eclipsed, at least in the world of poesy, that of his erstwhile
leader? Unfortunately there is no trace of there having ever
been a Robin or Robert Hood among the Earl's followers. It
therefore becomes almost irresistibly tempting to identify
Robin Hood with a Robert Hood who in the Pipe Roll of 1230
was described as a fugitive from justice. But all that the Pipe
Roll tells us of this man is that the Sheriff of Yorkshire was
accountable for his forfeited goods which were worth thirty-two
and sixpence; and nothing more is known of him. We must bear
in mind the plethora of Robert Hoods in the early fourteenth
century: it will need much stronger evidence than this, or for
that matter the entries in the Wakefield manor rolls, to identify
anyone with the Robin Hood of the ballads.

But if, as seems to be the case, we have to date back any
possible historical origin of the Robin Hood myth to the
thirteenth century, one important point does emerge. We have
seen already that the background scenery of the ballads belongs
not to the thirteenth but to the fourteenth and fifteenth cen-

turies. A Robin Hood of Simon de Montfort's time could not have used the longbow, for the longbow was not invented. The dominance of the theme of archery will therefore have to be deleted from the story. Equally he would be unlikely to be a yeoman or a yeoman's hero; for the unrest of the thirteenth century had nothing to do with the rustic poor, and the free peasant of the ballads was still a rare and fortunate individual. In the troubles of Henry III's and Edward I's reigns the question of forest grievances was indeed to the fore, but the particular points complained of were the extent of the forest boundaries and the unfair restrictions on clearing those parts of the forest which were actually wooded, grievances which the ballads do not mention. A historical Robin Hood of this period could therefore only be a very remote ancestor of the hero of the ballads. There is no reason to suppose that his career would particularly remind us of them, for though their incident is sometimes strikingly paralleled in the stories of earlier, genuine outlaws like Fulk Fitzwarin and Eustace the Monk, it is the fictional, not the factual episodes which establish the connexion.

It is surely beginning to look as though in this quest for a historical Robin Hood we are pursuing a will o' the wisp. With the area of our search now pushed back into the thirteenth century, we can no longer even be certain that if we met with him we would recognize him among the host of obscure Roberts whom medieval history throws up. The basic trouble is that the ballads are the only reliable source of information that we have, and the information which they supply is not of the kind which is useful for establishing historical identity. The events described in them are not distant echoes of real events. If they were, any sheriff in his right mind who had outlaws to deal with would clearly, with the awful precedents before him, have had every potter within a fifty-mile radius arrested on suspicion. It will not advance one to look for the shadows of real historical characters in men such as the Abbot of St. Mary's or the Sheriff of Nottingham, because the persons who in the ballads go under their name are not connected with history but with traditional legend. The absence of true personality from the sketches given of them in the poems stands revealed when we find the episodes in which they appear duplicated down to minute detail in the *Tale of Eustace the Monk*; their names have changed and they have become the Abbot of Jumiéges and the Count of Boulogne but the story has not changed at all. The apparently striking coincidence between the career of the Robert Hood of the Wakefield theory, who was first outlawed and then pardoned and taken into the King's service, and that of the hero of the *Geste*, loses its force when one finds that the career of this composite character is equally coincident in outline with that of Hereward, of Fulk Fitzwarin, of Gamelyn and of Adam Bell. Like the incidents, the recurrent plot of the story belongs not to history but to popular traditions which follow a plausible pattern of events.

One must not be misled by the apparent similarity between the earlier outlaw stories which have a historical basis and those of Robin Hood. In the former history and stock incident borrowed from traditional sources are mingled in a compound of fact and fiction. Their foundation in history betrays itself in detailed genealogy and in the particularized names of persons and places with whom and which the heroes of the stories were really associated; and by careful analysis it is possible to separate the substratum of fact from the superstructure of legend. But named characters who had a part to play in history, like Payn Peverel and Maurice Fitz Roger in the *Tale of Fulk Fitzwarin*, do not appear upon the scene in the ballads. Their abbots and sheriffs and monks are anonymous, stock figures who have acquired apposite titles. Their kings change their names with the changing times; their hero has no birthplace, no remembered ancestry and no childhood, all of which he acquires only in the spurious historical writings of the sixteenth century. Those who try to trace him back to a real ancestor are reversing the sequence of events in the growth of his story; the origin of the ballads is anonymous tradition, and the particularization of places and dates and names is what time has added thereto. Their stories remain remote and impersonal because they are still half formed only, and not because the clear cut outlines of historical memory have been blurred by the attrition of ages.

The name Robin Hood may possibly be derived from some dim memory of a forest bandit of the thirteenth century[1]. It may

[1] Mr J. C. Holt, in 'The Ballads of Robin Hood', *Past and Present*, No. 18 (November 1960), published since this book was sent to press, has strengthened the

equally echo the name of some figure of popular mythology; one cannot be dogmatic about its origin. But if either of these theories ultimately explains the name, it is clear that, whatever person went under it in the worlds of either myth or history, he has very little to do with the hero of the ballads. That individual is, as Professor Child put it, 'the pure creation of the ballad muse'. He is an ideal figure, and the incident of his tale is drawn from tradition to illustrate a moral—social justice. He embodies the wishful thinking of the common man: what he and Little John did to the sheriff was what the common man would have liked to have done. The appeal of the ballads lies in their presentation of their theme through vivid scenery and fast-moving incident, which contain the testament of an age and a class that expressed its aspirations most naturally in the embodied projection of narrative. Robin Hood is rightly called 'the people's Arthur', for his story enshrines their ideal just as the stories of the Round Table enshrine the ideals of knighthood. It is this that makes the ballads still compelling in an age when the outlaw stories which centre about characters drawn from history have become mainly literary curiosities.

case in favour of adopting the Robert Hood described as a fugitive in the 1230 Pipe Roll as the most likely candidate for a historical, and original, Robin Hood. The Pipe Roll of 1228 gives him a popular nickname, 'Hobbehod', suggesting local celebrity, and Mr Holt argues that he may well have been involved in the movement led by Sir Robert Thwing in 1231–2. Thwing's followers carried out systematic raids on the property of foreign monasteries, seized their granaries and sold the corn cheaply or even gave it away 'for the benefit of the many'. Such activities would suit a historical Robin Hood. If such a figure is essential, the claims of Hobbehod are probably the strongest; but the case remains unproven and the association with Thwing is only conjectural.

XIII

❖◇❖◇❖◇❖◇❖◇❖◇❖◇❖◇❖◇❖◇❖◇❖◇❖◇❖◇❖◇❖◇❖◇❖◇❖

The Outlaw in History

❖◇❖◇❖◇❖◇❖◇❖◇❖◇❖◇❖◇❖◇❖◇❖◇❖◇❖◇❖◇❖◇❖◇❖◇❖

A ROBIN HOOD who played his part on the stage of real life eludes the historians' pursuit. The quest seems fruitless, for there are woven into his myth too many strands of traditional story which are far older than the world from whose circumstances the ballad makers took their cue. But this does not mean that the ballad makers' world of the 'fair forest' where the outlaw king is master is a pure figment of popular imagination. Robin Hood is not just a Fulk Fitzwarin whose castle and whose noble ancestry have been forgotten because they do not suit the story of a yeoman; he stands a good deal nearer to life. If modern research has failed to unearth a man of flesh and blood from dusty medieval records, it has shown that the outlaw's legendary career does not lack verisimilitude.

Robin Hood the yeoman is not the kind of figure to catch the limelight of medieval historical writing. He has no part to play on the grand political stage; he is a forest robber of humble origins and his cause has to do with the conditions of the everyday social world, not with the melodramatic conspiracies which troubled the sleep of kings. We must seek therefore for men of his stamp not in the chronicles but in the records of everyday business, in the rolls of forest administration, in the king's orders to his sheriffs and officers, and in the decisions of antique

191

courts. Here it is if anywhere that we will hear of the doings of his prototypes, obscure bandits who had their hour of local fame and were then forgotten. For the early middle ages such records are scarce, and in consequence such outlaws as we do hear of are men of quite different standing, men of political power and social status, like Fulk Fitzwarin or Geoffrey de Mandeville, who had the misfortune to fall foul of the King. But from the thirteenth century onwards records become much fuller, and a little diligence can tell us a great deal of men whose lives, if less imposing, command no less interest than those of the turbulent barons of the reigns of Stephen or John, and resemble much more closely the fictional lives of the ballad outlaws.

The middle ages were violent times. Local knights and lords only too readily took the law into their own hands in their rivalries with their neighbours: and common thieves plied their trade in every part of the country. Armed bands of poachers wandered in the forests, and if foresters interrupted them, did not hesitate to resist with violence. Police measures were rudi-

Robin Hood meets a 'Ranger' of the Forest

mentary, and the government was not capable of dealing effectively with the disorderly elements in society. The lists of offenders presented before the forest courts are impressive, but they become less so when one examines how many cases actually came to trial; over and again the records tell of accused persons who 'did not come' or 'could not be found'. The same applies to the criminal law. It is clear, moreover, from the records of the commissions of trailbaston[1] empowered by Edward I to deal with the problem of local disorder that evil doers were often aided and abetted by local people. Where for this or other reasons a man could not be brought to book, there was nothing for it but to put him outside the law, and the sentence of outlawry was common enough. But the very existence of the sentence was, as has been said earlier, an implied confession of governmental inability to enforce order; if men could be found and brought to trial it would not have been needed.

We are looking, however, for something more than accounts of the acts of individual criminals or casual bands of poachers. The outlaws of the ballads worked in permanent bands under known leaders, and they had their own society with its own liveries and laws. Such men really did exist. We shall not be disappointed in our search for them, for they were enough of a menace to claim grave consideration in Parliament itself. When that body met at Westminster in March 1332, the King's Chief Justice, Geoffrey le Scrope, rose to tell 'how the King had heard . . . how divers persons, in defiance of the law, had risen in large bands and were preying on the King's leigemen, as also on the goods of the Holy Church, on the King's justices and others; and some they took and held their prisoners and made them pay heavy ransoms to save their lives'. He demanded that measures be taken to deal with these men. A hundred and fifty years later, at the beginning of Henry VII's reign, the government was still facing the same problem; a statute passed in his first Parliament spoke of 'divers persons in grete nombre' who 'have often tymes in late daies hunted, as well by night as by day, in divers forests, parkes, and warrenes in divers places of this Royalme . . . by color whereof have ensued in tymes past grete and heinous rebellions, insurrections, rioutts, robberies, murdres and other inconveniences'. The activities of bandits who worked in organized bands, frequently with tacit local support, seem thus to have remained a problem throughout the later middle ages and even after. At times, and especially in the

[1] Judicial commissions with special powers to deal with criminal cases; the word means literally 'carry truncheon'.

disorderly periods following political unrest, they were almost impossible to control. Such persons were the real life models for the outlaws of the ballads, and when one examines their deeds more carefully one will find that the similarity is sometimes very striking.

The story of Fulk Fitzwarin is based, as we have seen, on the career of a historical person who had a part to play in the troubles of the restless reign of King John. The long struggle of John's son, Henry III, with his barons and their leader, Simon de Montfort, brought forth a new crop of outlaws, the children of nearly seven years of unrest during which England was constantly on the verge of civil war. Twice, in 1263–4 and 1265, the smouldering embers of rebellion burst into the flames of open war. The changes of fortune favoured now one side, now the other; and each turn of her tide left stranded supporters of the defeated party who remained in arms, carrying on a local guerilla warfare. The King's final triumph at Evesham in 1265, where the great Earl Simon died, was very far from putting a final end to resistance. It was nearly a year later that those who were still fighting, and who had been outlawed and disinherited for their contumacious revolt, were finally admitted to his peace. The terms by which, under the Dictum of Kenilworth, they could obtain pardon and restitution were stern; their lands were only to be redeemed at a price, which it was calculated it would take seven years of their profits to pay fully. The *force majeure* of circumstances brought some men in directly, and others followed their example; their claims and counter-claims to forfeited lands brought a mass of litigation into the courts and was the cause of endless local disorder. A few preferred to remain at large, and lived as outlaws.

Many are the names of those who in these wild times at one stage or another took to the woods. One was the famous Sir John Giffard of Brimpsfield, whose story has reminiscences of that of Fulk Fitzwarin. From the pages of Robert of Gloucester's rhyming chronicle a series of fragments of what must once have been a poem or geste on its own concerning him can be pieced together. Like Fulk, he began as a baronial rebel but after de Montfort's victory at Lewes in 1264 he fell out with his leader and fled to the Forest of Dean where he gathered a band about him:

'To the Forest of Dene Sir Jon wende tho,
   And turnde age Sir Simonde and procurede other mo.'

He was in alliance with the Welsh princes and 'robbede mid his route' in the lands upon the border. After a while, says Robert, the Earl of Gloucester came to join him:

'Tho wende the Erl from Londene priveliche and stille,
   Ac to socori is lond age Sir Simondes wille
In the forest of Dene to gadere sone hii come,
   He and Sir Jon Giffard and stable conseil nome.'

On the King's victory, of course, both were reinstated. But the triumph of Evesham left a host of Simon's supporters at large, who took similar refuge in waste places, men like Robert de Ferrers and David of Uffington, and Sir John Deyville who held out in Hereward's old fortress of Ely. The most celebrated was probably Adam de Gurdun, who lurked with a band of armed outlaws in the forest of Alton, and raided all over Berkshire and into Wiltshire and Hampshire. It took a major military force to hunt him down, and he was finally worsted in single combat by Lord Edward himself, King Henry's son and heir.

From our point of view, however, by far the most striking of the baronial rebels who continued to resist was a much more obscure man, one Roger Godberd. He deserves special notice, both because he remained in arms as an outlaw long after the cause was hopelessly lost and almost all his fellows had been reduced or had surrendered, and because the scene of his activities was Robin Hood's own forest of Sherwood. Indeed much of his career is reminiscent of that of the ballad hero. We first hear of him at the end of 1265, when he came in to surrender and obtain a pardon under the Dictum with two others, Roger de Remes and Nicholas de la Mus. These two obtained pardon at once, but Roger and his brother William had to wait a month for theirs. The terms they obtained were not good, for they regained only some of their lands; and they were only given peace on condition that 'they stood by the award of Kenilworth with regard to their lands which the King had given to others'. Perhaps this soured Roger, or he may have had some other source of grievance; at all events he soon relapsed into outlawry. In 1267 the outlaws of Sherwood had again become a serious menace. Roger de Leyburn, the lieutenant of Reginald de Grey, the King's Constable at Nottingham castle, fought two quite large-scale engagements with them, one in the heart of the forest itself. He does not seem to have achieved much, and the horses which his men lost in the two fights were valued at sixty-three pounds.

Three years later, in 1270, Roger Godberd and his men were still at large. Loud complaints were reaching King Henry that 'through outlaws, robbers, thieves and malefactors, mounted or

Robin Hood and his men fight with foresters of Sherwood.

on foot, wandering by day and by night, in the counties of Nottingham, Leicester and Derby, so many and great homicides were done that no one with a small company could pass through most parts without being taken and killed or spoiled of his goods'. Another record states that 'no religious person . . . could pass without being taken by them and spoiled'. Surely there is an echo here of the *Tale of Gamelyn:*

> 'While Gamelyn was outlawed had he no cors;
>   There was no man for him ferde the wors,
>   But Abbots and prioris, monke and chanoun.'

The King ordered that a sum of a hundred marks be levied from the three counties concerned and paid to Reginald de Grey to hunt down these malefactors, and he 'pursued them manfully and captured one Roger Godberd their leader and master and delivered him to prison'. Our last trace of Roger is the King's order, given a month or two later, that he be brought to the castle of Bruges and detained there until further notice.

It is tantalizing that the records tell us so little of a career which, if it ended ignominiously, might yet prove one of the most fascinating in a period of crowded event. It is not clear from the records whether Roger's capture ended for the moment the troubles of Sherwood, but from an incident which occurred six years later it looks rather as if it may not have done. In 1276 John de Lascelles, the steward of Sherwood, caught two men with bows and arrows in the forest and took them to Bledworth, probably intending next day to hand them over to the sheriff at Nottingham castle. But in the night twenty men armed with swords and bows and arrows broke open the doors of the house where they were, released the prisoners and beat up John's servants who were guarding them. They then went to the steward's own house, where they broke the windows and shouted insults at him. When an inquest was held many of those involved seem not to have been found. This incident, which has a real ring of one of the countless rescue scenes of the ballads, could be an epilogue to the story of Roger Godberd. It is clear anyway that where the deep forest afforded them a refuge, the law was not capable of controlling the actions of disorderly men.

It is interesting to hear of outlaws of the time of de Montfort's rebellion, because it is to this period that Bower assigns Robin Hood, and Andrew of Wyntoun's date for him in the 1280's is not far off it. In the disorderly years which followed the political upheaval during which Edward II lost his throne, we hear again of outlaws whose doings bear a striking resemblance to those of the heroes of the ballads. These are doubtless the men of whom Chief Justice le Scrope told the Parliament of 1332. Affairs had by then come to a pretty pass. The commission of trailbaston issued as a result of Scrope's complaints stated that criminals had been virtually waging war against the King and addressing letters to their enemies 'in a style which was almost royal'.

The activities of a band led by the Folvilles of Leicestershire at this time have recently been closely studied by Professor E. L. G. Stones of Glasgow. Their career is therefore not hard to follow. It was spread over a period of some twenty years, and their leader, Eustace de Folville, died a natural death. That they were able to conduct their criminal affairs for so long a period unchecked was clearly partly due to the capital they made out of the political instability of the times, for the Folvilles more than once obtained pardon for their misdemeanours by backing the right party at opportune moments. After the triumph of Mortimer in 1327 and Edward II's deposition, their crimes in the reign of the late King were officially forgotten: in 1333 their leader, Eustace, again obtained forgiveness, in return for the services he had rendered against the Scots. One is reminded of the part played by the bowmen of Sherwood in the victory of Halidon Hill; it was the same kind of men who helped in this age to win England her famous victories in France and on the northern border, whose activities were the bane of good government at home, the independent yeomen and the county knights.

The Folvilles came of a family of good knightly standing in Leicestershire. The first we hear of their career of crime is in 1326; their leader, Eustace, died in 1346 and his death was considered by the Leicester Abbey chronicler, Henry Knighton, of sufficient interest to deserve mention in his annals. This is hardly surprising, for he had by then an impressive career outside the law behind him. His most melodramatic crime was also his first, the murder of Roger Bellers, a baron of the exchequer and a man of power and influence in the government, near Melton Mowbray in 1326. The Folvilles caught him in 'a little valley' near Reresby on the way to Leicester; there were three brothers there besides Eustace and they had a band of fifty men in their company. Proceedings were instituted against them, but it was the usual story: they could not be found and a sentence of outlawry was passed. The whole process came to nothing when, after the upheaval of Mortimer's rebellion and King Edward's deposition, they were pardoned for their crime. But this does not seem to have affected their manner of living much, and the new government was soon writing to the Sheriff of Nottingham complaining that two of the Folville brothers were roaming abroad again at the head of a band, waylaying persons whom they spoiled and held to ransom.

Their next most dramatic action was the capture on the 14th of January, 1332, of one of the King's Justices, Richard Willoughby. He was taken as he was travelling from Grantham to Melton Mowbray and was held to ransom for

1,300 marks. He was not released until this sum was handed over to the outlaws; meanwhile they carried him with them to obscure hideouts, 'from wood to wood' as one indictment declares. This naked defiance of the law roused the government to activity, but its efforts do not seem to have had much success. The outlaws merely shifted their ground; two at least of them are heard of in the wild district of the Peak in Derbyshire, but when the law set out in their pursuit they had timely warning from a local spy and made off. Once again a sentence of outlawry was recorded, but it remained a dead letter since none of the principals in the affair could be found and brought to justice. A year later when the focus of national attention was turned to the King's war with Scotland, Eustace de Folville again obtained a pardon.

The Folvilles continued their careers of crime on and off for years afterwards. One of them, the chaplain Richard, was finally run to earth with part of his band in his church at Teigh in Rutland in 1341. The forces of the law had to lay regular seige to the place where he had taken sanctuary and one man was killed and others wounded before he was taken. He was beheaded on the spot by Sir Robert de Colville, the keeper of the peace who led the men against him. But Eustace ignored his example; he was up to his old tricks again in 1345 when the King was abroad. He died in the next year, in peace which was unbroken by the law's intervention. By that time he had twenty years of successful crime behind him, and a host of minor robberies and offences to his credit besides two successful and melodramatic attacks on the King's officers.

The story of the Folville brothers has, however, more relevance to the Robin Hood ballads than merely to show that there is nothing incredible about open attacks on royal officials going unavenged. There are plenty of other respects in which they resemble the outlaws of popular poesy. Robin Hood's men had their own 'society', and so did the Folvilles' gang; Eustace was the 'leader of their brotherhood' (*capitalis de societate*). They had their sympathizers and even their admirers. When the law was on their heels they were warned of their danger by their spies, just as Adam Bell was warned by the swineherd's boy that Cloudisley was taken. For Henry Knighton the murder of Bellers was no more than a just retribution, for he was a great 'oppressor of the religious and his other neighbours whose lands and churches he coveted'. Willoughby, the Folvilles' other famous victim, was again a man of ugly reputation; when later he was accused of general corruption it was said that he had sold the laws 'like cows'. Knighton noted the death of Eustace de Folville not because he was a black villain convicted of blood guiltiness, but because he was a dashing, defiant man whose deeds deserved record.

From the same period as that of the Folvilles comes evidence even more striking that men of the stamp of the outlaws of the ballads were not unknown to history. In 1336 Richard de Snaweshill, chaplain of Huntington near York, received a letter which gave him pause. It read as follows: 'Lionel, King of the rout of raveners salutes, but with little love, his false and disloyal Richard de Snaweshill. We command you, on pain to lose all that can stand forfeit against our laws, that you immediately remove from his office him whom you maintain in the vicarage of Burton Agnes; and that you suffer that the Abbot of St. Mary's have his rights in this matter and that the election of the man whom he has chosen, who is more worthy of advancement than you or any of your lineage, be upheld. And if you do not do this, we make our avow, first to God and then to the King of England and to our own crown that you shall have such treatment at our hands as the Bishop of Exeter had in Cheep (Bishop Stapledon was murdered there in 1326); and we shall hunt you down, even if we have to come to Coney Street in York to do it. And show this letter to your lord, and bid him to cease from false compacts and confederacies, and to suffer right to be done to him whom the Abbot has presented; else he shall have a thousand pounds worth of damage by us and our men. And if you do not take cognizance of our orders, we have bidden our lieutenant in the North to levy such great distraint upon you as is spoken of above. Given at our Castle of the North Wind, in the Green Tower, in the first year of our reign.'

In this letter we hear across the centuries the authentic voice of a king of the outlaws. He speaks with authority, and his commands are given in order to right a wrong done. His 'rout of raveners' is an order with laws of its own which purport to represent true justice where the law has failed. How it has failed is made clear by the reference to the 'false compacts and confederations' made by Richard's lord; it is against the frauds and injustices of a law which is open to all the forces of corruption and influence that the leader of the men at the Castle of the North Wind threatens to invoke terrific sanctions. At the same time that he defies the law which has upheld Richard de Snaweshill's claim, he claims that he acts in the name of God and the King of England; he would be at one with the outlaws of Sherwood in the *Geste* who fell on their knees before comely King Edward in the forest when they discovered who it was that was with them in an abbot's disguise. The letter is not just an extravagant practical joke, for Richard de Snaweshill was frightened enough by it to seek the law's protection. No other letter like it has yet been found, but the talk in the commission of trailbaston of 1332 of evil-doers who write threatening letters to knights and abbots 'in a style which is almost royal' suggests that it was once far from unique. If it was then but one of many of its kind, as seems likely, it shows that not only were there men whose deeds had a certain similarity with those of the ballad outlaws, but also that they shared the attitude of righteous indignation of their literary counterparts. 'With its allusions drawn at one extreme from romance and at the other from the harsh realities of contemporary legal process,' writes Professor Stones, 'this is an extraordinary document. It shows that there were people who could not only persuade themselves that they were innocent victims of the law but could go on to represent acts like the murder of Stapledon in 1326 as acts of a rival system of justice.' The peasants who executed Archbishop Sudbury on Tower Hill in 1381 took the same line.

It is from this same period in which Eustace de Folville and Lionel, King of the rout of raveners, were going about their business that the *Tale of Gamelyn* comes. Professor Stone's description of the letter, in which he sees behind its romantic phrases a situation which arises from the harsh realities of the legal system, could just as well be applied to the poem, whose author was able to combine a talent for melodrama with a knowledge of the law. Professor Stone's study of the real outlaws of the fourteenth century shows that even in its most extravagant detail the *Tale* is not really trespassing beyond the bounds of credibility. We can parallel now from history a crowned king of the outlaws, the holding of a king's justice to ransom, and a threat from the outlaws to come to town in force, if they have to do so in order to set things to rights. When we now come on to the fifteenth century we shall find that not only the outlaws themselves but even the government's clerks who recorded reports of their doings were aware of their kinship with the legendary heroes whose ballads were by then being sung all up and down England.

In the year 1439 a petition to Parliament recalls in striking terms the activities of one Piers Venables of Derbyshire. Piers had been a fugitive from justice ever since he had taken part in the rescue of a prisoner who was being taken to Tutbury Castle, a deed which in itself recalls the event of more than one ballad. 'And after that tyme,' the petition continues, 'the same Piers Venables, having no liflode ne sufficeaunte goodes, gadered and assembled unto him many misdoers, beyng of his clothinge, and in manere of insurrection, wente into the wodes in that country, like it hadde be Robyn Hode and his meynee'. Once again the parallel with the ballads is very striking. Piers Venables began life outside the law with the rescue of a prisoner: we do not know what the circumstances were, but this could surely be represented as just that kind of act of defiant justice in which the ballad outlaws so often took a hand. Piers' refuge was the same as theirs, the wild wood where the law could not follow him. His men, like they, belonged to a brotherhood of their own, for they wore his cloth as a sign of their company and their allegiance. Perhaps this cloth may even have been the Lincoln green of legend.

Even more striking than the case of Piers Venables is that of the outlaw who in the reign of Henry V and later was calling himself after the legendary Friar Tuck. His real name was Richard Stafford; he was a Sussex chaplain, and his activities won him sufficient renown to earn him a mention in the *Annals* of the Tudor historian Stow. We first hear of him in 1416, when a commission was issued to Thomas Canoys, Thomas Poynynges and John Pelham 'to arrest one assuming the name of Frere Tuck and other evil doers of his retinue who have committed divers murders, homicides, robberies, and depredations etc. . . . in the Counties of Surrey and Sussex, and bring them before the King and Council'. The commission does not seem to have achieved much, for in the next year a new commission was issued to William Lasyngley and Robert Hull. This new report reveals Richard Stafford, like Robin Hood, as combining the roles of bandit and forest poacher who lives by the King's venison. The two commissioners were ordered 'to inquire into the report that a certain person assuming the unusual name of Frere Tuk and other evildoers have entered parks, warrens and chases of divers lieges of the King in the Counties of Surrey and Sussex at divers times, hunted therein and carried off deer, hares, rabbits, pheasants and partridges, burned the houses and lodges for the keeping of the parks and threatened the keepers'. In two years 'Frere Tuk' had clearly gathered a pretty tail of misdeeds to his discredit. But once again, and this time even in the Home Counties, the law seems to have been ineffective in its efforts to bring him to justice. He was still at large in 1429, when he was finally pardoned, both for new crimes and for the old ones done in Henry V's time. He had never appeared in the Courts to answer for any of these offences.

One would like to know a great deal more of the life of Richard Stafford, 'alias Frere Tuk'. With him, as with the robbers' king, Lionel, a figure whose rightful place is in the world of romance seems to have stepped on to the stage of history. The name which he bears as an outlaw he has borrowed from ideal legend. His men are bound together in a known company by the strong ties of retinue. His deeds are not limited to crimes such as robbery and homicide. He has set at open defiance the forest law and declared war on its officers; he has burned the keepers' houses and put them in terror of their lives. Here is a real echo from official records of the ballads' description of the forest misdeeds of Adam Bell and his companions who have killed the King's foresters.

> 'And broken his parkes, and slaine his deer;
>   Over all they chose the best;
> Such perelous outlawes as they were
>   Walked not by easte nor west'

Once more the history of obscure bandits reveals the outlaw ballads as true to life.

What these last two instances, those of Piers Venables and Richard Stafford, reveal is that men were consciously aware of

the similarity between the bands of robbers who lurked everywhere in waste places and the outlaws of literature. Since they
regarded the latter as popular heroes, it was impossible for
contemporaries to view the former as irredeemable villains.
The ballad makers have not strained their literary credibility
by idealizing graceless thieves who were the curse of a violent
age into upholders of social justice; their portrayal of Robin
Hood and the men of his ilk represents a genuine contemporary
attitude to those who have set the law at defiance. The very
existence of such men as outlaws was, as has been said, the
result of the law's inability to bring criminals to justice, and one
of the reasons for this was that, since the law was too corrupt
and uncertain to obtain respect, those outside the law could rely
on finding friends and sympathizers within it. When the
government acted to deal with the menace which the activities
of outlaws presented, no sigh of relief went up from a populace
that had suffered by their depredations. In this world where
'law goys as lordshipp biddeth hym' the general feeling was
that the trailbaston commissions had 'done more harm to the
good than to the bad'. In the Folvilles' capture of Willoughby,
Henry Knighton saw no more than an act of reprisal against
oppressive measures. 'In this year', he wrote in 1331, 'the
judges of trailbaston sat throughout England, and many persons
everywhere were outlawed. In consequence Justice Richard
Willoughby was taken by Richard de Folville . . . a fierce,
daring and impudent man.' This passage immediately calls to
mind Wat Tyler's demand at Smithfield in 1381 that 'sentence
of outlawry be not pronounced in any process at law henceforth.'
In the contemporary situation where the law's decisions all too
often were backed by no shadow of justice, the sympathy of the
common man inclined as much to the outlaw as to those who
sought to suppress him.

This attitude is put better probably than anywhere else in a
poem of the early fourteenth century called the *Outlaw's Song*.
It purports to have been written on a stray leaf of paper and cast
into the highway for whoever should pass to pick up, by a man
who had lost his land and been forced into the outlaw's life by
the tyranny of the judges of trailbaston. For all its hardships,
he declared, the life of the free forest is preferable to the uncertain world without where law rules, *car trop est douteux la*

comune ley. 'For this reason', he writes, 'I will remain in the forest, in its delightful shade; for there is no falseness and no evil law in the wood of Belregard, where the jay flies and the nightingale sings unceasing'. Faced with the law's tyranny, he will answer force with force; 'I will teach them their game of trailbaston; I will break them, arms and legs, backbone and crupper, and it will be but justice; I will cut out their tongues and their mouths together'. These ferocious menaces may seem to us to clash harshly with the pleasing description of the forest which precedes them, but it was one of the consequences of the corruption which appeared to have become an integral part of the legal system that the only road to fair freedom seemed to lie through violence.

The *Outlaw's Song* is not a popular poem. It is written in Anglo-French, a language which the peasant would not understand. But all this goes to show is that the attitude towards the law of which we have been speaking was not confined to that class. We should really have expected this, for after all members of the class of the local knighthood have their part to play in the outlaw ballads as well as the common people. Sir Richard atte the Lee held his lands freely, as his ancestors had done for a hundred years past, at the same time as being the friend of Robin Hood and of every poor yeoman. Gamelyn was 'born of a lady and gotten of a knight'. Eustace de Folville belonged significantly to this same class, the local gentry. The outlaw ballads show no hostility to social standing, as such, and the common people saw that there were those among their superiors who were suffering like them by the tyrannies of the law. There cannot, after all, have been all that much difference in economic status between the less prosperous of the local gentry and the richer yeomen, for all the latters' humbler origins. County knights and peasants fought side by side in Jack Cade's rebellion in 1450. Given the contemporary acceptance of a hierarchical social system, such men were the natural leaders to whom a discontented peasantry, which had no wish to arrogate to itself democratic rights to a share in government, might turn. There is nothing strange about the respect with which Robin Hood treated Sir Richard atte the Lee.

The situation in the outlaw ballads therefore reflects not only the genuine discontent with the working of the law in the age in which they were written, but also a genuine sympathy with those who had set it at defiance, which seems then to have been felt over a wide social field. One must, of course be careful to avoid making too much of the evidence. There is more than a touch of wishful thinking in the picture painted by the ballads. Though such men may have been able to colour their misdeeds with some shadow of justification, it is impossible in the end to portray people like the de Folvilles of Leicestershire as being in any true sense upholders of the cause of social justice. They could be hired every whit as easily as the law. In 1332 they destroyed a local landowner's water mill and they were paid twenty pounds in cash by two churchmen for doing so. This is the only occasion on which we hear of the Folville's being hired to commit felonies, but the wording of trailbaston commissions makes it clear that the practice was all too common. One cannot find much to admire here. When moreover one examines the careers of members of the Folville's band, one will find them not the victims of injustice but old and tried criminals. James Coterel, who was accused of having a hand in the capture of Willoughby, had outstanding against him convictions for murders done in Derby in 1329 and 1330; another who was arrested on the same charge, Roger Savage, had committed two murders and other unspecified offences, and had been in prison in London before he escaped to join the Folville's band. It is not easy to distort these men into generous outlaws of the stamp of the heroes of the ballads. These are not 'yonge men of price' but hardened desperate men, who rob for gain and will not stop short of bloodshed.

To urge this point as a criticism of their efforts would however be unfair to the ballad makers. The situations of real life can never be straightforward; those of fiction can. It is only in literature that we may look for black and white, instead of our common experience of a multitude of shades of grey. We must not ask too much of our authors; we must remember that they were simple men and that they sang for a rude audience. When they idealized the outlaws into heroes they were doing no more than translate circumstances into clear-cut terms which they and their audience could understand. It was beyond the limitations of a literary tradition which was aware of individuals only as type-cast characters to convey the full complexity of any given human situation. In medieval romance, which was interested in causes rather than psychology, and which saw personalities as representative rather than individual, a certain amount of distortion was bound to occur. No medieval knight ever loved as Lancelot did in story; and if he had done, the historian of the twentieth century would regard him as something less than a whole man. The middle ages admired him because he was the embodiment of a principle they revered. Robin Hood also embodied a principle, that of social justice; the ballad makers were using his story to put a case, and they should therefore surely be allowed the literary privilege of a little exaggeration.

Ultimately the verisimilitude of the ballads is more striking than the exaggerated idealization, and much more illuminating. What is interesting for the historian is that there were genuine circumstances which leant themselves to this treatment, that men like Eustace de Folville could command sympathy and that idealized versions of them could command the universal admiration of the populace. This helps him to diagnose the disease which was eating at the heart of the medieval system. That men who would ordinarily be regarded as the bane of society should be regarded as heroes is a sure indication that something is amiss. The reason for the outlaw's popularity was not that the upper classes of the later middle ages were worse than other men, for men are good and bad in every age and every station of society. They were merely the victims of the situation; the system had got so far out of hand that those who made their compromise with it could not avoid being tarnished with its corruption. Since the age could not conceive of any system but the one it knew, men regarded this corruption as a cancerous growth and demanded an operation in order that the body of society be restored to health. Thus it was that those who put themselves outside the law and defied it could justify their resort to force as an attempt to operate surgically on the diseased body politic. That the operation was no less fatal than the disease men failed to see. It was this blindness of uneducated persons who sincerely deplored corruption, but were too set in their ideas to perceive its root cause, which idealized the bandit into a figure typifying social justice.

XIV

<hr>

Conclusions

<hr>

THE historian is not, like the story teller, the master of his sources; rather he is at their mercy. If they will not furnish him with all the information he requires, he must resign himself to leaving questions open at the end of his tale. The basis of probabilities only goes a certain way to help him out of his situation. A fictional story may have its own internal logic, and if there are loose ends left over their outcome can sometimes be imagined by the application of this same logic. But the logic of history is confused; its events all too often deny all inherent likelihood, and it is dangerous to speculate unless the indications are very sure. There are problems concerned with the Robin Hood myth which it is impossible to solve on such evidence as is available. The story of his death cannot be interpreted in terms of the theme of social justice which seems to run through the other ballads; perhaps if the stanzas torn from the oldest manuscript of the ballad in question could be restored, we could come nearer to deciding whether this part of the story had any particular significance. But perhaps it was no more than a traditional episode grafted by endless repetition into the body of the legend. Similarly, it is impossible to establish precisely how the story of Maid Marian became associated with that of Robin Hood, or what was Friar Tuck's original part in the tale.

Finally, moreover, one is unable to give any convincing account of the origin of the name Robin Hood. He steps on to the stage of poesy as a fully formed hero of popular fiction, and neither myth nor antecedent history can endow him with any certain ancestry. He has his kindred, as we have seen, in the worlds both of fact and of imagination, but nothing that we know about them will tell us why it was in his story that the outlaw myth found its final and most perfect expression, and why his fame as an outlaw came in the end to eclipse that of all the others.

But if history will produce no clue as to the origin of the name, Robin Hood, what we have learnt from it will go some way to explaining just what is the relationship between his story and the similar tales recounted of other outlaws, and this in turn sheds light on the literary ancestry of his legend and its background. What we are faced with is a very striking similarity between the stories told of him and those told of other persons at an earlier date. This similarity is offset by certain important differences between their stories and his. Hereward and Fulk Fitzwarin were historical characters, famous in their day, who had roles to play in moments of political crisis; Robin Hood eludes all attempts to pin him down to any particular historical context, and, even if he did live, he clearly made little impact on the events of his own lifetime. Hereward and Fulk Fitzwarin were men of high birth, to whom deeds of chivalrous prowess were attributed; Robin Hood was a yeoman, and giants and dragons and fair women had no place in his story. Their stories, at least in the form in which they survive, are clearly written with an eye to an aristocratic public; his story belongs essentially to the common people, whose hero *par excellence* he was. Since these differences are so striking—almost as striking, indeed, as the similarities—their basis needs to be explained before one can make any general statements about the outlaw legends.

The heroes of the earlier outlaw stories made their names fighting for the cause of right against known oppressors. Behind the violence and bloodshed of the stories of Hereward and William Wallace lies the bitterness of two races to whom great injustices had been done. The outrages which the conquering Norman inflicted on the proud Anglo-Saxon people are well known; his lasting victory was founded in deliberate devastation, in mass expropriation, in the infliction by arbitrary power of unfamiliar laws upon an unwilling people. Similarly, history attests the bitterness and savagery of the struggle which resulted from Edward I's deposition of the Scottish King and his attempt to enforce his own rule against a nation's will. The stories of Fulk Fitzwarin and Eustace the Monk, though they have nothing to do with racial hatreds, have also their basis in the battle against tyranny. The case against Rainald of Dammartin as an oppressive feudal suzerain is set out clearly in the earlier parts of the *Romance of Eustace the Monk*; Eustace's rebellion is justified in the blood of his father and the Count's refusal to do justice upon his murderer. The case against King John and his Angevin predecessors, Richard I and Henry II, is set out in Magna Carta; Fulk Fitzwarin's rebellion is justified in its famous thirty-ninth clause, which set down for all time the rule that no free man should lose his inheritance without judgement. The conflicts in which these outlaws came to the fore can all, therefore, be represented in terms of a struggle between those who have ancient and inherent right on their side and those who, through naked power or naked corruption, are attempting to seize or suppress that right. The essence of the latter's villainy is their abuse of law; William the Conqueror and Edward I have laid claims to lands to which they have no legitimate title, John has twisted the law of England into the instrument of his tyrannical will. As these men all have power at their command, those who resist them, although they are enrolled on the side of justice, may from the point of view of existing power be called outlaws. This is essentially the self-same situation which is presented in the stories of Robin Hood.

It is the part they play in this situation which makes the earlier outlaws heroes of legend. The causes which they defended could all lay claim to some sort of popularity, whether it was the popularity of national resistance or of the baronial stand against royal tyranny. Popular acclaim acted always as a magnet to romance in an age when myth and history were barely distinguished. All sorts of traditional incidents quickly became attached to their stories. Some of these were purely romantic; these were the kind of tales which might be told of anyone who had performed enough memorable deeds in fact to justify the annexation of the leading role in a traditional fiction. Some were incorporated into the story as embellishment which would increase the hero's stature; that Fulk Fitzwarin spent his spare time dealing with dragons and saracens added greater significance to his part in the baron's war against King John. Others had a further purpose, to bring into clearer relief the rights and wrongs of the situation; Fulk's careful inquiry to insure that the merchants whom he robbed should not suffer personal loss, helped to contrast the scrupulousness of his conduct with that of John, whose justice could be bought with money or with the present of a white gerfalcon. Of these fictional additions some can be recognized at once because they occur in a mythical world of marvels and enchantments. Others are much closer to life, and their origin in popular imagination is only revealed because they are told over and again of different people. It might be possible to believe that William Wallace once spied on his enemies disguised as a potter, if Hereward and Eustace the Monk had not done so too. It is these incidents in particular that are told both of the earlier, historical outlaws and of the later, imaginary ones.

But however much is added to their stories, the earlier outlaws remain fixed in their historical contexts. The story of Hereward cannot be divorced from the story of the Norman Conquest, nor that of Wallace from the story of Edward I's hammering of the Scots. Forget King John, and the story of Fulk Fitzwarin ceases to exist as an intelligible narrative. These stories, for all their embellishment, centre round dramatic dates in the political history of the middle ages; 1066, and the death of the last Saxon king; 1199, and John's succession to the throne of his brother Richard; 1297, and the Scots triumph over the English invader at Stirling. If these dates are forgotten, the stories lose their point altogether.

Robin Hood, on the other hand, belongs to no one year or reign rather than another. To make nonsense of his story, one would have to forget not a single date but a century and a half of history. Herein lies the first important difference between his legend and those of the earlier outlaws. Like them, he is the hero of a struggle against tyranny and oppression. But the background of his story is not political but social history; his context is the general one of an age and a system, and not of any one particular crisis. It is from this first difference between the earlier and the later stories that the other major differences stem. The early stories have their origin in political history, and in the middle ages politics was a stage upon which only those who were qualified by birth and status could play a part. That the humble had no right to concern themselves in the affairs of government was not contested by the humble themselves; their only demand was that they be not misgoverned. Since those who took a part in political events were aristocrats, it was by fellow aristocrats that their part was most likely to be admired; so the stories which extolled their deeds and idealized their virtues made use of aristocratic literary conventions. The later stories have their origin in social history, and one did not have to be an aristocrat to resent the corruption and inefficiency of a system riddled with abuse. The lords, indeed, were the persons likely in the long run to gain from these abuses, and an indictment of the system amounted for them to an indictment of themselves. It is the exigencies of a social, instead of a political historical context, which excludes matter in the aristocratic tradition of chivalrous adventure from the stories of Robin Hood.

Political crisis called forth real leaders, about whose spectacular successes legend later grew up. The drawn-out agony of social discontent, on the other hand, failed to conjure up any real leaders and scored no spectacular triumphs. As long as a hierarchical system was accepted without question, this was bound to be so; the common man looked instinctively to the aristocrat as his leader, but the aristocrat could hardly sympathize with his cause because he had enjoyed the profits of social injustice for so long that he had come to regard them as his natural right. For him the discontented rustic was simply a man in whose heart the devil had sowed the seed of strife. Deprived of any natural leaders, and with his political horizons limited by the woods and fields of his immediate neighbourhood, the common man's occasional outbursts of violent anger were unlikely to accomplish much. His only weapon was violence, but as he was incapable of planning against victory, this was a weapon whose other edge was sure in the end to be turned against him. The Peasants' Revolt, Jack Cade's rising in 1450, the Cornish rising of 1497 and Ket's Rebellion in 1549 all alike ended in tragedy. Only the small-time rebel, who was protected by his own obscurity and the ineffectiveness of the law and who supported his protest against the system by preying on it, could look for a limited success. Eustace de Folville and Richard Stafford managed to avoid the downfall which overtook Wat Tyler and Jack Cade. It was therefore men of their stamp whose deeds the common man chose to celebrate. But because his complaint was against a general situation, not a particular one, he turned not to any historical figure, whose actual deeds might belie his professed intentions, but to an ideal one. Robin Hood was for him an idealized version of the whole tribe of Godberds and Folvilles and Staffords. These historical figures might cut sorry enough figures in heroic attire, but they were the only men whose protest against the social system was not foredoomed to failure, and the acute reality of the corruption within that system made their idealization easier.

By the time that the ballads came to be written, the outlaw hero was already a well known figure of traditional narrative. This is where the link between Robin Hood and Hereward the Wake comes out at last clearly. The ballad makers, it is true, were not inventive, but this does not mean that we need to look for a historical Robin Hood who inspired them. The outlaw hero was already familiar under more than one alias, as Hereward, as Fulk Fitzwarin, as Eustace the Monk. What the ballad makers did was to adapt his story to a context that was similar in many ways to those in which these earlier, historical outlaws achieved their renown, but which was not the same. They used stories which had come to be told of real persons and wove them into the story of a person who probably never existed, but whose imaginary career, in a different context, followed parallel lines. The material which they employed was almost purely traditional; its nature is revealed in the virtual anonymity, behind their titles, of the figures whom they set upon their stage, in the unparticularized context of their stories, and in the total absence of those episodes with a traceable historical basis in which the stories of the earlier outlaws abound. From the literary point of view this is pure gain. It gives the narrative free rein; in the ballads we are never bothered with the pother of genealogical information which dulls the tone of long passages in the romance of Fulk Fitzwarin, or with the endless details of place names and movements and military forces which clog Blind Harry's poem on William Wallace. Nor are we concerned by questions of historical accuracy or with the intricate rights and wrongs of particular situations. Robin Hood's outlawry is part of the general human protest against corruption, whose features remain perennially ugly through all changes of circumstance. His struggle is part of man's ageless war against abuse, and his story is more vivid and human than that of any participant in the struggles of, say, the Norman Conquest or the reign of King John, because it is more universal. We may question in the light of history just what epitaph we should write on the grave of Fulk Fitzwarin; but we may echo without hesitation the ballad maker's adieu to Robin Hood:

> 'Cryst have mercy on his soule,
>   That dyed on the rode;
> For he was a good outlaw,
>   And dyd pore men much good.'

Common experience, backed by a very small knowledge of the hardships to which the medieval system exposed those who had neither wealth nor influence, is sufficient to endorse this judgement.

Enough seems now to have been said of the ways in which the various outlaw legends differ from one another, and about what they have in common. Something general needs to be said now in conclusion about the three problems posed at the beginning of this book, their background, their origin, and their spirit.

The background of the outlaw legends is historical. The heroes of many of the stories are drawn from history itself; Hereward and his gang march through the pages of the *Anglo-Saxon Chronicle*; the pardon to Fulk Fitzwarin and his outlaws has been entered on the Patent Rolls of the Royal Chancery; Eustace the Monk on the Channel and William Wallace in Scotland in their time made English seamen and soldiers shake in their shoes. These men acted their parts on the grand stage of history. Robin Hood's world is the world of England in the later middle ages, and the description of it in the ballads rings true as the intimate account of contemporaries. If he himself is untraceable, we can find real men who are his prototypes walking the woods of fourteenth and fifteenth-century England. His situation in story is the result of abuses and anomalies of the system which really existed. The *Tale of Gamelyn*, with its close understanding of the law whose unjust course gives birth to the story, is probably the best example of this, but the ballads are true to life too. No doubt the ballad makers have taken liberties with fact; one suspects that the author of the *Geste* was nearer the truth than he realized when he said of Robin Hood:

> 'So curteyse an outlawe as he was one
> Was never non founde.'

But the very exaggeration is historically revealing; it shows how strong the reaction was to the everyday oppression to which the great mass of the common people was subjected. Robin Hood himself may be over painted, but the backcloth of his story, the harsh world in which the poor man is flogged from pillar to post by sheriff, justice and abbot, is not.

The origins of the outlaw legends are only partly historical. They are born of historical situations in which justice and the law have, by some irony of fate, found themselves in opposite camps. Outlaws such as we have been dealing with only exist where the law has become a tyrant. It is this that puts them into a special category in the annals of banditry; their closest literary relations are not 'gentlemen of the road', but those quite different figures of romance, the men who work for the cause of justice but outside its official scheme. They are rightly called outlaws, because they are outside the law, not against it. The inspiration behind their stories is the special historical circumstances, which gave men, whom the law had stamped as antisocial beings for whom no allowances could be made, a claim to popular affection.

But though it was historical circumstances that made them heroes, and though many of the legends cluster about the names of men who really existed, the stories themselves, or at least the most typical of them, are not founded in recorded fact. Is it enough to say they are traditional? Are not the origins of a great deal of tradition factual in the end? These are questions which it is hard to answer. The ballads of Robin Hood have been treated as popular epics centring around a traditional character. Folk-story such as this is created by the play of primitive imagination on the essential theme of narrative, conflict. Since primitive imagination sees conflict in terms of incident rather than character, it weaves its story around simple occurrences which have nothing inherently unlikely about them (as long, that is, as it is dealing with the ordinary affairs of men; in an enchanted world marvels will be as natural as misfortunes in a mortal one). A man who is reduced to a war of ruses by the power of his enemies assumes a disguise to spy on them because it is the natural thing for him to do; it is impossible to say whether an incident such as this is born of fact or fantasy. There is nothing incredible in the idea that some leader in dire straits at some time assumed the guise of a potter to escape the notice of his enemies, but such a simple expedient does not need a factual basis to explain it. The ultimate origins of tradition are part of a past which time has simply effaced from the historical map. It is impossible to say in the end whether the opening line of the forgotten ballad *Robin Hood in Barnesdale stood* represents an echo of some pictorial memory, or merely an association of concepts which has been hallowed by time.

Traditional sources tend to blur the outlines of narrative, to render it distant, impersonal, anonymous. What brings the outlaw legends alive is their vivid and fiery spirit. It is this that breathes life into the depersonalized incident of the outlaw stories. The justice of the tale of Gamelyn is a man for us, not because we know him as a person, but because we have heard his bones crack. The outlaws of Sherwood Forest may never be familiar to us, but we know that living adventure is enacted within its bounds. This adventure is born of a human situation which we can understand, even if the actors never appear as rounded human beings. Robin Hood lives in his violent deeds, in the downfall and death of the sheriff of Nottingham, in the robbing of the Abbot of St. Mary's, in all the actions which made men pray that:

> 'Such out lawes as he and his men
> May England never see again.'

Behind the trail of corpses with which his story is littered, behind the dead body of the little page and the mutilated face of Guy of Gisborne, we see the medieval desire to see retribution overtake injustice. To die by the hand of the outlaw was more disgraceful in the end than to die by the law's sentence, for such a death gave no cause for lament; it represented no more than the triumph of justice, who is too often reduced to roundabout means to achieve her end:

'It had been better for William a Trent
To hange upon a gallowe,
Then for to lye in the grenewode,
There slain by an arrowe.'

That is all the epitaph which the sheriff's man, whom Little John slew in the *Ballad of Guy of Gisborne*, earned himself. The heroes of the ballads are full-blooded men, and lives are at stake in their struggle with the law. Their worth is guaranteed, in spite of their crimes, by their championship of the cause of right and those who saw this knew how to value it, as the Queen told the King when she craved as a boon that Adam Bell and his companions be granted her as her servants:

'Ye myght have asked towres and townes;
Parkes and forests plentie.'
'None so pleasant to mi pay' She said
'Nor none so lefe to me.'

Their very ferocity was the outlaws' title to esteem in a violent age; at the risk of life and fortune they were prepared to wage war against injustice, and they neither gave nor expected quarter.

In part the violent spirit of the outlaw stories represents the attachment of a past age to the principle of retributive justice. In part it is a desperate remedy, the sole course left open for those who accept a system but not its defects. Intensely conservative in his social thinking, the common man of the middle ages could think of only one means to relieve himself of the burden of corruption and oppression, to cut out the rotting member. If there is only one system, as for him there was, those who abuse it must be removed, and the victory for the common interest justifies one's revelling in the sight of their running blood. But there is more behind the violence of the outlaw legends than the intemperate fury of conservatism which tries to hack the contemporary world into conformity with its mirage of a past golden age (though it was the hopelessness of just that effort which reduced the strivings of generations of medieval idealists to futility). Their violence is really part of the common

217

human reaction to unrelieved oppression. If you goad a submissive animal long enough, you will sooner or later unloose a fury. Injustice may be tolerated for a long while, but if it is sufficiently unjust, crime which is committed against the perpetrators will cease to be such. Ultimately it will acquire a halo of glory because, inhuman as it may be, it is perpetrated in the name of humanity and justice.

So the Irish rebels of 1798 who ravaged and burnt and murdered became national heroes in the eyes of subsequent generations who had suffered under the same oppressions. So those who in Russia destroyed the innocent with the guilty in a holocaust of bloodshed in 1917 became the heroes of a people which could remember all too vividly the barbarous cruelties of a condition still close to serfdom. Robin Hood's place in the affection of the common man of medieval England is therefore the indictment of the medieval English social system. Men whose real prototypes were villains of the stamp of Eustace de Folville could not have come to be generally admired if there was not something radically wrong with it. At this point it ceases to be relevant to say that the cure proposed was not the right one. When the enforcement of the law calls down exultant vengeance on its officers, things cannot be as they should. There is a warning in Gandelyn's cry over the dead body of the forester:

'Now xalt thu never yelpe, Wrennok,
   At ale ne at wyn
That thu hast slawe goode Robyn
   And his knave Gandelyn.'

It is a warning that injustice cannot be tolerated just because it is part of the system, for the anger which such injustice in the end awakens is unrestrained.

Appendix I

THE SUPPOSED MYTHOLOGICAL ORIGIN
OF THE ROBIN HOOD LEGEND

BECAUSE this is chiefly a historical book, I have concentrated in the text on the historical interpretations of the Robin Hood story, and for the sake of continuity have omitted discussion of the alternative mythological explanation. As a great many persons have at one time or another adopted this explanation of its origin, a word needs to be said about this theory, which, though attractive, does not seem to me very satisfactory. It appears basically to rest on four arguments.

Firstly there is a general similarity between Robin Hood and his outlaws, and the fairy people. They have the same haunts; the fairy people are wood-spirits, and Robin Hood's home is in the forest. They wear the same cloth; the outlaws' livery is green, and the fairies' traditional habit is the 'kirtle of the living green'. Robin is moreover a spirit name; it is the commonest of all the names given to familiars by witches, according to the accounts of their trials, and it is the name of the most famous of all the wood spirits, Robin Goodfellow. In addition, his pranks have a certain distant similarity with the deeds of Robin Hood; he too misled wanderers in waste places, and he too rewarded the poor and deserving, performing their labours for them and leaving sixpences in their shoes or on their doorsteps. Accordingly Robin Hood is said to be no more than Robin Goodfellow in a different guise. An alternative theory makes his name a corruption of that of a Teutonic wood-spirit, Hudekin.

Secondly, it is pointed out that various mythological elements have found their way into the outlaw stories. The story of the shooting of the apple off his son's head, which is told of William of Cloudisley in the ballad of Adam Bell, occurs also in the history of William Tell and in Norse legend. It is usually associated with the story of the blind Hodr, who, in the Scandinavian Edda, shot his brother Baldur, the God of Summer, in the archery contest of the Gods. Robin Hood's story, being associated with that of Adam Bell, is therefore associated with a Northern sun-myth; and the story of his death is said to represent the sacrifice of a victim representing the sun god, in a rite which symbolizes the recurrent conflict of the seasons. The tone of the death

219

ballad, Margaret Murray points out, suggests that it was known that Robin Hood was going to his death; whence the witch 'banning' him at the black water, and the group of mourning women who met him on his way to Kirklees. His death was symbolic and expected, because his whole story is symbolic and mythological, based in a heathen sunmyth.

This point connects conveniently with a third. Robin Hood, it is pointed out, was a traditional figure of the medieval summer festival, in particular of the May Day rites and of the Morris dance. This is certainly true of the fifteenth and sixteenth centuries; parish accounts of the time of Henry VIII and the letters of John Paston show that plays of Robin Hood formed part of the May Day festivities. Robin Hood's 'games' were condemned both by Bishop Latimer and by the Parliament of Scotland as 'lewde sportes'. All this might be interpreted as late coincidence, but it is suggested that the association of Robin Hood with rustic festival may be much older than this. Two peasant figures, Robin and Marion, appear in French pastourelles of the twelfth and thirteenth centuries. Their story, as given by Adam le Bossu in his *Jeu de Robin et Marion*, tells how Robin and his companions rescued Marion, his love, from the advances of a lustful knight. It has a vague similarity with the story told in the ballad of Robin Hood and Alan-a'-Dale. Given this similarity and the familiar name of Marian, and the fact that the rites of country festivals certainly did preserve a great deal of the less offensive of pre-Christian practice, it is suggested that Robin is a traditional figure, whose role in pagan rites has been preserved in the drama of seasonal rustic celebrations.

Robin Hood has also been associated with pagan myth because, like many pre-Christian heroes, he has lent his name to various natural features. He has barrows at Whitby and Guisborough; a great barrow near Ludlow was once known as his 'but'; a huge moorstone at Monstone in Lancashire was said to have been quoited by him from his bed on Blackstone Edge six miles away, and a druid stone near Halifax is another boulder which he is said to have amused himself by throwing at a distant mark. A stone near Nottingham was his chair, and in the early eighteenth century curious rites were still used to initiate persons into the 'brotherhood of the chair'. In this respect it cannot be denied that Robin is essentially similar to pre-Christian heroes. Woden gave his name to natural features, as the Wansdyke; Weyland's Smithy was located in the burial chamber of an open barrow on the Berkshire downs; while the Devil, who took over as a kind of residuary legatee a good many of the activities of heathen gods and spirits, has littered the English landscape with dykes, quoits and punchbowls. The similar traditions about Robin Hood, which raise him from the stature of a forest outlaw to that of a mythical giant whose arrowheads are megaliths of tons in weight, seem further to confirm the mythological origin of his story.

There are, however, serious problems about all these arguments. To the theory that Robin Hood is really a fairy it may be objected that the fairies are always essentially regarded as supernatural beings, and that Robin Hood is not only definitely a mortal, but also that the supernatural is markedly absent from his story. Lincoln green was a famous cloth, and patronized by corporeal beings in history, as well as by incorporeal beings out of it. Robin was a common name, and if familiars were sometimes called by it, it cannot therefore be held that anyone who was called by it was probably a familiar. Dr. Margaret Murray gets over this difficulty by suggesting that witches and fairies were the same people and both were human; but this is quite contrary to medieval opinion, which regarded witches as bad human beings, but did not look on the fairies as invariably bad and certainly did not regard them as human. In any case her theory that fairies (and witches) represent extensive surviving pockets of a neolithic people will not bear historical examination. In general, it seems unnecessary to credit with supernatural associations a person whose activities have ample historical parallels. Roger Godberd the outlaw was much more like Robin Hood than Robin Goodfellow ever was.

To the argument that Robin Hood's legend must have a mythological origin because some of the stories contain mythological material, it may be answered that this ignores the incorrigible habit of borrowing which beset all medieval authors. Even if the story of the apple shot from a boy's head was originally part of a sun-myth, it is not to be supposed that any story in which this incident occurs is to be lumped into the same category. In fact very few of the incidents in the Robin Hood story look as if they have anything to do with seasonal symbolism, or fertility cults, or anything of the kind. The sheriff of Nottingham is portrayed as a medieval sheriff, not the spirit of winter. The mythologists have here selected one or two incidents which are not typical and treated them as if they were the whole story, though in fact the material simply will not bear a mythological interpretation.

Robin Hood's part in country festivals is at first sight more striking. On the other hand, none of the references to this are particularly early, and in any case the Morris Dance, with which he is specially associated, was a continental importation, probably of the fourteenth century. As a result, much hinges on the interpretation put on the appearance of a Robin and a Marian in the early French pastourelle. This could have something to do with the origins of the story, but as Marian is not mentioned in any of the early ballads at all, it seems easier to believe that the story of this pair came, like the Morris Dance, from abroad, and that it was only later that this French Robin became associated and finally confused with the most famous of all English Robins, Robin Hood the outlaw.

The same sort of objections apply to conclusions drawn from the naming of natural features after Robin Hood. None of these names have so far been recorded at an early date (before the fourteenth century, that is). This is not the case with other persons, like Woden and Weyland, whose stories were part of the ancestral heritage of the Anglo-Saxon people; from the very earliest times there seem to have been place-names commemorating such figures of heathen legend, but the Dark Ages produce no similar place-names to commemorate anyone with a name remotely resembling Robin Hood. Some of the places which are associated with him seem clearly to have been named late; Robin Hood's 'but' is a name which would hardly be given by a generation which was not interested in archery. Medieval men were always ready to ascribe marvellous powers to the great men of the past. As there is nothing to suggest that the traditions of Robin Hood quoiting boulders or sleeping in barrows have any genuine antiquity, they may just as well date from a period after his fame as an outlaw as well known as from a previous age.

To sum up, it is just possible that Robin Hood's name, or part of it, may be derived from that of some folk-hero or wood-spirit of a heathen past. The evidence for this is quite inconclusive, however, and it is clear that his story, as it was known in the later middle ages, has no more to do with mythology than any other story of the life and death of a heroic human figure. One of the occupational diseases of the mythologists has always been to put a mythological interpretation on any traditional story whose pattern may be remotely connected with that of the seasons. As this is in fact the case with the pattern of human life, it is easy to class by analogy almost any story as a sun-myth of some sort, but much less easy to see how any story can be excluded from this category. This seems to be peculiarly the case with their interpretation of the Robin Hood myth, which seems unnecessary, as it is a story without obvious mythological implications, and with very clear connexions with the history of later medieval England.

Appendix II

SOURCES AND BIBLIOGRAPHY

As I have not used footnotes in the text of this book, I have tried in this appendix to give a reasonably full guide to the sources of the stories of the outlaws, and to the secondary works, both general books and learned articles, which I have used and which bear most importantly on the subjects discussed. (An up-date of the information below, compiled in 1961, is provided in Appendix III, Additional Bibliography.)

SOURCES

The sources for the earlier outlaw stories are mostly in learned editions. The best sources for the story of Hereward are the *Gesta* and Geoffrey Gaimar's *Estorie des Engles*, which are printed together in the Rolls Series. The romance of Fulk Fitzwarin is printed, with a translation, in the Rolls Series edition of the *Chronicon Anglicanum* of Ralph of Coggeshall. The romance of Eustace the Monk lacks a modern editor; I have used that produced by F. Michel in 1847. Blind Harry's *Schyr William Wallace* was edited for the Scottish Text Society in 1889 by J. Moir.

Editions of the later poems are more readily available. The 'Tale of Gamelyn' is printed in Bell's edition of the *Canterbury Tales* (London, 1854), and also in Hale and French, *Middle English Metrical Romances*; there is a further edition produced by Skeat in 1894. Easily the best collection of the ballads is that in F. J. Child's *English and Scottish Popular Ballads*. The collections of J. Ritson (*Robin Hood*, London. 1795) and Gutch (*Robin Hood*, London, 1847) are still more complete, but their arrangement is less good, and a great many of the ballads printed in them are late variants on earlier models. 'The Little Geste', the ballad of 'Adam Bell', and a useful selection of others, are all to be found in the *Oxford Book of Ballads*.

BIBLIOGRAPHY

T.R.H.S.   *Transactions of the Royal Historical Society.*
E.H.R.   *English Historical Review.*
Hereward, Fulk and Eustace. On both Hereward and Eadric the biographical notes in Volume IV of E. A. Freeman's much abused *Norman*

Conquest are most useful, and quote all the important original authorities. On the historical background of racial discontent in the post-Conquest period there is very little in print. F. M. Stenton's article on 'English Families after the Norman Conquest' (*T.R.H.S.* 1944) stands more or less alone on the historical side, apart from the references in the general surveys of the period. On the literary side, a great deal is to be learned about works in English which have not survived from E. Wilson's *Lost Literature of Medieval England.* On the question of the value of the literary evidence there is debate: the two possible views are best put on the one hand by Chambers, *The Continuity of English Prose*, and on the other by Professor V. H. Galbraith in his article 'Nationality and Language' (*T.R.H.S.* 1941). Painter in his *King John* gives in detail the historical evidence for the career as an outlaw of Fulk Fitzwarin; that of Eustace the Monk is reviewed by Walker in the *E.H.R.* 1912.

Gamelyn. Skeat's introduction to his edition of the Tale is the best commentary on it. Besides this, there is Linder's article in *Englische Studien*, 1879, mainly devoted to linguistic analysis. E. F. Shannon's article, 'Medieval Law in the Tale of Gamelyn' (*Speculum*, 1951) is most useful and demonstrates the knowledge of law revealed in the Tale.

Robin Hood. On Robin Hood there is naturally an enormous literature, though only a little of it is of any real value. The two most illuminating interpretations, in my view, are those of H. C. Coote, 'The Origin of the Robin Hood Epos' (*Folk Lore Journal*, 1885), and of R. H. Hilton, 'The Origin of the Robin Hood Myth' (*Past and Present*, 1958). Both are unfortunately rather brief. The identification of Robin Hood with the Robert Hood of Wakefield Manor was first put forward by Joseph Hunter in 'Robin Hood, Great Hero of the English Minstrelsy' (*Historical Tracts*, No. 4, 1852). He has been supported by Dr J. Walker in his 'Robin Hood Identified' (*Journal of the Yorkshire Archaeological Society*, 1944), and by P. Valentine Harris in his book *The Truth about Robin Hood.* The mythological interpretation of the Robin Hood story was put by Thomas Wright in his *Essays of the Middle Ages* in 1847; the most important restatement is that of Dr Margaret Murray in her *Witch Cult in Western Europe.* Neither of these is very convincing, but they are much less intemperate and dogmatic than most other folk-lorists.

Ballads and Balladry. The classic work on the ballads is still Child's introduction to his *English and Scottish Popular Ballads.* Gummere's *Beginnings of Poetry* is also useful, while Professor W. J. Entwhistle's *European Balladry* and M. J. C. Hodgart *The*

Ballads are probably the best modern works. E. K. Chambers' *English Literature at the Close of the Middle Ages* and the *Cambridge History of English Literature* both give useful brief surveys of the subject.

The Agrarian Background. A good general work on the agrarian history of England in the later middle ages is lacking. G. Goulton *The Medieval Village* and M. Beresford *The Lost Villages of Medieval England* are both well worth consulting. Otherwise the most useful works are local surveys, such as R. H. Hilton *The Economic Development of some Leicestershire Estates in the 14th and 15th Centuries* and E. A. Levett *The Black Death on the Estates of the See of Winchester*, and works dealing with specific subjects, such as B. H. Putnam *The Enforcement of the Statute of Labourers*. On the Peasant's Revolt there are however a number of excellent works, especially A. Réville *Le Soulèvement des travailleurs en Angleterre*, C. Oman *The Great Revolt of 1381*, and E. Powell *The Rising in East Anglia in 1381*. The best chronicle accounts are those in the *Anonimalle Chronicle* (ed. V. H. Galbraith), in the continuation of the *Chronicon Henrici Knighton* (Rolls Series) and in Walsingham's *Historia Anglicana* (Rolls Series). On the influence of literature on popular attitudes, G. R. Owst *Literature and the Pulpit in Medieval England* is invaluable.

The Forest. Manwood's *Forest Laws*, written in the sixteenth century, is still the only general survey. G. J. Turner, *Select Pleas of the Forest* (Selden Society), with an excellent introduction, is most illuminating. The chapters on the forest in C. Petit-Dutaillis *Studies Supplementary to Stubbs' Constitutional History* are the best comprehensive modern account, and alone deal with the forest in the later Middle Ages. M. L. Bazely's article 'The Extent of the English Forest in the Thirteenth Century' (*T.R.H.S.*, 1921), and the short account of forest administration in A. L. Poole's *Domesday Book to Magna Carta* are also useful.

Historical Outlaws. There is no general book of any value on the outlaw. There is a little information in Jusserand *English Wayfaring Life in the Fourteenth Century*. The activities of the 'disinherited' of 1265–6 are discussed in F. M. Powicke *King Henry III and the Lord Edward* and J. E. Morris *The Welsh Wars of Edward I*, who also deals with the development of archers as a fighting arm. J. H. Round in *Peerage and Pedigree* discusses the evidence for a lost epos about John d'Eyvil. Far and away the most useful information on the subject of historical outlaws is however to be found in Professor E. L. G. Stones' article 'The Folvilles of Ashby Folville' (*T.R.H.S.* 1957), which I have found invaluable.

Appendix III

ADDITIONAL BIBLIOGRAPHY

A spate of new work has rendered the original bibliography to this book out of date. I have endeavoured below to indicate the most important publications since 1961 under appropriate headings.

1. *General.* D. C. Fowler has discussed expertly the ballad form, in which so many outlaw stories appear, in *A. Literary History of the Popular Ballad* (Durham, N. Carolina 1968). Two illuminating discussions of the outlaw hero as a literary theme and its socio-logical significance are E. J. Hobsbawm, *Bandits* (New York 1969), and (more specialised) I. Benecke, *Der gute Outlaw: Studien zu einen literarischen Typus im 13 und 14 Jahrhundert* (Tubingen 1973).

2. *Hereward.* Two important articles have substantially added to our knowledge of Hereward, Cyril Hart's 'Hereward the Wake and his companions', chapter 24 of his *The Danelaw* (London 1992); and J. Hayward, 'Hereward the Outlaw', in *The Journal of Medieval History*, vol. 14 (1988). M. Swanton has published a translation of the *Gesta Herewardi* in his *Three Lives of the last Englishmen* (New York 1982); this is reprinted in T. H. Ohlgren (ed.), *Medieval Outlaws: Ten Tales in Modern English* (Stroud 1998).

3. *Fulk FitzWarin and Eustace the Monk.* The careers of these two historical outlaws are carefully surveyed in the introductions to Glyn S. Burgess's translations of the romances concerning them, in his *Two Medieval Outlaws: Eustace the Monk and Fouke FitzWaryn* (Cambridge, Brewer 1997). Fulk's historical career is also examined in J. Meisel, *Barons of the Welsh Frontier: the Corbet, Pantulf and FitzWarin Families* (Lincoln, Nebraska 1980). There are modern scholarly editions of the original texts of both romances, with useful introductions; *Fouke le Fitz Waryn*, ed. E. J. Hathaway, P. T. Ricketts, C. A. Robson and A. D. Wilshere (Anglo-Norman Text Society 1975), and *Li Romans de Wistasse le Moine*, ed. D. J. Conlon (Chapel Hill, N. Carolina 1972). Both romances

are also translated in T. H. Ohlgren, *Medieval Outlaws*, above §2.

4. *William Wallace.* Blind Harry's poem on Wallace, the principal source for his career as an 'outlaw', has been edited, with a masterly and informative introduction, by M. P. McDiarmid, in his *Hary's Wallace* (Scottish Text Society 1968). A version of the story in modernised English is offered in T. H. Ohlgren, *Medieval Outlaws*, §2 above.

5. *Gamelyn.* The *Tale of Gamelyn* has been re-examined in two highly illuminating articles; R. Kaeuper, 'An historian's reading of the *Tale of Gamelyn*', *Medium Auvum*, vol. 52 (1983), and J. Scattergood, 'The *Tale of Gamelyn*: the Noble Robber as Provincial Hero', in Carol M. Meale (ed.), *Readings in Medieval English Romance* (Cambridge, Brewer 1994). A modernised English version of the *Tale* is offered in T. H. Ohlgren, *Medieval Outlaws*, §2 above.

6. *Robin Hood.* The Robin Hood story is exhaustively and illuminatingly surveyed in J. C. Holt, *Robin Hood* (London 1982). R. B. Dobson and J. Taylor, in *Rymes of Robyn Hood* (London 1976) bring together an edition of the principle ballads concerning him, with a very full and valuably discursive introduction. The subject is also examined in J. G. Bellamy, *Robin Hood: An Historical Enquiry* (Indiana 1985).

Among numerous discussions of Robin Hood in learned journals the following are of particular interest:

Peter Coss, 'Aspects of Cultural Diffusion: the early Romances, Local Society and Robin Hood', *Past and Present*, no. 108 (1985).

David Crook, 'Some further evidence concerning the dating of the Origins of the Robin Hood Legend', *English Historical Review*, vol. 99 (1984).

R. B. Dobson and J. Taylor, 'The Medieval Origins of the Robin Hood Legend: a Re-assessment', *Northern History*, vol. 7 (1972).

Douglas Gray, 'The Robin Hood Poems', *Poetica*, vol. 18 (1984).

J. C. Holt, 'The Origins and Audience of the Ballads of Robin Hood', *Past and Present*, no. 18 (1960).

—— 'Robin Hood: some comments', *Past and Present*, no. 19 (1961).

J. R. Maddicott, 'The Birth and Setting of the Ballads of Robin Hood', *English Historical Review*, vol. 93 (1978).

Colin Richmond, 'An Outlaw and some Peasants: the possible

significance of Robin Hood', *Nottingham Medieval Studies*, vol. 37 (1993).

All the above articles have been collected and reprinted, together with other useful papers, in Stephen Knight (ed.), *Robin Hood: an Anthology of Scholarship and Criticism* (Cambridge, Brewer 1999).

7. *Historical Outlaws.* Historical outlaws and their activities are discussed by J. C. Holt, by R. B. Dobson and J. Taylor, and by Peter Coss (§6 above); by R. Kaeuper and by J. Scattergood (§5 above); as well as by Glyn S. Burgess (§3 above), and J. Hayward (§2 above) for the earlier period. E. L. G. Stones opened up a new dimension to this aspect of the subject of outlaws in his article, 'The Folvilles of Ashby-Folville, Leicestershire, and their Associates in Crime', *Transactions of the Royal Historical Society*, 5th series, vol. 7 (1957). J. G. Bellamy has carried the line of inquiry there suggested further and most revealingly in three studies; in his *Crime and Public Order in England in the later Middle Ages* (London 1973), and in two important papers; 'The Coterel Gang: an anatomy of a band of fourteenth century criminals', *English Historical Review* vol. 79 (1964) and 'The Northern Rebellions in the later years of Richard II', *Bulletin of the John Rylands Library* vol. 47 (1965).

Appendix IV
ROBIN HOOD IN RECENT HISTORICAL WRITING
(1977-86): A POSTSCRIPT

When a revised edition of this book appeared in 1977, the publishers kindly allowed me to write a new introduction, in order to explain where I thought I had misinterpreted the evidence when I wrote originally, in 1961. Since 1977, the subject of Robin Hood and his legend has continued to draw the attention of scholars. What has been written more recently has not induced me to change my views again; but there is the opportunity now to bring the state of the inquiry up to date, and it should not be missed.

Since 1977 four works have appeared that seem to me to deserve specific mention. One of these, D. Wiles' *The Early Plays of Robin Hood* (Brewer, Cambridge, 1981), surveys a subject that is in large measure tangential to the themes that I have tried to pursue in this book — the way in which Robin Hood the outlaw became associated with the May King in popular games and plays celebrated at the coming of summer, around Whitsuntide, in the fifteenth and sixteenth centuries. Two points that he makes deserve mention here, however. First, he is able to show that Robin's association with the May games—a context quintessentially popular, rather than genteel—is earlier than has often been allowed (his first firm reference is to a playing before the Mayor of Exeter in 1427); and he argues persuasively from certain incidents in the *Geste* of Robin Hood that this association must have been already well known when that ballad was put together in its present form. The second is that these popular summer games and plays of Robin Hood appear to be a southern and western English development. In the northern homeland of the legend Wiles has found no trace of them (except across the Border, in Scotland), and there, it appears, Robin remained stamped in men's minds and memories as

229

the outlaw captain of the ballads, rather than as a 'Lord of Misrule' in summer revelry.

The three other works that I must mention focus on topics that have been central in this book. In his *Robin Hood* (London, Thames & Hudson, 1982), Professor Holt has restated and expanded his views on the subject in a masterly survey. For me, one of his most exciting discoveries must be what seems to be the earliest recognition of what I called in 1961 'the matter of the Greenwood' as a coherent body of stories, in the fictitious surnames that a facetious clerk supplied for the sureties for the members of Parliament returned for Wiltshire in 1432. Read vertically these emerge as Adam, Belle, Clyme, Ocluw (of the Clough), Willyam, Cloudesle, Lytel, Joon, Muchette, Millersson, and so on—a galaxy of greenwood heroes—and also encapsulate in the process a ballad couplet:

> Robyn hode inne grenewode stode, (Robyn, hode, Inne, etc.)
> Godeman was hee.

In the briefer compass of an article in the *English Historical Review* for 1978 (vol. 93) on 'The birth and setting of the ballads of Robin Hood', John Maddicott has suggested identifications of a series of principal figures in the *Geste* of Robin Hood with known individuals who were prominent in Yorkshire and Nottinghamshire in the second quarter of the fourteenth century. Finally, Professor Bellamy, in his *Robin Hood: An Historical Inquiry* (Indiana University Press, 1985), has restated at length and with further elaborations the case, first put by Joseph Hunter in 1852, for identifying Robin Hood with a Robert Hood of Wakefield who lived in the time of Edward II (see above, pp. 183-9).

Holt is concerned principally with the legend of Robin Hood and its origins, Maddicott and Bellamy with the historical identities of figures that appear in the legend. I am not convinced by either of these efforts at identifications, though those proposed by Maddicott undoubtedly have attractions. The legend of Robin Hood must have grown up in the early fourteenth century, he argues; that is the context suggested by the *Geste*'s references to livery and main-

tenance and its 'bastard feudal' vocabulary, and by the fact
that it is in the late fourteenth century that we first find
explicit evidence that 'rhymes of Robin Hood' were widely
known. On this chronological assumption, something more
than accident must, Maddicott suggests, underlie the coincidence in the 1330s of three (almost certainly interwoven)
careers, each of which in its individual way offers striking
analogues with what is told of certain principal figures in the
Geste. The first career is that of Thomas Multon, Abbot of St
Mary's, York, from 1332 to 1359, who can be shown, like the
Abbot of St Mary's in the *Geste*, to have been engaged in
lending money, and also to have been in contact with genuine
bandits. The second is that of Geoffrey le Scrope, Yorkshire
landowner and Chief Justice of the King's Bench from 1324 to
1338, who acted on commissions with Multon and was very
likely feed by him (as was the justice in the *Geste*), and who
certainly on occasion used his office unscrupulously. The
third career is that of John de Oxenford, sheriff of
Nottingham from 1334 to 1339, who was unpopular as a
stranger to the county and who earned himself a reputation
for corrupt and oppressive practice that was notably
unsavoury even by fourteenth century shrieval standards
(this ultimately cost him his job). Attractive as the argument
is, difficulties remain with regard to these identifications. The
coincidences are on consideration not quite as striking as
they at first seem. The corrupt justice is a recurrent figure, in
both fact and fiction, in the story of medieval England. It is
improbable that Multon was the only Abbot of St Mary's,
York, who lent money on behalf of himself or his convent.
And a number of earlier sheriffs of Nottingham had careers
which would fit them quite as well as Oxenford to be
candidates for the original of the legendary villain. Moreover,
Maddicott's identifications will not square with the hypoth-
esis, which has been convincingly argued on literary grounds,
that the story of Robin Hood, the knight and the abbot and the
story lampooning the sheriff of Nottingham had separate
origins (see above, p. xv). Perhaps most important of all, Holt
has now brought forward fresh evidence (see below) to show
that Robin Hood's name was already well-known, at least in
some localities, in the late thirteenth century, which makes

too late the early fourteenth date for the origins of the story, for which Maddicott argues so trenchantly.

This same objection, that the dating is too late, applies equally to Professor Bellamy's restatement of the case for identifying Robin Hood with Robert Hood of fourteenth century Wakefield. This case has always had attractions, first because Wakefield is absolutely in the right area, close to Barnsdale (Professor Holt himself feels that there must be *some* connection between Robin Hood and the Hoods of Wakefield), and secondly because, as Hunter showed, the progress of Edward II in 1323 through the royal forests of Yorkshire and Lancashire and on to Nottingham is the only genuine royal itinerary that fits with that ascribed to 'comely King Edward' in the *Geste*. As I have explained above (pp. 183-9) the argument in detail rests on identifying Robert Hood, a tenant of Wakefield mentioned in the Court Rolls of 1316 and 1317, with the Robert Hood who appears in 1324 as a *valet de chambre* in the royal household accounts. Robert Hood of Wakefield, it is suggested, was outlawed for taking part in the revolt of Earl Thomas of Lancaster in 1322 (as a number of Wakefield tenants certainly were, though it cannot be proved that he was among them). Then, when Edward II came to Nottingham in November 1323, he came in and was pardoned, and was taken into the royal service (Robin Hood in the *Geste* comes into Nottingham with King Edward, is pardoned, and taken into the royal service). After this he served in the royal household for about a year, before returning to his outlaw life (Robert Hood the *valet* was laid off at the end of 1324; Robin Hood of the *Geste* returned to the forest after a twelvemonth at court). There have always been a number of difficulties about this seemingly plausible piece of identification, as I have explained in Chapter XII, the principal one being that there is no proof that Robert Hood of Wakefield and Robert Hood the *valet* were the same man, or that either was ever an outlaw. But a more overwhelming objection now arises because Holt, by subjecting a faded MS ledger to ultra-violet light, has been able to show that Robert Hood the *valet* was already on the payroll of the royal household in April 1323, *before* Edward II came to Nottingham; in consequence the sequence of events and coincidences ceases to fit the story told in the *Geste*. Professor Bellamy has buttressed his and Hunter's central case with a number of further identifications of figures that he has found in northern and central records with figures from the legend, but this obstacle remains insuperable, in my view, and some of the new identifications are anyway a little far-fetched. This seems to me to be particularly the case with his attempt to link the composition of the *Geste* with the circle of Sir John atte (or de la) Lee of Hertfordshire, Steward of the royal household in the 1360s. The suggestion is that someone in the royal household, who had there met men who could remember Robert Hood the *valet* and the outline of his career, wrote the poem and brought in Sir Richard atte Lee as a friend of Robin Hood as a compliment to his patron, Sir John. A rather tenuous northern connection is provided by the fact that an uncle of Sir John's, a genuine Richard, was briefly parson of Arksey, near Doncaster and not far from Barnsdale, from 1318 to 1321, and Bellamy considers also that there is a significant connection between the reference in a sixteenth century ballad to Sir Richard (of legend) as being of Gower's blood and the fact that Sir John had some dealings with Gower the poet (though he does not seem to have been related to him). The connections here involved seem to me far too loose and hypothetical to carry the case built on them, and in any case I find it very hard to believe that the *Geste*, with its strong ring of the north country, can have been first composed for the royal household, which had no particularly strong northern bias.

The strong northern bias of the early ballads is one of the principal themes of Professor Holt's magisterial survey of the legend in his *Robin Hood* (1982). He has here explored, in more detail than anyone previously, the precise geographic references in the *Geste*; pinpointing the 'Sayles', for instance, on the modern map of Yorkshire close to Wentbridge, and overlooking the fourteenth century line of Watling Street a few miles from Barnsdale (Little John in the *Geste* goes 'up the Saylis, And so to Watlynge Street'). He also focusses attention on some very precise Lancashire place names that appear in early versions of the Robin Hood story: Wyresdale, Gisburn and Plumpton. As Holt goes on to show, this appearance of Lancashire names in a story based on Yorkshire and Nottinghamshire will bear a very significant explanation. Wyresdale was part of the honour of Lancaster, and lay close to Clitheroe: in the late thirteenth century both Clitheroe and the honour of Pontefract, in which Barnsdale lay, were held by the Lacy family, until in 1292 the marriage of Thomas of Lancaster to the heiress Alice Lacy secured that eventually all of these places would come into the same hands. The geography of feudal lordship thus appears to provide the crucial link between the precise references in the early ballads to places physically quite far apart. This in turn suggests that the growth and dissemination of the legend may be connected also with feudal geography. This suggestion dovetails very neatly with the argument that Holt had earlier advanced and which he expands in his book, that we must look for the origins of the popularity of the Robin Hood legend to the households of the aristocracy, and of the northern aristocracy and gentility specifically (see above, pp. xiv-xv).

There is dovetailing here also with another very significant point to which Professor Holt draws attention; that is, the appearance in the thirteenth century of the name Robinhood as a surname. One early figure who bears this surname is Gilbert Robinhood, who in 1296 appears as a tenant of Thomas of Lancaster's liberty of Lewes—and so we encounter another connection with the same lord whose feudal influence and marriage linked the Lancashire and Yorkshire areas with which the Robin Hood stories are associated. In addition, this use of the surname Robinhood suggests—and very strongly—that the outlaw's name and story were already well known, in some areas at least, by the late thirteenth century.

Gilbert Robinhood is not, in fact, the first bearer of that name that can be traced in the thirteenth century records. D. Crook, in a note in the *English Historical Review* for 1984 (vol. 99), reports an earlier reference, from the Memoranda Roll of the King's Remembrancer in the Exchequer for 1262, to one William 'Robehod', a fugitive whose chattels were seized (improperly) by the Prior of Sandleford in Berkshire; and who proves to be identical with one William son of

Robert Le Fevere, the seizure of whose chattels by the Prior is recorded on the Eyre Roll for Berkshire from which the Memoranda Roll information was derived. It seems clear that at some point in the process of transmission from the one record to the other a clerk consciously altered the name of the fugitive of the Eyre Roll from William son of Robert to William Robehod, and this can only have been because he associated 'Robehod' with the status of fugitive and out-law—in other words, because he knew a story of Robin Hood. We do not, of course, know what part of England that clerk came from, but his acquaintance with Robin Hood makes the case for a thirteenth century origin to the story, for which Professor Holt has so consistently argued, effectively watertight.

There is much more in Professor Holt's magisterial book than I have space to allude to here. A major review, by Professors R. B. Dobson and J. Taylor, has appeared in *Northern History* (vol. 19, 1983). Their most important critical suggestion is that Holt may have overemphasized the significance of aristocratic households as the centres for the dissemination of the legend, and have underestimated the significance—from an early date—of Robin's esteem with the more popular minstrelsy of the market place. They would also leave room to make Robin, and in early days, just a little more of a social rebel than Holt allows. With this last point I have a little sympathy, though I would rather talk of protest than of rebellion and I believe that the word 'social' may in the context have misleading twentieth century overtones. In general, Holt's approach to the Robin Hood story and to its historical significance for the medievalist seems to me the surest that has appeared to date. Clearly, though, the debates about the significance of that story are not ended; and the quest for the original Robin will no doubt continue too, even though he has so far proved quite as infuriatingly elusive to nineteenth and twentieth century researchers as the Robin of legend proved to be for the Sheriff of Nottingham.

Index